BUSINESS ORGANIZATIONS

BUSINESS ORGANIZATIONS

Practical Applications of the Law

PETER C. KOSTANT

Associate Professor of Law
Roger Williams University School of Law

Little, Brown and Company
Boston   New York   Toronto   London

Library of Congress Catalog Card No. 96-75590

ISBN 0-316-50249-9

MV-NY

Published simultaneously in Canada by
Little, Brown & Company (Canada) Limited

Printed in the United States of America

*To the memory of my parents, George and Beatrice Kostant,
and to the memory of Jonathan Mandelbaum, M.D.
and James W. Deer, Esq.*

Summary of Contents

Contents

Chapter 7.   Control Issues for Closely Held Corporations   125

PART III.   THE PUBLIC CORPORATION   153

Chapter 8.   Securities Law Practice   155

Acknowledgments

There are many people who helped with the development and preparation of this book. At the University of Missouri-Kansas City School of Law, Professor Edwin T. Hood taught a business planning course with me that served as a basis for parts of this book, and he read and commented on several chapters. Professors Robert Downs, Edward Richards, Ray Warner, Joan Mahoney, and Chris Hoyt were also generous with their help.

At Roger Williams University School of Law in Bristol, Rhode Island, all my colleagues have been helpful and supportive. I especially want to thank Dean John E. Ryan for his encouragement and for the summer research grant that I used to complete the manuscript.

Many students contributed to the book by participating in my courses, Business Planning/Corporate Drafting at UMKC and Business Organizations at RWUSL. Student research assistants provided invaluable assistance. I'd like to thank UMKC students Janet Jacobs, Ted Corless, Janet Kalt O'Bannon, and Karen Weber. Students at RWUSL whose comments were especially helpful include Les Rich, Ed Medici, and Kimberly Tanaka. Dianne L. Izzo consulted on organization and editing of the manuscript. She designed the book and converted raw text files to finished form.

I am forever indebted to RWUSL secretaries Cheryl Meegan and Theresa Kruczek.

Professors Larry D. Soderquist of Vanderbilt Law School and Eric Lustig of New England School of Law commented on the entire manuscript and helped me make it as accurate as possible. Professor Miriam Albert of Widener University School of Law provided valuable assistance with Chapter 9. Professor John Humbach of Pace University School of Law also provided constant support and encouragement. All four professors deserve credit for much of what is good in the book.

I am grateful to practicing lawyers Dwight Sutherland, Jr., John Jennings (currently visiting professor in the Czech Republic), and Jeffrey Stoler (who was especially generous with materials for Chapters 8 and 9).

Special thanks are due to my editors at Little, Brown and Company, including Carol McGeehan, Elizabeth Kenny, Michelle Sullivan, Joan Horan, Bob Caceres, Kim Silverman, and Anne Starr.

I owe a special debt of gratitude to Heather M. Paxton for editorial assistance and encouragement.

I would also like to thank Ruth Stone of CT Corporation System for all her help.

I gratefully acknowledge the following sources, which granted me permission to reprint exceprts from the works listed below:

Charging Order, Supermajority Provision for Shareholder Action, Supermajority Provision for Board of Directors Action, Employment

Agreement, Voting Trust Agreement, Cross-Purchase Agreement with Buy-Sell Provisions, Agreement and Plan of Merger, and Articles of Merger are reprinted with permission from *The Missouri Corporate and Partnership Forms Handbook* © The Curators of the University of Missouri (1994).

The Limited Liability Company Operating Agreement is reprinted by permission from *Organizing and Operating Michigan Limited Liability Companies: A New Business Entity*, published by the Michigan Institute of Continuing Legal Education and the Business Law Section, State Bar of Michigan. Operating Agreement copyright © 1993 by James R. Cambridge. All rights reserved.

Class Voting Provision for Articles of Incorporation (Form 4:69), Cumulative Voting Provision for Articles of Incorporation (Form 4:71), and Shareholder Agreement for Pooled Voting (Form 7:08), are reprinted with permission from Fogelman, *West's McKinney's Forms, New York Business Corporation Law* (1984). Copyright © 1984 by Martin Fogelman. All rights reserved.

BUSINESS ORGANIZATIONS

PART I
SOME BASICS FOR BUSINESS PRACTICE

Chapter 1

Comments on the Nature of Corporate Practice and Pointers for Effective Drafting

The American legal system is based upon English common law. Our law is to a large degree made by judges ruling upon actual disputes and strictly following the precedents set by prior decisions, while subtly adapting them. Supreme Court Justice Robert Jackson[1] compared this grand and complex result to a coral reef, which he admitted was in fact a collection of dead things.

In addition to judge-made law, the other primary sources of legal authority are statutes, constitutions (which are like very basic and general statutes), and ordinances (local statutes). Executive regulatory agencies also produce regulations and administrative rulings. Accordingly, as first year law students we learn to work with "The Law," these cases, statutes, constitutions, ordinances, regulations and rulings.[2] Law students spend much of three years briefing, analogizing and distinguishing cases, construing and interpreting statutes and arguing in general about all of the above. This is time well spent, and no competent lawyer can be without these skills.

What law school does not adequately reflect is that a major portion of the law that affects clients does not come from these primary sources of cases, statutes and regulations. This portion is not made by judges, legislatures or administrative agencies. It is private law made by lawyers for clients in the context of business transactions. The process by which this law is made is non-adversarial. The lawyering involved is "preventive." The object is not to win in court; it is to stay as far away as possible from courts and arbitrators. The need for formal dispute resolution is a badge of failure. Law school does not adequately emphasize this practice area, which requires clear writing and precise drafting.[3]

The purpose of this book is to introduce law students taking Business Organizations survey courses to what business lawyers really do. To accomplish this, basic representative legal documents are analyzed. Students learn document analysis and drafting by following certain rules and learning the reasons why provisions in the various forms were prepared in a certain way. Document analysis is the crucial precondition for effective drafting.

In Business Organizations survey courses, students mostly read cases. A good deal of their analysis involves matters that had to be litigated to determine what was intended by the parties or who would prevail. This book is intended to supplement that focus and to stress preventive law. It provides basic and realistic examples drawn from the host of different legal instruments necessary for business transactions. Ideally, it builds on what students have already learned in the Business Organizations survey course and applies that knowledge to what they will be expected to draft as soon as they enter practice and work on real "deals."

If lawyers do their jobs effectively, and practice preventive law, they avoid making law. The bulk of law student study involves reading appellate cases in casebooks. It is fair to say that many of these cases would not have evolved into lawsuits if the original lawyers had done their jobs competently. A good business organizations lawyer should recognize from the beginning that clear legal analysis, planning, document analysis, and drafting will obviate disputes and reduce the need for judicial intervention.

This book demystifies corporate document preparation and enables students to become comfortable with the critical and imaginative use of forms. A wise corporate lawyer once said, only half in jest, that 90 percent of successful corporate practice is starting with the right form. Forms are indeed the building blocks of business law practice. Shifting metaphors, forms are to business deals what oil paints are to paintings. The use of either by a novice does not generally yield a pretty result. While mastery, alas, is a lot to ask of either a painter or a lawyer, basic competence with legal forms is not difficult to achieve. Lawyers should begin learning this process in law school Business Organizations courses.

There are good reasons for this. Once a law student knows how to adapt legal forms, which are often a kind of checklist of what needs to be addressed, business law becomes fun. It does not seem fair that future litigators experience the thrill of argument in moot courts but future business lawyers do not usually get the satisfaction of planning and preparing the components of creative and profitable deals in law school. If more law students got a taste for corporate practice in law school, fewer would start practice as litigators.

Second, the well-trained student who has experience in drafting will be more effective in serving corporate clients. Less of the expense of wasted effort will be paid for by clients or swallowed by partners in law firms.

Significantly, students make a quantum leap in understanding business organizations law when they begin to prepare realistic legal documents. For example, there is a deeper understanding of how S corporations can be used when a student does not merely write in an examination blue book, "Only one class of capital stock is permitted," but must actively apply these rules while drafting Articles of Incorporation for an S corporation and preparing the provision which authorizes the capital stock.

Working with the full array of business entities, including general partnerships, limited partnerships, limited liability companies and S and C corporations, increases issue recognition and problem solving skills. Problems of control and deadlock, triggering events and valuation for transfer of ownership interests, liability and indemnification, and potential risks and rewards are leitmotifs that run through the entire book. The same basic transaction is done using each of the business entities. Accordingly, these materials should not be viewed as a mere "form book" to help prepare a lawyer for practice. Rather they should help instill a deeper appreciation for the basic principles of corporate practice.

A baseball analogy to the use of forms in this book may be helpful.[4] Preparing legal documents by understanding the use of forms is like hitting a baseball. It is harder than it looks, but infinitely satisfying to the one who can do it.

Law students often believe that corporate lawyers just spend tedious days filling in the blanks on forms. Not true. Many different skills need to be mastered and applied to mold the diverse forms that, combined with other elements, become the corporate instruments that form a business entity or consummate a deal. As baseball's greatest hitter, Ted Williams, once said about hitting a round ball with a round bat: "Does anyone realize how hard it is to do this?" *Cf. Flood v. Kuhn*, 407 U.S. 258 (1972). Law students must recognize the difficulties of what good corporate lawyers really do, to develop the tools that will help them do it well when they come up to bat.

Throughout this book, four key attributes of business organizations are constantly balanced or adjusted. These are limited liability, continuity of life, centralized management, and transferability of ownership rights and interests. Look for these common threads throughout the following chapters, as the world of corporate practice unfolds.

A. THE NATURE OF CORPORATE PRACTICE

Lawyers who handle business transactions are generally called "corporate" lawyers even though much of their work involves not only corporations but also general and limited partnerships and limited liability companies. Depending on the size of the law firm or legal department of a corporation, corporate lawyers may do much or little securities work. Lawyers who do mostly securities work also generally need to assist with corporate housekeeping in connection with securities financings and the preparation of disclosure documents. In a small firm or corporate legal department, corporate lawyers may need to have a good deal of tax expertise. In larger firms and corporate legal departments there are generally lawyers who specialize in tax law. Corporate lawyers may also handle commercial transactions involving the Uniform Commercial Code.

Effective corporate practice is preventive law. Corporate lawyers ideally see judges only on the golf course and at bar association dinners. The last thing that a corporate lawyer wants to do is to "make law," or to even need judicial intervention to indicate what a document means or what will be enforced. Much of what is taught in law school has only limited application to corporate practice. Formal adversarial advocacy is not part of a corporate lawyer's work as a planner in a generally non-adversarial context.

Corporate lawyers look at transactions prospectively.[5] They generally do not aspire to create new legal doctrines. They are not Thurgood Marshall (before he went on the bench) or Ralph Nader. Instead they take the law as given and structure transactions and prepare documents to avoid any possible violation of the law. An excess of caution is expected; "belt and suspenders" is the correct garb for their work product.

Newly minted corporate lawyers are often told that they are paid as much to be careful as to be smart. They must be extremely conservative about avoiding risks. It is important to know in advance exactly what is necessary and to use checklists to be fully prepared. For example, on the day that a corporate transaction will close, the lawyers will have arranged for official telegrams or in some cases, electronic facsimiles (faxes) to be sent from the offices of the secretary of state, of the state of incorporation and all states in which the corporation does business, confirming the good standing of the corporation as of that very day.

The practice is generally collegial and non-adversarial. While various clients involved in a business transaction will have differing interests, their lawyers must work together without friction while advancing and protecting those interests so that the deal moves forward. Even when problems arise and tempers grow short, it is unprofessional to get angry. The challenge is to understand the concerns of the other lawyers so that a plan can be agreed upon that is satisfactory to all. Corporate lawyers need to understand what is important to the different players. Effective transactions are never based on trickery. Everyone at the conference table must understand and approve of the terms if long term success is to be achieved.

This last point raises another that is closely related. There is a strict limit to what corporate lawyers have to sell. Our capital is our professional reputation for competence and integrity. If we deplete it, it may never be replenished. Corporate lawyers need to be constantly conscious of possible ethical problems. These will often occur because the entities we may represent, corporations and partnerships, are intangible and can only act through their human agents. Nevertheless, when we represent a corporation our fiduciary duty is to that entity rather than to the officer who hired us on behalf of the corporation and who signs the checks that pay our legal bills.

Issues of legal ethics will be discussed throughout this book. Consider one example here. Louis M. Brown suggests the dangers of not correcting an error made by counsel for another party that may be favorable to one's client.[6] First, if and when it is discovered, it will show bad faith and jeopardize the deal. It may be a violation of the Model Rules of Professional Conduct,[7] and it may give rise to an action to correct the mistake or for some other remedy.

It is also important to know the substantive area of law in which you are drafting or analyzing a document prepared by another lawyer. A simple "corporate" transaction may involve numerous different areas of law. For example, if stock in a corporation is being issued for property or services, there will be valuation problems. Tax analysis may be necessary to structure the deal most effectively. The restricted nature of the securities being issued will raise securities law concerns. The nature of business that the corporation will transact may raise labor and environmental law questions. Special licenses may be required and there may be patent and trademark questions. Thus, a corporate lawyer must have familiarity with a wide range of legal areas to identify issues, and know when to seek expert advice.

Drafting is not done in a vacuum. For example, you overreach by drafting an employment agreement with an unreasonably long or broad non-compete clause, because many states' courts will not enforce the unreasonable portion and may not enforce the provision at all. Similarly, if you leave an "out" in a contract that favors your client, a court may find that the agreement lacks mutuality and is unenforceable.

B. KOSTANT'S 14 POINTS FOR CORPORATE PRACTICE

1. We are lawyers so let's always start with the law. Is there a statute or a case on point? Exactly what does it say? What are the relevant regulations or rulings? Track the operative language from the legal authority and avoid unnecessary paraphrasing.

2. There is no such thing as a standard form. That a form is printed means nothing. Almost all forms (including the printed ones and those prepared by the most famous law firms) have at least small mistakes. A large part of corporate practice is finding, understanding, and adapting the right forms. It is often necessary to take provisions from different forms, but be very careful to make then consistent both in substance and in style. This is an additional and important step. A good place to begin to find forms is in your law firm's "form file," which may already be stored in a computer database. You can also use as forms similar transactions that you or your firm have handled. In addition to looking at your own, and your firm's, files, ask other lawyers for forms or documents they have used; refer to form books and treatises from the nearest law library; ask corporate service companies such as CT Corporation Systems[8] for model forms applicable for the relevant state; or purchase forms from commercial providers (such as Blumberg's). An important corollary is to always keep a copy of everything you draft, carefully indexed, for future use.

3. Even if it sounds impressive, never include anything from a form that you do not understand and cannot explain.

4. Do not reinvent the wheel, or design a square one. Before drafting a provision, try to find some established language before beginning from scratch. It is almost always better to build upon something that already exists. When using an existing docu-

ment (from your firm's files or those of another lawyer) as a form, try to understand the transaction for which this form was used. What were the special circumstances or concerns?

5.   When asked a question by a client or partner for whom you work, begin with "I'll have to look this up to be certain." Then you can give your tentative answer if you are fairly confident that it is correct.

6.   Always be completely accurate and honest in filling out your time sheets and billing your time. Keep track of everything you do while you do it, or you will forget. Clients are much more willing to pay bills when they know exactly what you did for them. Therefore, include what you researched; drafted; revised; the letters you wrote; the responses from other lawyers that you reviewed; and all conferences and telephone conferences in which you participated on behalf of your client.

7.   If you are asked to take on more work than you can handle, explain to the assigning partner exactly what you are doing. If more than one partner is involved, it is the partners and not the junior associate that should prioritize. As a rule of thumb, you lose far more points for missing a deadline than for candidly explaining that you may be too busy to take on an additional assignment.

8.   When preparing a legal memorandum, it is good professional practice to state exactly what you have considered and what is beyond the scope of your research. In that way the partner in charge may authorize you to expand your work, but no one will inadvertently rely on your research for more than it covers.

9.   If you make a careless or foolish mistake that is pointed out to you, say "Thank you, good catch." This converts what could be negative energy to positive energy. You make someone else look good and avoid looking bad yourself.

10. Always carry a pad to meetings with lawyers, judges or clients. Always take notes, especially of phone conferences. Include the date, time and who participated. The most junior lawyer generally is expected to take notes at meetings where documents are negotiated and will generally prepare and revise the drafts. Use a pencil and carry an eraser when you mark up a draft at a meeting because people will keep changing the language and you can go nuts if you write in ink.

11. In dealing with clients, corporate lawyers need to show creativity and tact. In the technical world of corporate practice, clients will often ask for things that the law may not allow. Rather than just telling a client why something cannot be done, it is always better to suggest an alternative way of legally reaching the desired result. There was a partner at a Wall Street firm who was known as "Dr. No" because he always had ten reasons why

everything the client wanted could not be done. He was valued by the firm for his brilliance but carefully kept away from the clients. In the same way, it is a good idea to always be ready to suggest what you think is the best idea whenever asking a question of the partner for whom you are working. In this way, even if you ask troubling questions, you will still be viewed as part of the solution rather than as part of the problem.

12. Never get angry except on purpose, and that should happen very rarely. It is easy to become frustrated while working on a high pressure transaction but crucial to remain focused and tactful. The greatest challenge in moving a complex deal to completion is not refuting the arguments of the other parties, as it would be in litigation or a law school moot court, but finding creative and constructive solutions to everyone's problems. To do this, always try to understand the basic objectives and concerns of all the parties.

13. Be very careful about everything. Proofread every word and count every page of every draft. Use a dictionary. You cannot rely on your computer's spell checking program because it will not catch common errors like "principle/principal," "their/ there" or "its/it's." Assume that anything that *can* go wrong, *will* go wrong. Remember, Murphy was an optimist!

14. If you are the only lawyer present representing your client and you are in over your head and are asked to agree to something— just say "There may be tax consequences that we'll have to check," and then shut up. This suggestion is partially, but not entirely, a joke.

C.   POINTERS FOR EFFECTIVE DRAFTING

A brilliant computer hacker who prefers to remain anonymous once suggested that "writing is God's way of telling us we do not think clearly." Probably at least 75 percent of poor writing is the result of not fully understanding the material about which we are writing. The other 25 percent flows from not having said what we meant because of a lack of precision. Legal writing is probably one of the more difficult types of writing. Nonetheless, a disciplined approach and careful work will yield an acceptable result.

There are really two overlapping types of legal writing. One is the usual careful and precise prose of letters and memoranda. The other is the drafting of legal instruments. Similar techniques apply to both, but this book will primarily involve the latter.

Good legal writing is a process. Outline the results of your analysis before you begin to write. Do not start to write until you have a clear idea of your conclusion and the steps that lead to it. Jot down all your ideas and impressions as you read through the source material that is being analyzed. Only after you are well into your analysis will you be able to evaluate the validity and relative importance of your ideas. What may have seemed like key points may turn out to be tangential or even irrelevant. What first may have seemed to be off the wall ideas may turn out to be central, brilliant or subtle. (This is rare.) Include all your ideas in the outline without fear; it is easy to delete rejected ideas and no one else need ever see them. There are exceptions to this method. One Wall Street lawyer is known to consistently make ten arguments, of which two are brilliant and eight are ludicrous. Unfortunately, he is unable to distinguish between them and needs the help of his colleagues.

Write down as questions everything that you do not understand, or with which you do not agree. Do not try to hide your confusion from yourself. It is by answering these questions that you will do most of your best analysis and reach your clearest and most supportable conclusions. By referring to your changing list of questions you will find gaps and inconsistencies in your analysis.

After you complete your outline and begin to write, start with a thesis paragraph telling your reader exactly what you will be discussing and what your conclusion will be. If you are unsure, go back to your outline and do not begin to write until you know what you are going to say.

When you write, use well-organized paragraphs so that your analysis is easy to follow. Begin each paragraph with a topic sentence. Make all the sentences in the paragraph relate to the topic sentence. If a sentence does not relate, it belongs in another paragraph. Avoid using short, choppy paragraphs because they jar and distract the reader. Very long paragraphs are also distracting because they contain too much information for the reader to digest.

Once you have completed a draft, try to put it aside for a period of time. If you are working under a pressure deadline (all too frequent an occurrence in the practice of law), at least stop for a cup of coffee or a quick walk around the office. After this hiatus, re-read your work critically and with an open mind. Pretend someone else wrote it and ask yourself the following questions.

1. Is the organization logical? Should sentences or paragraphs be moved? Have you included each logical step in your analysis? Use transition words or phrases such as "accordingly," "nevertheless" and "on the other hand" so that the reader knows where you are going and how the pieces fit together.

2. Does each sentence actually communicate what you intended to say? If not, rewrite it. Are there any unnecessary words, phrases, sentences or paragraphs? If so, delete them.

3. You may recognize points about which your analysis is confusing because you did not fully understand what you were writing. You may also notice counter-arguments which have not been addressed. Jot down these points and then go back to your outline. Relax and try to answer the questions that you have raised and consider the new counter-arguments which you recognized. Analyze to the best of your ability (which may require additional research) and revise your draft.

4.   Is your conclusion clearly stated and supported by your analysis? If not, revise it.

5.   Have you accurately introduced each topic to your reader? While you should not begin to write until you understand what you are going to say, after you have completed a draft, your ideas will undoubtedly be clearer. Accordingly, revise your thesis paragraph and topic sentences to utilize this clearer focus. Remember there is no such thing as good legal writing. It is really good legal rewriting.

6.   Objectively re-read your draft. Clarify what a reader unfamiliar with the material might not readily understand. Read the draft as though you were grading student work, or challenge it as though it were written by your adversary in a lawsuit. Note all weaknesses and then rewrite to cure them.

7.   Finally, proofread as though you have never seen these materials before. Read backwards (from the last word to the first) so that you will not get caught up in the brilliant logic of your analysis and thereby miss errors. Again, use a dictionary and do not rely on your computer's spell check program.

D. CORPORATE DRAFTING AND DOCUMENT ANALYSIS

Corporate lawyers spend a great deal of time drafting, commenting upon and revising legal documents. Professor Larry Soderquist of Vanderbilt Law School wrote, "A lack of interest in care and precision will keep an associate from ever being accepted as a corporate lawyer."[9]

Corporate drafting requires clarity. Ambiguity and vagueness both cause a lack of clarity. An ambiguity will be unclear because it will have more than one possible meaning. One favorite example is the instruction given to workers at a nuclear reactor on their first night shift, when they are told that they "cannot put too much water in the cooling system." Lives could depend upon which of the two meanings was actually intended for that ambiguous statement.

Vagueness occurs when the specific meaning of a provision is not clear. While it is always a mistake to draft a provision ambiguously, on rare occasions one will intentionally draft vaguely because the parties are not yet certain about how they want a provision to apply. Sometimes the parties will want to wait and see, and will intentionally use a vague term like "reasonable."[10]

Before a lawyer begins to draft, it is necessary to learn exactly what the client wants. Learn about the client's business in detail. Lawyers should prepare clear and well-thought out questions for client interviews. The lawyer should then try to provide for every possibility that may occur, and provide clear remedies. Frequently, by following this process the lawyer will raise questions that the client never considered. This is generally a good thing. There are, however, situations in which asking too many questions can "spoil the deal." This can happen if the lawyers focus on irreconcilable problems or the gory details of exactly what will happen when a deal fails. Experience gives lawyers a better understanding of when and how far it is appropriate to push. Lawyers must balance the need to focus on the potential for future problems against the danger of frightening the client or other parties to the transaction.

There are also limits to the extent that it is feasible to specify provisions in detail.[11] In some other cultures, lawyers recognize this difficulty more than we do. For example, in Japan written contracts are usually short and broadly worded. The parties rely more on good faith during performance than to specific provisions in their written agreements.

Part of knowing the law in the area in which you are drafting is to know the extent to which statutes, regulations and case law can be modified by the parties in their private agreements.[12] In this book we will see how relevant statutes like the Uniform Partnership Act contain default provisions which govern in the absence of express provisions between the parties.[13] Included among these default provisions are many that the parties would not have intended.

The best forms are often past deals that you or lawyers in your office worked on. At the conclusion of a major transaction bound volumes containing all the documents are often prepared for all the participating lawyers. These not only look great on your office bookshelf, they also give you ready access to prior deals.

Professor Robert W. Hamilton of the University of Texas Law School has observed that while lawyers with a background in business and finance do well in corporate practice, so do lawyers whose first exposure to business comes in legal practice.[14] I hope that by working through this book, students will get an idea of the scope and inherent interest of corporate practice.

I recommend that students look at several excellent supplementary books: Robert W. Hamilton, *Fundamentals of Modern Business* (Little, Brown and Company, 1989); Robert W. Hamilton, *Money Management for Lawyers* (Little. Brown and Company, 1993); Robert C. Clark, *Corporate Law* (Little, Brown and Company, 1986); William A. Klein and John C. Coffee, Jr., *Business Organization and Finance* (6th ed., Foundation Press, 1996); and Larry D. Soderquist and A.A. Sommer, Jr., *Understanding Corporation Law* (treatise).

E.   EIGHT RULES FOR GOOD DRAFTING

In *Drafting Contracts*,[15] Professor Scott Burnham provides some excellent drafting rules to follow. If a lawyer follows these eight rules, adapted from Professor Burnham's work, the result will be a well-drafted legal document. Students are well advised to rely upon Professor Burnham's handy paperback text.

1. Use recitals, the "whereas" clauses, to show the intent of the parties but do not include substantive representations and warranties in them because this section of an agreement is not legally binding.

2. If a term will be used more than once in an agreement, define it either in a separate definition section at the beginning of the document, or in the document the first time that the term appears. An example of this use of definition is the Kent Clothing Company, Ltd. (hereinafter the "Company"). Each time that you refer to the Company, it will have this meaning. When you refer to a different company, the letter "c" will not be capitalized. A long and cumbersome phrase can be defined into a word or two, and then used briefly and easily. For example, in preparing the Operating Agreement for a limited liability company, certain types of transfers of ownership interests have particular tax requirements. A relevant Internal Revenue Service Treasury letter ruling specifies that "transfers by reason of death, divorce, dissolution, liquidation, merger, or termination" are an exception to the general rule requiring consent by a manager. All of these transfers can be defined as "Permitted Transfers" and it will no longer be necessary to keep listing all six types of transactions each time the term is used.

   Another example of a clarifying use of definition would be to define "net income," to avoid controversy as to whether it means "before taxes" or "after taxes." Often it will be on your second draft of a document that you will decide upon additional terms to define.

3. Avoid elegant variation. To achieve this, never use the same words to mean a different thing, or different words to mean the same thing. Doing so is not only unclear, but it also gives other parties a basis for arguing in the future that the same thing, or something different, was intended. For example, as discussed above in (2), if you define "transfers by reason of death, divorce, dissolution, liquidation, or merger" as "Permitted Transfers," always refer to them as such. If you use the full Treasury letter ruling definition but carelessly leave out one element (e.g. "liquidation"), it could be argued and possibly litigated that something different was intended.

4. Generally avoid use of the passive voice. It is wordy and can also be unclear because it often does not express clearly who is to act. Remember: "The passive voice is often disdained by the good drafter."

5. Draft in the present tense and use "shall" to indicate obligation and not future tense.

6. Consistently use language of obligation (that is, "shall" for what must be done, "may" for what is authorized but not mandatory, and "must" for conditions upon which action is contingent).

7.   Avoid legalese and jargon. Include no superfluous language.

8.   Avoid sexist language. Rather than saying the "obligor must pay within three days of receipt by him," it is better to use "receipt by the obligor" or "when he or she receives."

After you have drafted a document, apply the eight rules to improve it. Make sure that the language and numbering are consistent. Before a document leaves your office, count the pages and proofread very carefully.[16]

F.   LAWYER'S BILLING TIME SHEET

Law firms are generally compensated for their efforts by one of two standard methods. They either accept payment of fees on a contingency basis or they bill clients based on an hourly rate. The latter is the usual method of compensation for corporate law firms. "Billing Time Sheets" are documents lawyers use to record all time spent on behalf of each client.

In practice, you will use one time sheet (or more) per day, making a separate entry to indicate the amount of time spent working on each client matter you tackle. If a firm handles more than one matter for a client, each separate matter will be given a different matter name and billing number. Different matters for one corporate client might include a joint venture, merger, public offering, private placement, advice on doing business in another country, and defense of a derivative action. You will seldom work on just one matter for one client at a time, and you must carefully keep track of your time. If you take a call on a different matter than the one currently open on your desk, note the different name and number, and time spent, on your daily time sheet. When you are working on a project that is continued over for more than one day, make a new entry each day, even if it is for the same client on the same matter. If these sheets are not prepared on a daily basis, billable time gets lost. This will not please the partners in your firm.

The law firm is owned by the partners, who are "members" of the firm. The lawyer-employees, called "associates," are paid a salary and are neither owners of the firm nor are they liable for the firm's contractual obligations. An associate may be offered partnership after six to nine years. The partners' profits generally come from legal fees clients pay for the partners' billable hours and from the profit taken on billing of associates' hours.

One rule of thumb holds that one third of an associate's billings will cover the associate's salary, one third covers the firm's overhead expenses, and one third is profit for the partners. A ratio of one partner to one associate is fairly high. One partner to two or even three associates would yield greater profits for the partners.

Each lawyer is generally given a billing number. This number may change if and when the lawyer becomes a partner. Time is usually billed in six-minute intervals, representing tenths of an hour. If you make a

Form 1: Lawyer's Billing Time Sheet

SANTORO, RYAN & KOSTANT
ATTORNEYS AT LAW

DATE: _____

ATTORNEY: _____

ATTORNEY NUMBER: _____

CLIENT: _____

MATTER: _____

CLIENT NUMBER: _____

MATTER NUMBER: _____

TOTAL HOURS: _____

SERVICES RENDERED: _____

_____

_____

_____

CLIENT: _____

MATTER: _____

CLIENT NUMBER: _____

MATTER NUMBER: _____

TOTAL HOURS: _____

SERVICES RENDERED: _____

_____

_____

_____

Note: Each client of the firm will have a name and billing number. If a firm handles more than one matter for a client, each separate matter will be given a matter name and billing number.

Note: Learn the abbreviations that your firm uses. Some examples are:

c	conference
tc	telephone conference
r&r	receipt and review
rev	revision
I/L	investigation of law, i.e., legal research
att. tc	attempted telephone conference
pr	professional reading

phone call for a client and just leave a message, and then begin work for another client, the attempted phone call will usually be billed as ".1 hours."

Professional reading is a good example of time that will not be billed to a client. Professional reading to learn and keep up with the law is generally billed to "office general." Some or all of the time that you spend learning the law for a specific client may be billed either to the office or to the client. That determination should be made by the partner in charge. Of course, you should never inflate the time you spend on a client matter. Moreover, the associate should not reduce the amount of time spent. Again, that is a financial decision for a partner to make.

Drafting Exercise 1:

Billing Time Sheet

Associates are usually expected to provide seven to eight billable hours a day. This may require ten to twelve hours of time in the office.

For one week, maintain billing time sheets to keep a record of your "billable time," by "matter," as if you were working in a law firm now. Include time spent attending classes and meetings, preparing for classes, doing research and writing memoranda, briefs and articles; and record any time spent in the field, working in clinics or other employment. Be as specific as possible in maintaining your records.

Practical Pointers

1. Keep a record of what you do for each client and how long it takes, while you are doing the work. In that way time will not be lost. Clients are much more willing to pay bills when they can see exactly how much was actually done for them each day. Time sheets are compiled and used in computing client bills and showing what was done. If clients complain about bills, remind them that if you pay peanuts, you get monkeys. One large New York law firm would hold a lawyer's paycheck if time sheets were not submitted each week. The firm record for holding a check was 14 months!

2. Never inflate or reduce the time you spend on a client matter. If your work has been inefficient, the billing partner may cut down on the number of hours billed, but that decision should be made by the partner.

3. You will often "revise" but never "correct" your drafts. Revision makes them better, but why should a client pay you to correct your own mistakes?

Notes

1. Robert Jackson, 1892-1954, served on the U.S. Supreme Court from 1941-1954 and wrote with great clarity and eloquence.

2. *See, e.g.,* Wren & Wren, The Legal Research Manual at 3-10 (2d ed. 1986); Dernbach & Singleton, A Practical Guide to Legal Writing and Legal Method at 2-4 (Rothman 1981).

3. *See generally* Robert MacCrate, Preparing Lawyers to Participate Effectively in the Legal Profession, 44 Journal of Legal Education 89 (1994); Brown and Dauer, Planning for Lawyers (Foundation Press, 1978).

4. Baseball and law have a close kinship. Read, for example, Justice Blackmun's list of the greatest players in *Flood v. Kuhn,* 407 U.S. 258, 261 (1972), or consider Justice Holmes' belief (now being seriously questioned after the cancellation of the 1994 season) that baseball and antitrust law do not mix. *See Federal Baseball Club v. National Lawyers,* 259 U.S. 200 (1922).

5. *See* Larry D. Soderquist & A. A. Sommer, Jr., Corporations (Michie 1991, 3d ed.) (hereafter "Soderquist & Sommer") at 15-18, for an excellent discussion of the distinguishing features of corporate practice.

6. *See* Louis M. Brown, Reviewing and Revising Draft Transactional Documents, The Practical Lawyer Vol. 36, No. 4.

7. *See, e.g.,* ABA Model Rules of Professional Conduct, Model Rule 4.1.

8. Corporate Service Companies are referred to in Chapter 7.

9. Soderquist & Sommer at 15.

10. Scott Burnham, Drafting Contracts (2d ed. 1993), §7.4 at 96.

11. William A. Klein & John C. Coffee, Jr., Business Organization and Finance, at 78 (5th ed. Foundation Press 1993).

12. Id. at 4.

13. Id.

14. Robert Hamilton, Fundamentals of Modern Business at 1-2, (Little, Brown and Company, 1989).

15. *See generally* Burnham, Drafting Contracts.

16. *See* Burnham, Drafting Contracts, Chapter 16, Operative Language at 233-246, and Chapter 17, The Language of Drafting at 247-260. *See also* Brody, Rutherford, Vietzen & Dernbach, Legal Drafting (Little, Brown and Company, 1994).

PART II

SELECTION AND USE OF APPROPRIATE BUSINESS ENTITIES

Chapter 2

The Sole Proprietorship

There are numerous ways to set up a for-profit business. The methods discussed in this book, each utilizing a different business entity, are: Sole Proprietorship, General Partnership, Limited Partnership (with or without a corporate general partner), Limited Liability Company, and Corporation (Type S or C). Each of these business entities is discussed in Chapters 2 through 5. It would be a good idea for the reader now to read the introductory sections of each of these chapters, to glean an overview of the advantages and disadvantages of each entity.

The Sole Proprietorship is the simplest structural form of business entity. The name describes it exactly, an unincorporated business owned and operated by one person. By definition, a sole proprietorship cannot have more than one owner.

The sole proprietorship is primarily subject to the laws of agency and contract. The sole owner is the principal. There is no limit on the number of agents that the principal may hire. Liability issues, however, present a great drawback to this form of business organization. From a legal standpoint, the principal is vicariously liable for any tortious act an employee performs within the scope of employment.

Thus, the potential liability of the principal can be enormous. The principal has unlimited liability not only for his or her own acts but also for the acts of the employees. It may however make a certain amount of sense to operate a business as a sole proprietorship when the owner will be doing all of the work, since the owner will always be personally liable for his or her own torts.

The principal will also be liable for her own contracts in a sole proprietorship. In a limited liability entity like a corporation or limited liability company, she would not have personal liability for the contracts of the entity.

In the typical business context in which employees do much of the work, the owner would be vicariously personally liable for employee torts committed within the scope of employment, and for contracts into which the employee had the authority to enter. As a practical business matter, the tort liability can be catastrophic. All of the principal's wealth (including assets that have nothing to do with the business) would be subject to judgments resulting from these kinds of employees' acts. Insurance can provide some protection.

The sole proprietorship is the most numerous type of business entity in the United States, but it represents only a small proportion of the economy when numbers of employees and accumulations of assets are figured. The operation of a business as a sole proprietorship depends only on the intent of the owner. It is casual, generally does not require any government approval to organize, and significantly, does not require any services to be performed by an attorney.

Professor Soderquist has correctly observed that many sole proprietorships exist because lawyers were not involved in their establishment.[1] For many of these businesses, the owner is unknowingly and unnecessarily at risk.

To establish a sole proprietorship, investigate the practical steps necessary in the local area. Steps may include obtaining appropriate business licenses, business name registration, secretary of state filings, local business tax filings, state sales tax collection notices, quarterly anticipated income tax filings, and application for an Employer Identification Number from the Internal Revenue Service (using IRS Form SS4).

Because sole proprietorships can have only one owner, and are likely to have many liability problems, this book contains very little further discussion of this business entity.

Note

1. *See* Larry D. Soderquist & A.A. Sommer, Jr., Corporations (Michie 1991, 3d ed.) at 25.

Chapter 3

The General Partnership

A. SOME ADVANTAGES

The partnership form is appropriate when the business is to have more than one owner, and the owners want to participate actively in the management of the enterprise. Every state except Louisiana adopted the Uniform Partnership Act of 1914 ("UPA"), so the general partnership is a good entity for a business that is active in many different states. Recently, the Revised Uniform Partnership Act of 1994 ("RUPA") was completed, but it has not yet been widely adopted. The discussion in this chapter will focus on the UPA which remains the law in many states. Some differences between the Acts are addressed in the Practical Pointers at the end of the chapter.

There may be important tax reasons for using the partnership form.[1] Partnerships receive flow-through tax treatment which avoids the problem of double taxation for some corporations. As discussed in Chapter 6, corporations of the C type are subject to double taxation, which means that they are first taxed on their profits as an entity and then the dividends paid to shareholders, which are not deductible business expenses of the C Corporation, are again taxed as income to the shareholders. Corporations that qualify for and elect Subchapter S status generally receive flow-through tax treatment, avoiding double taxation. Moreover, no double tax will occur on the sale or liquidation of a partnership business, unlike a C corporation.

While Subchapter S corporations and general partnerships receive flow-through treatment for federal income taxes, it is often possible to do business as a general partnership when the Subchapter S corporation form would not be available. For example, partners could be corporations or non-resident aliens, and there could be more than one class of equity interests issued to partners thereby giving certain partners a preference in connection with their partnership interests. (See Chapter 6 for more details of the stringent requirements of Subchapter S status.)

Partnerships are very useful in tax planning. In setting up general partnerships, there is considerable flexibility in allocating partnership income, loss, deductions or credits. Partners can utilize partnership losses to offset their active or passive income.

When a new enterprise will experience losses during the start-up period it should be organized as a flow-through entity whenever possible. The losses should flow directly to the individual investors, that is, the partners of a partnership or the shareholders of a Subchapter S corporation. The losses should not remain in the entity, as they must in a C Corporation, where they can only be carried forward and deducted against future profits (if any) in later years. Many new businesses will experience losses initially. Losses may be due to start-up expenses, or to the need to operate for a while before the company's enterprise becomes profitable, or because of "paper losses," such as immediate depreciation (sometimes accelerated) of business equipment and property.

The tax treatment may be somewhat more advantageous for a partner than a shareholder of a Subchapter S corporation because "unlike a partner . . . an S corporation shareholder does not increase her basis for any share of an indebtedness owed by the S corporation to a third party. A partner's basis determines the amount of income tax they will pay upon sale of the partnership interest or dissolution of the partnership. An S corporation shareholder's basis will be increased only if there is an actual economic outlay by the shareholder. In some cases, this difference could result in larger current deductions for losses being available to the owners of the business if it is operated as a partnership."[2]

Non-tax advantages of the general partnership form of business include ease of operation and flexibility.

B.   SOME DISADVANTAGES

The general partnership is a mutual agency arrangement in which each partner has the power to bind the partnership and the other partners when acting within the scope of the partnership business.[3] Each partner has unlimited liability for the debts and obligations of the partnership. In the event that the partnership is liable in tort, such as for product liability, the exposure of each partner could be enormous. A partner will also be liable for the payment of taxes on his distributive share of partnership income even if no distributions are made to him.

Unless otherwise provided, the partnership automatically dissolves upon the death, bankruptcy, or withdrawal of any partner. Upon dissolution, partners could lose the going concern value of the enterprise.

There are also restrictions on the alienability of partnership interests. A partner cannot transfer his partnership rights without the consent of all the other partners. These disadvantages may make it difficult for a partnership to attract outside capital. Nevertheless, as discussed more fully in the section on drafting partnership agreements, many of these problems can be solved by careful planning and drafting.

What can be done to limit the disadvantages of using a general partnership in connection with unlimited liability, automatic dissolution upon the occurrence of certain events, inability to transfer partnership interests, and the requirement of participation in management?

First, it is possible to purchase insurance against many, but not all, risks from unlimited liability. A general partnership may be a good business entity to choose when the business holds substantial insurable assets, like real estate, but a bad choice for high risk businesses like construction, demolition or recreational bungee jumping. While partners can agree to indemnify each other, these provisions are not binding on third parties to whom each partner is liable to the full amount of the partnership liability.

Second, some of the problems caused by automatic dissolution can be avoided. The partners can agree that the remaining partners will continue the business and execute a partnership continuation agreement. A well-drafted partnership agreement will provide for continuation of the business and contain clear buy-sell and valuation provisions.

Third, partners are not free to transfer the bundles of rights and obligations that comprise their partnership interests. Unless there is agreement to the contrary, a partner can assign his rights to receive partnership distributions. The assignee does not become a partner or have a partner's rights without the consent of all the partners. Nevertheless, partners could agree, under certain circumstances, to allow for the substitution or admission of new partners. Again, buy-sell and valuation provisions are very useful.

Finally, general partners can delegate management responsibilities to managing partners or a management committee and can hire professional managers.

C. THE NECESSITY FOR A WRITTEN PARTNERSHIP AGREEMENT

A partnership is formed when two or more persons agree to own a business together for the purpose of sharing profits. No written agreement is necessary but in the absence of an agreement, numerous default provisions of the Uniform Partnership Act ("UPA") control. Accordingly, it is extremely desirable to have a written partnership agreement because without contrary provisions, pursuant to the UPA, the following provisions are in effect.

1. All partners have the equal right to participate in the management of the partnership and each partner gets one vote regardless of percentage ownership interest. (UPA §§9, 18(e)).

2. Partners may not transfer their rights as partners without the consent of all partners. (UPA §18(g)).

3. In determining the sharing of profits and losses, each partner is first repaid her share of capital contributions and will then share equally in the surplus remaining after all liabilities, including those to partners, are satisfied, and each partner must contribute to losses, whether capital or otherwise, sustained by the partnership according to her proportional share in the profits. (UPA §18(a)).

4. A majority vote of partners will resolve differences in connection with managing the affairs of the partnership, but no action can be taken in contravention of the partnership agreement without the consent of all partners. (UPA §18(h)).

5.   Any partner may dissolve the partnership at will, without being liable for damages, unless there is an express or implied agreement as to the term of partnership existence. (UPA §31).

6.   The partnership is subject to abrupt and unexpected dissolution for death, bankruptcy, or expulsion of any partner. (UPA §31).

Written agreements also satisfy the statute of frauds for a contract that involves more than a certain amount of money (an amount which varies from state to state) or for ownership of real property, and for agreements with a term of more than one year. By preparing a written agreement, lawyers force their clients to think through and clarify their business intentions. This helps to avoid misunderstandings and litigation.

Some issues that must be addressed in a partnership agreement include: what happens upon death, disability, retirement or withdrawal; how are profits and losses to be divided; must partners contribute additional capital (and if they do, what percentage interest in the partnership assets will they receive); what are provisions for purchase or sale of partnership interests; may or must the partnership or other partners purchase the interest of a deceased or withdrawing partner, and how will the price be determined; and are partners to receive salaries and if so, do salaries offset income distributions. A partner's ownership of the partnership interest may be his or his estate's largest asset. Because the interests are not freely transferable (even if there is an agreement permitting sale it is not likely that there will be a market), it is very important to have a clear buy-sell agreement.

There are aspects of partnership status which cannot be modified, even by agreement between the partners. For example, partners are liable for the debts of the partnership (but not the debts of other partners as individuals) and are liable for torts and breaches of trust committed by the partnership or by partners in connection with the business of the partnership. If a partner becomes insolvent, the other partners will be liable for her share of partnership obligations.

D.   HOW TO DRAFT A PARTNERSHIP AGREEMENT

Partnerships are governed by the law of agency, contract and the common law of partnership as generally codified in the UPA.

Generally among the most important issues to consider are the treatment of capital accounts, profits, losses, voting percentages and salaries. The following are some business issues that should be carefully considered before preparing a general partnership agreement.

1.   Term

Unless the partnership agreement is for a definite period of time, or to complete a specific purpose, it is a partnership at will and can be dissolved at any time by a partner without penalty. It is possible that a specific term may be implied so that a partnership is not at will.

Partners always have the right to dissolve a partnership at any time, but to do so in breach of the partnership agreement will subject the partner to liability for damages for breach of contract. The reason for this rule is that given the otherwise unlimited liability of a partner for partnership obligations, no one can be *required* to become a partner, remain a partner, or acquire a third party as a partner, against her will.

2.   Capital

In settling accounts after dissolution, the rules for distribution under UPA §40 are: payment to creditors other than partners; debts to partners; repayment of partners' capital contributions; and any residual profits. In the absence of an agreement, UPA §18(a) requires that partners contribute funds to satisfy losses in the same proportion as they would share profits. If a partner is insolvent or refuses to pay, the other partners must contribute the additional amount in the same proportion as their pro rata interests in the partnership profits.

Profits and losses are generally shared in accordance with percentage interest based on capital contributions. Often, a value is placed on services being contributed by a partner. For service industries like law, a formula is often used which includes billable hours, new client development and management work for the firm.

Cash flow is very different from profits. There may be situations in which a partner is liable for income taxes on partnership profits without having received cash distributions to pay the taxes. It is also possible for a partnership to have "bookkeeping" losses and still have funds available to distribute to the partners. For example, a real estate venture may immediately begin to show losses due to depreciation while generating positive cash flow from receipt of rent payments.[4]

Partners may agree to pay a salary to partners which may or may not be deducted from their share of profits. Advances to partners from partnership revenues are called draw.

3.   Management of the Partnership

Unless there is an agreement to the contrary, all partners have equal right to management. UPA §18(e).

Each partner has authority to bind the partnership in transactions in the usual course of the partnership business unless the partner has no actual authority and a third party has knowledge of this fact. UPA §9(1). Under UPA §§13, 14 and 15, partnerships and other partners are liable for acts of any partner within scope of business and certain breaches of trust.

Unless there is an agreement to the contrary, a majority of the partners will decide any differences arising in the ordinary course of the partnership. UPA §18(h). But no act may be done in contravention of the partnership agreement without consent of all partners. Accordingly, a unanimous vote is necessary to make a change which would be in contravention of the agreement. This may give each partner a veto power, and the resulting risk of deadlock must be balanced against a written provision to the contrary that would give partners less protection. This problem is comparable to supermajority provisions for corporations discussed in Chapter 7.

4.   Title to Partnership Property

A partner's interest in partnership property is personal property, even as to real property that partnership owns. UPA §26.

The partnership agreement should clearly state whether real property is owned by the partnership or by individual partners. For example, it is possible that a partner might own real property which he leased to the partnership, perhaps treating the market value of this lease as a capital contribution. Upon the death of a partner, real property and personal property might pass to different distributees. If the real property was owned by the partnership, it would pass as personal property. If the partner owned it, it would pass as real property.

5.   Assignment and Transfer

Unless the agreement provides otherwise, a partner may assign his partnership interest but not his rights as a partner, so the assignee does not become a partner and the partnership is not dissolved. The assignee can only become a partner with the consent of all the partners.

The assignee may effect dissolution under UPA §32(1) under circumstances that would render a dissolution equitable; for example, if profits were being unreasonably withheld from distribution. Under UPA §32(2) an assignee could also effect dissolution if the term of the partnership expired, just as if the assignee were a partner, or at any time if the partnership was at will.

6.   Dissolution

"Dissolution," "winding up," and "termination" all have different meanings. Under UPA §29, dissolution is the change in the relation of the partners caused by any partner ceasing to be associated in the carrying on of the business. Under UPA §30 after dissolution the partnership is not terminated, but continues until the winding up of partnership affairs is completed.

Under UPA §31 dissolution is caused without violation of the agreement "By the termination of the definite term or particular undertaking... [b]y the express will of any partner when no definite term ... is specified ... [b]y the express will of all the partners who have not assigned their interests or suffered them to be charged for their separate debts... [and b]y the expulsion of any partner from the business bona fide in accordance with such a power conferred by the agreement between the partners...." Any partner can dissolve a partnership in contravention of the agreement but would be liable for damages resulting from this breach of the partnership agreement.

Dissolution would also be caused by any event that makes the partnership business unlawful; or by the death of a partner; by the bankruptcy of the partnership or any partner; or by decree of a court pursuant to UPA §32.

7.   Buy-Sell Provisions and Valuation

Buy-sell provisions and valuation present important problems that affect all business entities. The analysis will be similar whether the entity is a general partnership, limited partnership, limited liability company or Subchapter S or C corporation.

The ready susceptibility of partnerships to dissolution would seem to make them too unstable to be a satisfactory entity for transacting business. In fact, by careful planning and drafting this instability can be avoided for the most part. A well-drafted partnership agreement includes provisions for the continuation of the business, as well as buy-sell provisions and some form of valuation mechanism. Planning and drafting buy-sell provisions is complex and interesting. Some questions to consider would include the following.

a.   Should the partnership survive the death, incompetency or withdrawal of a partner? If the partnership is to survive the death of a partner, how should the deceased partner's estate be paid and to whom should the partnership interest be transferred?

b.   To the remaining partners pro rata? To the partnership? To third parties?

c.   May or must the partnership or partners purchase the interest? Where will the funds come from? Life insurance?

d.   What if a partner wishes to retire or becomes disabled? What if a partner wants to withdraw because of a personal financial crisis or divorce?

e.   What if there is dissension over how to run the business or whether to distribute profits that may be needed for expansion?

f.   Should different rules govern death, disability, unforeseen emergencies or business disputes?

It may be extremely important to avoid dissolution and the winding up of the partnership business, with liquidation of its assets, since a large portion of the value of the business may be its goodwill as a going concern which would then be lost. It may also be important to insure that disgruntled partners are not able to threaten or force the sale or dissolution of the partnership and liquidation of its assets.

There are two basic types of buy-sell provisions which may apply to general partnerships, limited partnerships, limited liability companies, C corporations and Subchapter S corporations. The first type is the redemption agreement, in which the entity may or must buy the departing owner's interest, and the second type is the cross-purchase agreement, in which some or all of the remaining owners may or must buy the departing owner's interest.

Generally, redemption agreements, in which the partnership entity purchases the departing partner's interest using the entity's funds, are often the easiest way to deal with partnerships with three or more partners. In cross-purchase agreements, the partners may agree to acquire one another's interest, either pro rata or according to a formula, and the remaining partners generally use their own funds for the purchase. This method can become cumbersome if there are multiple partners. Sometimes the methods are combined, with the partnership as a whole having a right of first refusal, followed by individual partners.

Agreements may be mandatory or optional for either the buyer or the seller. For mandatory agreements there is often a need to provide for funding the purchase.

Purchase rights or requirements may be triggered by death of a partner or by retirement, disability, expulsion, or voluntary withdrawal. Where death is the triggering event, life insurance proceeds are usually the designated source of funds. Optional plans not triggered by death of a partner, and not covered by life insurance policies can be risky since there is often no assurance that purchase funds will be available.

Buy-sell provisions and valuation methods are discussed in greater detail in Chapter 7.

Form 2: General Partnership Agreement

GENERAL PARTNERSHIP AGREEMENT

THIS PARTNERSHIP AGREEMENT (the "Agreement") is made this ____ day of _____ , 19___, between _____, _____, and _____ (hereinafter referred to collectively as the "Partners" and individually as a "Partner").

NOW, THEREFORE, the parties hereto agree as follows:

1. *Name and Business.* The parties do hereby form a New York general partnership (the "Partnership") to operate under the name of "_____" to (purposes to be stated here) and for the purpose of engaging in any and all businesses that a general partnership may lawfully engage in under the New York Uniform Partnership Act. The principal office of the business shall be at _____, New York, or at such other place as the managing partner shall select from time to time.

2. *Term.* The Partnership shall begin on the day and year first above written, and shall continue until terminated as herein provided.

Q: Would it be a good idea to provide a section of recitals, which are sometimes called "whereas" clauses? What might be included? That the partnership entity would be bound? That all partners were signing? That it was intended that any future partners would sign? When may a statement of the intent by the partners be useful?

Note: Be careful to name all parties correctly.

Q: Are any of the parties entities other than natural persons?

Note: Refer to each of the numbered provisions as sections or paragraphs and be consistent.

Q: In naming the partnership, will it be necessary to file a fictitious name certificate? Is the name deceptively similar to that of any other business?

Q: How specific should the purposes of the partnership be? Consider using very broad language.

Note: A vote of all partners will be necessary to do something in contravention of the express terms of the partnership agreement and this would include changing the partnership purposes.

Note: Be careful that the partnership does not commence doing business until any necessary licenses or permits are obtained.

Note: Cross index to sections of agreement which will provide for definite term. While a definite term may be express or implied, if none exists there is an "at will" partnership. The result is that

Form 2: General Partnership Agreement (continued)

any partner can dissolve the partnership without penalty, and the valuable going concern value of the enterprise can be lost. Coordinate term provisions with later transfer, buy-sell and continuation of the business provisions.

Q: Will any of the partners be making capital contributions other than in cash, i.e., "in kind"? How will such property or services be valued?

Note: The percentage interest is very important since many agreements will provide that voting power varies with percentage interest.

Note: The percentage interest will determine the partners' distributive share of profits and losses.

Q: Would there ever be any reason to allocate losses differently than profits?

Note: There is no requirement that partners must make additional capital contributions. What will happen if the business goes badly and more capital is required to avoid substantial loss of the initial capital? If one partner, perhaps the wealthiest, agrees to provide additional capital, how should this affect that partner's percentage interest for the purposes of voting rights and rights to profits? What about upon dissolution? Remember, it may not be fair to use the initial formula in determining what each additional dollar is entitled to because if the entire business was not worth less there might not be a need for additional capital.

3. *Capital.* The capital of the Partnership shall consist of cash contributions of Partners as follows:

PARTNER	CAPITAL CONTRIBUTION	PERCENTAGE INTEREST
_____	$_____	_____%
_____	$_____	_____%
_____	$_____	_____%
TOTALS:	$_____	100%

The Partners shall have such percentage interest in Partnership property, profits, losses, tax credits and other benefits and liabilities as is set forth beside their names above.

If at any time or times hereafter, the Partners should determine that further capital is required by the Partnership and that the capital of the Partnership should be increased, the additional capital required shall be contributed by the Partners as the Partners may agree and the percentage interests of the Partners shall be adjusted accordingly.

Form 2: General Partnership Agreement (continued)

4. *Accounts.* (a) A separate capital account should be maintained for each Partner, which shall be reflected on the books of the Partnership. The capital account of each Partner shall consist of each Partner's initial capital contribution increased by any additional contributions to capital.

(b) A separate income account shall be maintained for each Partner. Partnership profits and losses shall be charged or credited to the separate income account of each Partner. If a Partner has no credit balance in his, her or their income account, losses shall be charged to his, her or their capital account. At any time that a Partner shall have a negative balance in the Partner's income account the Partnership by vote of a majority in interest of the Partnership may require that the Partner pay all or any portion of such amount to the Partnership.

(c) No interest shall accrue on any capital or income account.

Q: Should the agreement provide for what will happen if a partner fails to make additional capital contributions?

Q: Is it a good idea to require that the partners vote unanimously to require additional capital contributions?

Q: What would be the practical effects of changing the percentage interests?

Q: Should the agreement provide for the separate treatment of loans to the partnership from a partner?

Note: It would be a good idea to specify more clearly what is meant by "as the partners may agree." This probably should mean by the vote of the partners owning a majority of the percentage interest of the partnership.

Note: There are two sets of equity accounts: Capital Accounts and Income Accounts. The Partnership assets minus Liabilities equals the sum of the partners' equity accounts.

Q: Should partners be allowed to make withdrawals from their capital accounts during the life of the partnership, or must this money remain available to the partnership for working capital? If the agreement provides that withdrawals cannot be made, would a unanimous vote of the partners be necessary to allow a partner to make a withdrawal? See Section 6 about "substantial matters and changes."

Note: Income accounts are really income and loss accounts. Profits and losses are allocated periodically to each partner's income

Form 2: General Partnership Agreement (continued)

account, generally according to each partner's percentage interest.

Note: A partner may be liable for income tax on his distributive share of profits even if no money is actually distributed. Cash flow and allocated profits are not the same thing.

Note: Each partner is liable for the obligations of the partnership to third parties. If one partner pays more than her share, she is entitled to contribution from the other partners according to their percentage interests. If they are judgment-proof, she is out of luck. How would this be reflected in capital accounts? Could a partner's capital account be negative?

Q: Why might it sometimes be a good idea to pay interest on income accounts?

Q: Should a partner always be allowed to withdraw the credit balance of an income account?

Q: What is the difference between salary and draw? Will any partners require regular payments or draws for their living expenses?

Note: By providing for managing partners it is possible to centralize much of the management.

Q: Are "substantial matters and change" overly vague? Would it be better to provide a list of non-exclusive exceptions?

Note: A vote of a majority in interest of the partnership is necessary for action within the ordinary course of business but unanimity is necessary for actions in

5. *Salaries and Draws.* No salaries shall be paid to Partners, except upon a written agreement signed by a majority in interest of the Partnership. Each Partner may, from time to time, withdraw the credit balance of his, her or their income account.

6. *Management of the Partnership.* (a) _____ and _____ shall be the initial managing partners and as such shall have exclusive day-to-day control of the business management of the Partnership. All "substantial matters and changes" relating to the business or affairs of the Partnership shall be determined by agreement of the Partners. Each managing partner shall devote substantially all his or her full time to the business of the Partnership. All matters specified as occurring on the basis of the agreement, permission, determination, or approval of the Partners shall be determined by vote of a majority in interest of the Partnership. A "substantial matter or change" shall be one which alters the ordinary affairs of the Partnership from the manner in which they had previously been carried on. It is the intent that the managing partners shall have the authority to conduct the ordinary and usual business of the Partnership. Each Partner

Form 2: General Partnership Agreement (continued)

shall have one vote for each percentage point representing his or her interest in the Partnership.

The managing partners shall conduct each vote, by soliciting the vote of each Partner either in writing or orally, and shall record the question voted upon and the tabulated vote on each issue in the Partnership records. In the event of a managing partner's resignation, removal or incapacity to act for any reason, the Partners shall by agreement name a successor managing partner.

Nothing shall authorize the managing partner or any other Partner to do any act detrimental to the best interests of the Partnership, or which would make it impossible to carry on the ordinary business of the Partnership. No Partner other than the two managing partners shall, without the approval of the other Partners, endorse any note, or act as an accommodation party, or otherwise become surety for any person.

(b) In the event of death, removal or inability to act of a managing partner, the successor managing partner shall be selected by a majority in interest of the remaining partners. Any managing partner may be removed at any time by the vote of a majority in interest of the Partnership.

(c) Each Partner other than a managing partner may have other business interests and may engage in any other business or trade, profession, or employment whatsoever, individually or in partnership with others or as an employee of, or as an officer, director of shareholder of any other person, firm or corporation, and such Partner shall not be required to devote his entire time to the business of the Partnership.

7. *Banking.* All funds of the Partnership shall be deposited in Partnership name in any checking account or accounts as shall be selected by the managing partners. All withdrawals therefrom are to be made upon checks signed by the managing partner or his designee. The managing partners are authorized to execute a partnership certificate required by a banking institution.

8. *Books and Records.* Accounts, books, and records shall be maintained at the principal office of the Partnership and be open for inspection by the Partners. The books of account shall be kept in accordance with generally accepted

---

contravention of the agreement. Unanimity is necessary for action on "substantial matters and changes."

Q: Does this result in an unacceptable risk of deadlock since it gives each partner a veto power?

Q: Are "substantial matters and changes" overly vague? Would it be better to provide a list of nonexclusive exceptions?

Q: What is an accommodation party? When might the partnership become a surety? Should there be a dollar limit?

Q: Each partner owes a fiduciary duty of loyalty to the partnership and the other partners. Here, since the nonmanaging partners may have other business activities, when might they compete with the partnership? Could this be clarified by using specific examples of the facts for a client? Would a non-compete provision be enforceable? What if it was in a law firm's partnership agreement?

Q: Should one managing partner be able to sign checks to make withdrawals regardless of amount?

Q: Are these rights any different from those provided in the statute?

Form 2: General Partnership Agreement (continued)

Note: Partners are fiduciaries and have rights to access books and records (UPA §19); true and full information (UPA §20) and are accountable as fiduciaries for any benefit received without the consent of all the partners (UPA §21) and have the right to an accounting (UPA §22).

Q: Will any real property be owned by a partner and leased to the partnership?

Note: Each partner owns an individual interest in all the partnership property, including real property, as tenants in partnership. A partner's partnership interest is always personal property.

Q: In the absence of this provision, what is a partner's statutory right of assignment?

Q: What is the legal effect, if any, of this provision?

Q: Does this provision assure that the partnership is not one at will? Does it assure that the enterprise will continue so that its value as a going concern cannot be lost by the owners?

Q: Must the vote to continue be unanimous?

Q: Do we need to provide for the possibility that a partner's income account might show a negative amount? Would this mean the amount of the capital account should be reduced?

Q: By not receiving any value for goodwill, is the retiring partner getting a fair return?

accounting principles. The fiscal year of the Partnership shall be the calendar year. The books will be closed and balanced at the end of each fiscal year of the Partnership. Each Partner will be entitled to receive within ninety (90) days after the expiration of each fiscal year a statement of receipts and expenses prepared by the Partnership's accountants, together with a statement showing the profits or losses of the Partnership for federal and state income tax purposes and the allocation thereof to each Partner determined by the certified public accountant regularly employed to service the Partnership.

9. *Title to the Partnership Property.* The title to any property owned by the Partnership shall be held in such manner as the Partners may determine.

10. *Assignment and Transfer.* (a) A Partner shall not mortgage, pledge, encumber, hypothecate, assign, sell or transfer all or any part of its interest in this Partnership without the prior written consent of a majority in interest of the other Partners.

(b) Any other purported sale or transfer by a Partner, other than those by operation of law, shall be null, void, and of no force and effect.

11. *Withdrawal, Death, and Retirement.* (a) Upon the withdrawal or retirement of any Partner, the Partnership shall not be terminated but shall continue. Any Partner may withdraw or retire from the Partnership at the close of any fiscal year. Upon such withdrawal or retirement, the remaining Partners shall have the right to continue the business of the Partnership under its present name by themselves, or in conjunction with any other person or persons they may select, but they shall pay to the withdrawing or retiring Partner the value of its interest in the Partnership as provided in subsection (b) of this Section 11. If the remaining Partners desire to continue business, but not together, the Partnership shall be liquidated in accordance with the provision of Section 13 below.

(b) The value of the interest of a retiring or withdrawing Partner as of the date of the withdrawal shall be the sum of
    (i) Partner's capital account, plus
    (ii) Partner's proportionate share of accrued, undistributed net profits which may be the balance set forth in his income account.

Form 2: General Partnership Agreement (continued)

If a net loss has been incurred by the Partnership to the date of withdrawal, the withdrawing or retiring Partner's share of such loss shall be deducted from the Partner's accounts. No value for good will or firm name shall be included in any computations of a Partner's interest under this Section 11.

12. *Dissolution and Termination of the Partnership.* The Partnership shall be deemed to have voluntarily dissolved upon the death, disability or insanity of a partner; or at any time that all remaining Partners shall agree to dissolve the Partnership, in which event the managing partners shall liquidate the Partnership.

13. *Liquidation.* On any voluntary dissolution, the Partnership shall immediately commence to wind up its affairs. The Partners shall continue to share profits and losses during liquidation in the same proportions as before dissolution. The proceeds from liquidation of Partnership assets shall be applied first to pay or provide for all debts of the Partnership, other than to Partners; then to pay or provide for all debts of the Partnership to Partners; then amounts owed to Partners for undistributed net profits; and finally the capital contributions of the Partners as reflected in their respective capital accounts. Any gain or loss on disposition of Partnership properties in the process of liquidation shall be credited or charged to the Partners in the proportion of their interests in profits or losses. Any property distributed in kind in the liquidation shall be valued and treated as though the property were sold and the cash proceeds were distributed. The difference between the value of property distributed in kind and the book value shall be treated as a gain or loss on sale of the property and shall be credited or charged to the Partners in the proportions of their interest in profits and losses. Should any Partner, including the estate or trust of a deceased Partner, have a negative balance in its capital amount, whether by reason of losses in liquidating Partnership assets or otherwise, such balance shall represent an obligation from him or her to the other Partners, to be paid in cash within six (6) months after written demand by the other Partners.

14. *Arbitration.* Any controversy or claim arising out of or related to this Agreement shall be settled by arbitration in accordance with the rules then obtaining of the American Arbitration Association, and judgment upon the award rendered may be entered without notice and enforced in any court having jurisdiction thereof.

Q: Is there any way to assure that the partnership will have liquid funds available to pay an outgoing partner the amounts in capital and income accounts?

Q: Shouldn't the remaining partners be able to continue the business?

Q: Should the partnership purchase life insurance on the life of each partner so that funds might be available to make payments to the deceased partner's estate?

Q: Is it possible to keep the deceased partner's interest out of the probated estate?

Q: Should managing partners be responsible for winding up?

Note: This assumes that no partner has made any withdrawal from a capital account.

Q: Are these provisions different from those set forth in the UPA?

Note: Much blood and ink have been spilled over whether to include an arbitration clause. The conventional wisdom is that arbitration is cheaper and quicker than litigation. It may be possible to agree to select an arbitrator

Form 2: General Partnership Agreement (continued)

with specific technical expertise and sophistication and the arbitration process may be less adversarial so that it may be easier for the parties to continue to work together in the future if that is necessary.

On the other hand, arbitration may be slow if the arbitrators decide to spread hearings over a long period of time. It may be necessary to go to court to enforce the arbitration agreement. The process of selecting an arbitrator may be slow and contentious. Paying for the arbitrator's hearing and preparation time may be very expensive, especially if there is a panel of more than one arbitrator. The informality of the process results in the loss of some procedural safeguards and arbitrator's awards cannot be judicially challenged on the grounds of mistakes applying the relevant law or facts. (See Norman Solovay, *The Business Break-Up* 28-29 (Practising Law Institute 1973)).

Note: These six miscellaneous provisions are standard and useful "boilerplate." Omitting any of them could at least raise the issue of whether the parties actually did not intend for them to apply.

15. *Miscellaneous.* (a) Any amendments or modifications of this Agreement, in order to be effective, must be in writing and executed by the Partners.

(b) Section headings herein are inserted only for convenience of reference, and shall in no way define, limit or prescribe the scope or extent of any provisions of this Agreement.

(c) Subject to the provisions hereof, the benefits of this Agreement and the burdens hereunder shall inure to and be binding upon the heirs, representatives, successors and assigns of the Partners.

(d) This Partnership Agreement shall be construed and interpreted according to the laws of the State of New York and specifically the provisions of the New York Uniform Partnership Act, except to the extent modified by the provisions hereof. In this regard, the Partners hereby waive any rights to seek a court decree of a dissolution or to seek the appointment of a court receiver for the Partnership.

Form 2: General Partnership Agreement (continued)

(e) All notices provided for under this Agreement shall be in writing and shall be sufficient if sent by registered or certified mail to the last known address of the party to whom such notice is to be given.

(f) The parties hereto covenant and agree that they will execute any further instruments and that they will perform any acts that are or may become necessary to effectuate and to carry on the Partnership created by this Agreement.

IN WITNESS WHEREOF, the parties hereto have hereunto set their hands the day and year first above written.

Witnesseth:

s/_____
GENERAL PARTNER

s/_____
GENERAL PARTNER

s/_____
GENERAL PARTNER

Q: What is the legal effect of the signatures under "Witnesseth?"

Q: Must the signatures be verified or acknowledged? What is the difference in meaning between these two terms?

Drafting Exercise 2:

Prepare a General Partnership Agreement

The Kent General Partnership

Henry Kent is a long time client of our firm. He is very wealthy and we have assisted him with many matters. Henry wants us to help him form a new general partnership to import, manufacture and sell clothes. The business will be managed by Henry's niece, Donna, and Linda Chen, who was Donna's roommate at the Harvard Business School. The partners will be:

> Henry Kent - age 60
> Donna Kent - age 30
> Linda Chen - age 30
> Otto Chen - age 60
> Hugo Chen - age 55

We do not yet have many details about the deal but we know the following:

1. Donna and Linda will be managing partners and will each be paid $30,000/year.

2. Henry will invest $100,000. Donna will invest $50,000.

3. From the Chen group, Linda, Otto and Hugo will each invest $50,000.

4. Henry will loan the partnership $150,000 on reasonable terms. He wants some security for the loan.

5. Henry has substantial passive income from other investments. This venture will have losses for at least two years and Henry would like to use these losses to offset his income. The other partners are not in this position.

6. Hugo is a 60-year-old retired business man and Otto is a 55-year-old accountant. Both are citizens of Hong Kong, but Otto lives in San Francisco.

7. The business will be operated in New York.

Use Form 2, General Partnership Agreement, as a starting point. Some important areas to think about include Capital (Section 3), Accounts (Section 4), Management (Section 6), Withdrawal, Death and Retirement (Section 11), Dissolution (Section 12), and Liquidation (Section 13).

The Chens will not be hiring their own attorney, and Henry wants us to prepare an agreement that is "fair to all parties." Will there be ethical problems with having the partnership entity? Are there any steps that we should take to be careful?

Practical Pointers

1. It is a good idea to include recitals, which need not take the form of "whereas" clauses. They help to cure possible ambiguity. It may also be useful to restate the terms of a prior oral partnership agreement under which a partnership may have been operating, and to ratify prior actions.

2. The way this form has been prepared, it is probably not a partnership at will, and can only be terminated with the consent of all the partners. See Section 12 of the agreement.

3. The allocation of loss differently than gain is more generally encountered with limited partnerships used for what were once called "tax shelters." These are now much less important than they were prior to 1986 because the amended Internal Revenue Code severely limits their availability. (See Chapter 4.) If losses are allocated differently, they must have substantial economic effect. If a partner is allocated a larger share of losses, and is able to deduct them against income tax liability, that partner's capital account will be reduced to indicate these losses and the partner will receive a smaller share of any profits upon dissolution unless there is a gain charge-back provision in the agreement.

4. As a practical matter, changing the partnership percentages will often engender bad feelings. It may be a better idea for wealthier partners to loan additional funds to the partnership. These loans can be secured by partnership assets.

5. It is possible to agree that the partnership or other partners will have a lien on the partnership interest of a partner who fails to make required contributions.

6. Partnership draw is not the same as salary. The Internal Revenue Service W-2 form must be prepared for employees who receive a salary, and deductions for payroll taxes and other items must be withheld. In contrast, a partner's draw is generally against future profits. If these are not realized, the future draw can be adjusted downward or the income account can be reduced.

7. "Substantial matter or change" in Section 6 is pretty vague. When you know the exact nature of the partnership business, it is a good idea to use more specific examples based upon a prediction of what might actually happen.

8. Carefully check the applicable state law to find out the extent to which non-competition agreements are enforced. Generally, only agreements with reasonable provisions are enforced and there is great disparity among states as to what is reasonable. Non-competition agreements among lawyers are unenforceable.

9. It is often a good idea to require more than one partner's signature for large checks.

10. Section 11, concerning withdrawal, death, and retirement, will cause the partnership to continue after events that would otherwise result in dissolution. It abrogates many of the provisions of the UPA. By using a provision like this, it is possible to establish reasonable continuity of existence for the partnership entity and avoid the loss of value of the entity as a "going concern."

11. Not including "going concern value" in determining the value of a partnership interest will often cause the interest to be undervalued.

12. It is possible to assure that funds will be available to buy out the interest of a deceased partner by purchasing insurance on the partner's life or by placing a share of profits in escrow for that purpose.

13. Check carefully to see to what exent the Revised Uniform Partnership Act of 1994 (RUPA) has been adopted in the relevant jurisdiction. While adoption of the new act may not change the result, there are areas of significant difference.

    a. RUPA treats the partnership as an entity and provides for certain public filings. This further underscores that an attorney may be the lawyer for the partnership entity and would have the duty, pursuant to ABA Model Rules of Professional Conduct, to the organization as the client, including the conflicts of interest under Rule 1.7 and the duty to report conduct in violation of the law which could be imputed to the organization, to the organization's highest authority under Rule 1.13. RUPA §201.

    b. The general partnership entity has become more stable and "dissolution" has been in part replaced by "dissociation" of a partner which does not yield the absolute right to demand a winding up of the partnership business.

    c. Fiduciary duties among partners have been somewhat reduced, especially in connection with formation, and made more specific.

    d. Individual partners have greater protection from the liabilities of the partnership. With certain exceptions, judgment creditors must first exhaust partnership assets before going after the assets of individual partners. RUPA§307(d). Partners are also now joint and severally liable. RUPA §306.

    e. Partnership property ownership interests have been simplified. See RUPA §203.

Drafting Exercise 3:

Prepare a Letter to General Partners Disclosing Potential Conflict of Interest

Prepare a letter to the members of the Kent and Chen groups of potential general partners (introduced in Drafting Exercise 2) who have asked you to prepare a Partnership Agreement for them. Assume that in the past you have only represented Henry Kent and that you have handled many matters for him, for many years.

Explain your potential conflict of interest and the conditions under which you can represent the partnership and not each individual partner.

How is the style and tone of client correspondence different from that of formal legal instruments such as partnership agreements, or memoranda prepared for lawyers, or briefs prepared for courts?

E. COLLECTING AGAINST AN INDIVIDUAL PARTNER FROM PARTNERSHIP PROPERTY: THE PARTNERSHIP CHARGING ORDER

If a judgment is taken against an individual partner personally but not against the partnership, the judgment creditor may seek to satisfy the judgment from the partner's share of the business, called the partnership interest.

A charging order is a statutorily created means for a judgment creditor to reach the debtor partner's beneficial interest in the partnership without risking dissolution of the partnership. The creditor becomes entitled to partnership distributions that would be made to the judgment debtor partner. The creditor has no direct right to the assets of the partnership. UPA §28. The judgment creditor petitions a court to issue a charging order which the creditor prepares for the judge to sign. The charging order is served on the partnership.

The order charges the interest of the debtor with payment of the unsatisfied portion of the judgment. If necessary, the court may appoint a receiver to collect the debt. At any time prior to foreclosure, the other partners may buy or redeem the debtor partner's interest, and they would have a fiduciary duty to pay fair value for their partner's interest. UPA §28(2). By giving the partners this opportunity, they can protect the partnership from unnecessary disruptions caused by the individual acts of partners.

The creditor need not pursue a partner's other assets before seeking a charging order. In the drafting exercise that follows a very angry judgment creditor is especially interested in charging her ex-spouse's partnership interest in order to embarass him professionally.

Form 3: Charging Order

Note: Seeking a charging order against a partnership interest after obtaining a judgment against a partner should not be confused with the doctrine of marshalling assets pursuant to which partnership creditors must satisfy a partnership's debts from partnership property before going after the partners individually.

Note: One must already be a judgment creditor to seek a charging order.

Note: Under RUPA §504(b) the charging order constitutes a lien.

CHARGING ORDER

On the _____ day of _____ of 19___, Plaintiff herein, presented a petition for a charging order; and the Court having considered the same finds: that on the _____ day of _____, of 19___, Plaintiff recovered in this cause a judgment against the Defendant in the sum of _____ together with costs and an attorney's fee in the amount of _____ which judgment draws interest on the entire judgment from the date thereof at the rate of nine percent (9%) per annum until paid; that such Judgment has now become final; that such Judgment has not been satisfied and the Plaintiff is entitled as a matter of right to a charging order against any interest of the Defendant in any partnership or joint venture in which he may be engaged, that Plaintiff's application alleges that Defendant is a partner with _____, a resident of _____ County, Missouri, in a partnership known as _____ ;

It is hereby Ordered by this Court that the interest of _____ as a partner in _____ and/or the interest of _____ in any other partnership or joint venture in which _____ has an interest be and the same is hereby subjected to a charging order pursuant to section 358.280 of the Revised Statutes of Missouri in favor of and for the benefit of _____.

It is Further Ordered by the Court that on or before the Monday following the expiration of ten days from the date of service of this order that _____and/or _____ shall file with the Clerk of this Court a sworn answer reporting to the Court all amounts distributable or payable at the time of the service of this Order and at all intervening times to _____ by _____ and/or _____ attributable to any interest of _____ in _____ and/or any other partnership or joint venture in which _____ has an interest with _____, and in such sworn answer and report to state the value at the time of the service of this Order, and at all intervening times, of both the capital and income and surplus account attributable to the interest of _____in said and/or any other partnership or joint venture in which _____ has an interest with _____ .

It is Further Ordered by the Court that _____ shall appear before this Court at a hearing set for the _____ day of _____ 19_____, at _____o'clock __.M., for the purpose of showing cause, if any, why an order of this Court should not be entered requiring him to pay over to _____ such amounts as may from time to time become payable or distributable to by reason of his interest in _____ and/or be reason of any other interest _____ may have in any other partnership or joint venture in which _____ now holds an interest or may hereafter hold an interest.

Form 3: Charging Order (continued)

It is Further Ordered by the Court that at the time of such hearing _____ produce a copy of the partnership agreement which may in anywise affect the interest of _____ as a partner in _____ and/or as partner in any other partnership or joint venture in which _____ has an interest.

It is Further Ordered by the Court that the Clerk issue a writ to serve notice of this Order on _____ personally and on _____ by leaving a copy thereof at the usual place of business of _____ at _____ .

Entered this _____ day of _____ , 19_____ .

_____
JUDGE

Note: It is possible that under RUPA §801(6)(ii) the judgment creditor is less likely to obtain termination of the partnership than under the 1914 act.

Drafting Exercise 4:

Prepare a Charging Order to Collect a Partner's Debt

Wong Child Support Collection

Linda Chen divorced her husband Sidney Wong on October 27, 1989. The divorce decree was filed on that date in Wyandotte County District Court, Kansas City, Missouri. Linda was awarded child support for her two children, Karen and Janet, in the amount of $600/month.

Sidney is a partner in the law firm of Wong, Davis & Wong. The firm has five partners and four associates. Their offices are located at One Grand Avenue, Suite 1419, Kansas City, Missouri.

As of September 1, 1994, Sidney has not paid child support for six months and is $3,600 in arrears. Sidney has ignored our letters and not returned our telephone calls. Linda Chen has asked us to prepare a Charging Order to be served on Wong, Davis & Wong.

Practical Pointers

1. The charging order is used to go after a general partner's partnership interest. It can only be used by a judgment creditor.

2. There is no requirement that the judgment creditor go after any of the general partner's other assets first.

3. Under RUPA it may be more difficult for the judgment creditor to force the eventual dissolution of the partnership. As a practical matter, even under the UPA, if payment to the judgment creditor of the partnership distributions that would have been paid to the judgment debtor partner are not sufficient to satisfy the judgment, the other partners would generally force some settlement. Under the UPA, partnership dissolution was seldom ordered by a court after a charging order was issued.

Notes

1. Hood & Mylan, Federal Taxation of Closely Held Corporations ch. 1 (CCH 1991) provides an excellent discussion of choice of entity issues.

2. Hood & Mylan, §1.05 at 20.

3. Liability exposure is unpredictable because it may be difficult to anticipate which of the acts that a partner performs will be found by a court to be within a partnership's business. Law firms, which traditionally were organized as general partnerships, faced tremendous malpractice liability after the savings and loan debacle (in which such eminent firms as Kaye, Scholer, Fierman, Hays & Handler and Jones, Day, Reaves & Pogue paid settlements of $41 million and $51 million, respectively). As a result, some states, beginning with Texas, allowed firms of professionals to pay a fee and register as Limited Liability Partnerships (LLPs) in which

partners are generally not liable for the malpractice of other partners in transactions in which they play no part. Malpractice insurance is often required. Currently, 18 states provide for registered limited liability partnerships, but not all these states allow professionals to utilize this entity.

4. Klein & Coffee, Business Organizations and Finance at 81 (5th ed. 1993).

Chapter 4

The Limited Partnership

A.   INTRODUCTION

The limited partnership does not exist at common law. It is entirely a creature of statute. The requirements for formation of a limited partnership vary from state to state, but they always involve filing with the state and payment of a fee. To insure limited liability in all relevant jurisdictions, it is also necessary to file in each state in which the limited partnership plans to do business. The certificate of limited partnership may contain a long list of information which must be disclosed. The modern trend, however, is away from detailed disclosure.

In a limited partnership there are two classes of partners. There must be at least one general partner, and any general partner is liable for partnership obligations. There can be one or more limited partners whose status is strictly that of investor, and whose liability for partnership debts and torts is limited to the amount of the limited partner's investment (unless the limited partnership agreement provides for a "capital call" pursuant to which additional investment by limited partners may be required).

B.   LIMITED LIABILITY AND TAX TREATMENT

In selecting an entity through which to do business, two preeminent concerns are the avoidance of personal liability and the avoidance, wherever possible, of double taxation. Accordingly, investment by limited partners can be attractive because these two goals are achieved. Two major drawbacks of the limited partnership are that there must be a general partner whose liability cannot be limited, and limited partners who participate in control of the partnership may become liable as general partners. The latter may not be a problem for limited partners who intend to act strictly as investors and do not intend to be involved in managing the business.

Traditionally, it was risky for limited partners to play any role in management. This problem, as well as the problem of the unlimited liability of the general partner, has been substantially ameliorated by the Revised Uniform Limited Partnership Act ("RULPA"). Great care is needed in relying on this uniform act because, unlike the Uniform Partnership Act ("UPA"), it has not been adopted by state legislatures in a consistent fashion. In addition, some states continue to rely on their adoption of the earlier Uniform Limited Partnership Act. Where strictly adopted, RULPA allows substantial safe harbors for activities by limited partners that do not result in their unlimited liability. The statute also makes clear that limited partnerships may use corporations as the sole general partner, thereby mitigating the problem of unlimited liability.

Pursuant to RULPA §303(a), a limited partner does not become generally liable for partnership obligations unless the limited partner is also a general partner, or she participates in the control of the business. Section 303(b) clarifies what activities do not constitute control. These include being an independent contractor, agent, or employee of the limited partnership; being an officer, director or shareholder of a general partner that is a corporation; consulting with or advising a general partner; acting as a surety for the partnership; bringing or pursuing a derivative action on behalf of a corporate general partner; requesting or attending a partnership meeting; proposing or approving or disapproving, by voting or otherwise, partnership actions including dissolution, sale of substantially all the partnership assets or borrowing not in the ordinary course of business; change of business or removal of a partner.

RULPA §303(a) also substantially reduces the liability exposure of limited partners who participate in control by providing that a limited partner who participates in control is only liable to persons who do business with the limited partnership reasonably believing that the limited partner is a general partner.

When organizing a corporate general partner, the normal precautions must be taken to avoid possible "piercing of the corporate veil." A separate concern is to make certain that the corporate general partner is sufficiently capitalized so that the limited partnership will not be taxed as a corporation, and thereby subject to double taxation. In Rev. Proc. 92-88, the Internal Revenue Service has stated that if the sole general partner is a corporation, its net worth must equal or exceed 10 percent of the total contributions to the limited partnership.

C.   LIMITED PARTNERSHIPS AS TAX SHELTERS

Prior to the 1986 changes in the Internal Revenue Code, limited partnerships were often used as a vehicle for tax shelters. Limited partnerships worked as tax shelters when an enterprise initially generated losses which could be allocated pro rata to limited partners and deducted against their other income. These losses were often merely "paper losses," since they may have been derived from devices like depreciation for ventures that may even have had positive cash flow. In the later, profitable years of the enterprise, the partnership's earnings were passed through to the limited partner investors without taxation at the limited partnership entity level, or even better, the limited partners could offset these profits with new passive losses from other limited partnership ventures.

After 1986, the tax code was changed so that each category of loss can only be deducted against income of the same category. There are now three categories of losses: active loss, portfolio loss (i.e., stocks and bonds) and passive loss (like losses by a limited partner in the limited partnership investment). Therefore, now most passive losses can only be deducted against passive income (from similar investments), thereby greatly reducing both the availability of tax shelters and the number of limited partnerships formed for that purpose.

Passive investors in ventures like real estate development, cattle and farming operations, and oil and gas exploration could at one time use limited partner status to get the benefits of both limited liability and the immediate write-off of their pro rata share of the entity's initial losses. This benefit was not available to corporate shareholders in a similar venture.

Form 4: Limited Partnership Agreement

LIMITED PARTNERSHIP AGREEMENT

THIS LIMITED PARTNERSHIP AGREEMENT (hereinafter the "Agreement") is made this day of _____, 19_____, by and among _____, of _____ (hereinafter "General Partners"), and _____, of _____ (hereinafter "Limited Partners").

The parties hereto, being desirous of associating themselves together, hereby form a Limited Partnership business (hereinafter the "Partnership") under the laws and State of New York under the following terms and conditions:

ARTICLE 1
Place of Business

1. The Partnership shall commence as of the day and year above written and shall continue until _____, or until earlier termination as provided herein.

2. The business of the Partnership shall be carried on under the name of _____, with such variations or changes therein as may be necessary in order to comply with the statutory requirements of the various states in which the Partnership does business.

3. The purpose of the business shall be to engage in the business of _____.

4. The principal place of business of the Partnership shall be at _____, and such other place of business as may from time to time be determined by the General Partners.

ARTICLE II
Capital Contributions and Accounts

1. _____ and _____ shall be the General Partners, and _____, _____, and _____ shall be the Limited Partners.

2. The General Partners shall contribute an aggregate of $_____ to the capital of the Partnership, as follows:

Q: Would it be helpful to include this information in the form of "Recitals?"

Q: If Henry Kent is only a limited partner, is it misleading to call this the Kent Limited Partnership? Does it make any difference that Donna Kent is a general partner? (*See* RULPA §303(8)(d)).

Note: To preserve limited liability, it will be necessary to research and satisfy the filing requirements for each state in which the entity does business.

Q: Do the limited partners desire a more narrowly drawn purposes clause to limit the power of the general partners?

Note: If appropriate, add that "the General Partners shall devote substantially all their time to management of the Partnership."

Note: Different provisions will be necessary if any partner's capital contribution will be property or services.

Form 4: Limited Partnership Agreement (continued)

_____ $_____
_____ $_____.

and the Limited Partners shall contribute an aggregate of $_____ to the capital of the Partnership, as follows:

_____ $_____
_____ $_____
_____ $_____.

Note: Consider putting a cap on the amount of additional capital that may be required. Also, perhaps greater than a majority vote should be necessary for a mandatory capital call.

3. Each General or Limited Partner shall make additional contributions to the capital of the Partnership in cash in such amounts as may from time to time be agreed upon by the vote of a majority in interest of the Partners.

4. An individual Cash Capital Account shall be maintained for each Partner to which shall be credited or debited his cash contributions or withdrawals and his undistributed share of net profits less his share of net losses.

Note: To avoid sexist language, replace "his" with "each Partner's." Be careful to be consistent throughout the document.

5. An individual Tax Capital Account shall be established and maintained for each Partner and shall be credited with the amount of each Partner's capital contribution to the Partnership. Any Partner whose interest in the Partnership is increased, by means of the transfer to such Partner of all or part of the interest of another Partner, shall have a Tax Capital Account that has been appropriately adjusted to reflect such transfer. Each Partner's Tax Capital Account shall be determined and maintained throughout the term of the Partnership in accordance with the requirements of Section 704(b) of the Internal Revenue Code of 1986, or its counterpart in any subsequently enacted Internal Revenue Code, and of the Treasury Regulations promulgated from time to time thereunder.

6. No Partner shall be entitled to interest on the Partner's capital contribution, or to withdraw any part of such contribution, or to receive any distributions from the Partnership, except as specifically provided in this agreement.

Note: Consider adding a provision covering loans by Partners to the Partnership.

ARTICLE III
Management, Salaries, Books of Account

1. The General Partners shall manage the Partnership business. Checks drawn on any Partnership bank account shall be signed by both the General Partners.

Q: What would happen if there were two general partners who could not agree? It is necessary to specify that the general partners vote equally or in proportion to their percentage ownership interest.

Q: In case of a deadlock of the general partners, may the deadlock be broken by vote of a numerical majority or majority in ownership interest of the limited partners? Would this right subject the

Form 4: Limited Partnership Agreement (continued)

limited partners to unlimited liability as having the right to participate in management or control or is it protected under the safe harbor provision, §303 of the RULPA?

Note: General Partners who are professional managers will require a salary which may either be drawn from Partnership profits, or which may be an expense of the Partnership to be deducted in determining the amount of profits.

Note: As provided in Article VI, Section 2, approval of a majority in ownership interest of the limited partners will be required for some partnership actions.

2. The General Partners shall not receive any salary.

3. The Limited Partners shall not take part in the management or control of the business or transact any business for the Partnership, and shall have no power to sign for or bind the Partnership. No salary shall be paid to the Limited Partners.

4. Proper and complete books of account of the Partnership business shall be kept by or under the supervision of the General Partners at the principal place of business of the Partnership and shall be open to inspection by any of the Partners, or by their representatives, at any time during the regular business hours.

ARTICLE IV
Fiscal Year, Statements of Account, Profits and Losses

1. The fiscal year of the Partnership shall be the calendar year. As of the close of each fiscal year, the General Partners shall make or cause to be made and distributed to the Limited Partners a full and detailed statement showing the operation of the Partnership business during such fiscal year, together with a true and correct statement of all income and disbursements during such year. For the purpose of determining net profits and losses of the Partnership, Partnership accounting shall be carried out in the same manner as for Federal income tax purposes and in accordance with generally accepted accounting principles.

2. The net profits earned by the Partnership during each fiscal year, including securities received by the Partnership, valued at fair market value, shall be allocated as of the close thereof among the partners in the following proportions:

Name	Ownership Percentage
_____	____%
_____	____%
_____	____%
_____	____%

Form 4: Limited Partnership Agreement (continued)

Before the net profits are so allocated, they shall first be credited to the Cash Capital Account of any Partner to the extent that, and in the order in which, such Accounts were previously debited because of net losses and have not been previously restored by allocations of net profits. Net profits in excess of the amounts required in the opinion of the General Partners for the operation of the Partnership business shall be distributed at the close of each fiscal year to the Partners in their respective interests as hereinabove set forth; but no distribution shall be made which would impair the capital of the Partnership. Undistributed net profits shall be credited to the respective Cash Capital Account of each Partner.

3. Net losses incurred by the Partnership during any fiscal year shall be allocated among the Partners in the following manner:

Losses shall first be debited in an equal amount to each Partner against any undistributed net profits in the Cash Capital Account of each Partner. If the undistributed net profits in the Cash Capital Accounts shall then be reduced to zero, any remaining net losses shall be debited against the remaining Cash Capital Account of the Limited Partners. Any remaining net losses shall then be debited against the remaining cash capital accounts of the General Partners, in an equal amount. Finally, any remaining net losses shall be allocated equally to the General Partners and shall be debited to their Cash Capital Accounts to create deficits therein.

Notwithstanding any of the foregoing to the contrary, no net losses shall be allocated to the Limited Partners that would cause a deficit in the Limited Partner's Cash Capital Account. In order to preserve, to the extent possible, the partners' economic arrangement, an under-allocation of net losses to the Limited Partners due to the foregoing limitation shall be taken into account in making subsequent allocation of net profits and net losses so that, to the extent possible, the total of all such allocations shall be equal to the amounts that would have resulted had such under allocation not occurred.

4. The Limited Partners shall not be personally liable for any debts of the Partnership or for any losses thereof beyond the amount contributed by them to the capital of the Partnership.

Note: "Notwithstanding any of the foregoing to the contrary...." may sound like classic legalese, but it is a cautious way to make certain when drafting that the provision it introduces will take precedence over any conflicting language in the document. Really careful drafters need not use it because they know that there is no contrary language in the agreement. Nevertheless, it can be used as a "belt and suspenders" provision for very important concerns.

Note: This language will not avoid liability for limited partners that are deemed to have participated in the control of the business. Note that in jurisdictions that have adopted it, RULPA §303(a) limits the general liability of such limited partners to third parties doing business with the partnership who reasonably believed that the limited partner was a general partner.

Form 4: Limited Partnership Agreement (continued)

Note: It may not be a good idea to allow dissolution without a provision for continuation of the business by vote of some percentage of the remaining partners.

Q: Under RULPA §704, what are the rights of the assignee of a limited partner's interest?

Note: For limited partnerships which are primarily tax-oriented, provisions for distributions and allocations of income, loss and cash flow may be very complex and varied. Ratios may also shift after limited partners have received a certain return on their investment. (See Robert W. Hamilton, Fundamentals of Modern Business at §13.5.1, at 311-312.)

ARTICLE V
Withdrawal, Death, Dissolution

1. Any Partner may withdraw from the Partnership at will.

2. The withdrawal, death, or insanity of any Partner shall cause the immediate dissolution of the Partnership.

3. Upon the dissolution of the Partnership for any reason, its liabilities and obligations to creditors shall be paid. A proper accounting shall be made of net profit or loss of the Partnership from the last previous accounting to the date of dissolution, and the net profit or loss shall be allocated as provided in Article IV. A property accounting shall be made of the Cash Capital Accounts of each Partner, and the assets of the Partnership shall be distributed to the Partners in accordance with their positive Tax Capital Account balances.

ARTICLE VI
Miscellaneous

1. No Partner shall assign any interest in the Partnership to any person without the consent of all other Partners. No person may be admitted to the Partnership without the consent of all the Partners.

2. The General Partners may not, without the consent of a majority in ownership interest of the Limited Partners:

(a) Assign, transfer, or pledge, any of the claims of, or debts due to, the Partnership except upon payment in full;

(b) Make, execute, or deliver any assignment for the benefit of creditors, or any bond, confession of judgment, security agreement, deed, guarantee, indemnity bond, surety bond, or contract to sell all or substantially all of the property of the Partnership;

(c) Amend this Agreement;

(d) Arrange the sale, lease, or other transfer of all or substantially all of the assets of the Partnership other than in the ordinary course of business;

(e) Incur indebtedness by the Partnership outside the ordinary course of business;

(f) Change the nature of the Partnership business;

(g) Remove a General Partner.

Form 4: Limited Partnership Agreement (continued)

IN WITNESS WHEREOF, the parties hereto have set their hands on the day and year first above written.

_____, General Partner

_____, General Partner

_____, Limited Partner

_____, Limited Partner

_____, Limited Partner

Drafting Exercise 5:

Prepare a Limited Partnership Agreement

Using the facts from Drafting Exercise 1, prepare a limited partnership agreement with Donna Kent and Linda Chen as general partners and Henry Kent, Otto Chen, and Hugo Chen as limited partners.

Redraft Article IV so that Henry Kent will be able to take advantage of all partnership losses for the first two years, and then recapture these losses when profits are eventually achieved.

Drafting Exercise 6:

Prepare a Limited Partnership Agreement with a Corporate General Partner

(To be used after Chapter 6 on forming corporations and Chapter 7 on control issues of corporations.)

Prepare a Limited Partnership Agreement with Henry Kent, Donna Kent, Linda Chen, Otto Chen, and Hugo Chen as limited partners and a corporate general partner managed by Donna Kent and Linda Chen. Include certain appropriate veto powers for the other limited partners in order to protect their investment and the balance of power between the Kent and Chen groups.

Practical Pointers

1.   It is necessary to satisfy filing requirements that vary from state to state. Generally, a Certificate of Limited Partnership must be filed with the Secretary of State or clerk of the county in which the limited partnership has its principal office. The certificate

generally includes the partnership name, character of the business, amount of capital contributions and information about the rights of the partners. Some states, including New York, have a publication requirement.

2. The form of the Limited Partnership Agreement was drafted pursuant to the provisions of RULPA, especially in connection with the powers of the limited partners. Check carefully to see if RULPA has been adopted in the jurisdiction in which the limited partnership is to be organized, paying particular attention to §303. RULPA, unlike UPA, has not been adopted consistently in many jurisdictions.

3. A general partnership may add limited partners when trying to attract investments from persons who do not wish to be involved in managing the partnership business. Also, retiring general partners who no longer want to be involved in management may wish to become limited partners and continue to participate in partnership profits.

4. In the Kent Partnership, Henry Kent is the only investor with passive income against which he can write off the limited partnership's projected losses for its first two years. As discussed in Chapter 3, Practical Pointer 3, these loss allocations must have "substantial economic effect." If we expect the venture to lose money for its first two years of operation, we can allocate to Henry Kent, in Article IV, all of the partnership losses for the first two years of operations, and doing so will have substantial economic effect because his cash capital account will be reduced by these amounts. Once the venture is profitable, this account will be replenished pursuant to a "Loss Recapture Provision" and Henry will have taxable gains in the future. Nevertheless, he will have the losses now, and he may be able to shelter the gains in the future by offsetting them with other passive losses. At the least, he will be effectively receiving an interest-free loan from the government by not having to pay these taxes now.

Sample language could be:

For the first two years of operations, all losses shall be debited against the cash capital account of Henry Kent, but not below $0.00. Losses in excess of Henry Kent's cash capital account shall be charged against the remaining Partners in the manner provided for in this Agreement for years other than the initial two years of operations.

A loss charge-back provision should also be included, pursuant to which profits would first be credited to Henry Kent's cash capital account to reimburse him for losses he took at the outset.

Chapter 5

The Limited Liability Company

A.   LIMITED LIABILITY COMPANIES

The limited liability company is a new business entity of enormous importance that is entirely a creature of statute. As of October 1995, only three states have not yet adopted legislation allowing formation of limited liability companies. Limited liability companies can provide flow-through tax treatment, like partnerships, but all the investors can retain limited liability and the right to be involved in management and operations. When the author began teaching business planning four years ago, the limited liability company was scarcely worth a mention. Within five years, it may largely replace closely held corporations and partnerships as the business entity of choice.

The continued vitality of the limited liability company became clearer in early 1995 when the Internal Revenue Service issued Rev. Proc. 95-10 providing guidelines for the taxation of limited liability companies as partnerships. The Internal Revenue Service has ruled that business entities that have more than two of the following four corporate attributes — (1) liability limited to the entity's property, (2) free transferability of interests, (3) continuity of life and (4) centralized management — will be subject to corporate taxation. *See* Treas. Reg. §301.7701-2.

Because limited liability companies are formed to provide limited liability to investors, called "Members," planners must be careful that the entity not have more than one of the three remaining corporate attributes. Some states, such as Colorado and Virginia, have adopted statutes that require unanimous approval of remaining Members, after losing a Member, in order for the company to continue in business, and unanimous approval of Members before a transferee of a Member's interest is entitled to membership and management rights. This type of statute is called "bullet proof" because there is no flexibility for planners and the companies will always lack continuity of life and free transferability of interests. Limited liability companies in these states will always lack these corporate attributes and will not be taxed as corporations.

The limited liability company's existence generally begins when the document titled Articles of Organization (in Delaware, "Certificate of Formation") is filed with the Secretary of State. This document is very similar to corporate Articles of Incorporation. In addition to this public document, a private Operating Agreement, something like a cross between a general partnership agreement and corporate bylaws, is executed by all the Members. Many states, including Delaware and Michigan, have enacted flexible statutes. Planners forming the companies can select which two corporate attributes they desire when preparing these documents.

Lawyers must carefully examine each state's statute to determine what must be included in Articles of Organization and what may be provided in the Operating Agreement. Many of the same concerns are addressed in drafting these documents as in drafting partnership agreements, but there is the additional concern, under non-bullet proof statutes, of not including more than two of the four corporate attributes.

Unlike general partners, limited liability company members' exposure is limited to the amount of their investment, but they get the same tax advantages as general partners. Limited liability companies are taxed as flow-through entities, and investors avoid the problem of double taxation, first at the entity and then at the individual investor level. In a general partnership, each partner is an agent who can bind the partnership and the other partners for activities within the scope of the partnership business. This is not true for Members of a limited liability company. Another important advantage is that a limited liability company Member who withdraws will not be liable to creditors the way a withdrawing general partner is.

Unlike limited partners, all the investors in a limited liability company can have the right to participate in management, and there is no requirement that there be a person, like a general partner in a limited partnership, who is exposed to unlimited liability. There is also little danger that Members of a well-planned limited liability company could lose their limited liability.

Of great importance, the limited liability company is not subject to the rigid restrictions on the number and type of investors that apply to S corporations. Members may be corporations, trusts, and foreign nationals. It is possible effectively to have more than one class of equity security. It is also possible to make flexible partnership-type tax allocations.

Form 5: Certificate of Formation for a Delaware LLC

CERTIFICATE OF FORMATION
OF

_____

1. The name of the limited liability company is

_____

Note: In Delaware, the name must include "Limited Liability Company" or "L.L.C." It may contain the name of a Member or Manager. (§18-102).

Note: It is possible to reserve a name. (§18-103).

2. The address of its registered office in the State of Delaware is _____

_____

The name of its registered agent at such address is

_____

Note: Corporate service companies like CT Corporation System can be hired to supply an address in Delaware, and to act as registered agent. The address need not be the same as the LLC's actual place of doing business.

(Use the following paragraph only if the company is to have a specific date of dissolution.)

3. The latest date on which the limited liability company is to dissolve is _____.

Note: The Operating Agreement may specify a dissolution date, or dissolution shall occur 30 years from the date of formation. (§18-801).

Note: The LLC may carry on any lawful business, purpose or activity except insurance or banking. (§18-106).

3 or 4.

(Insert any other matters the Members determine to include herein. For instance, this Certificate may be made effective on a date or time later than that of filing. If a later effective date is desirable, set forth as an additional item: "This Certificate of Formation shall be effective on _____ (date).")

Note: The Articles of Organization once filed are public documents. Information not required by the state statute for inclusion in the Articles, when set forth in the Operating Agreement, can remain confidential.

Form 5: Certificate of Formation for a Delaware LLC (continued)

Note: The Certificate must be signed by a "person" defined as "a natural person, partnership (whether general or limited and whether domestic or foreign), limited liability company, foreign limited liability company, trust, estate, association, corporation, custodian, nominee or any other individual or entity in its own or any representative capacity." (§18-101).

Note: One signed original must be filed with the Secretary of State, together with a fee of $50.00. (§18-1105).

Note: "Substantial compliance" is recognized.

Q: Must the filing be verified? Must it be acknowledged?

Q: Can there be a limited liability company formed in Delaware with only one Member?

IN WITNESS WHEREOF, the undersigned have executed this Certificate of Formation of

_____

this _____ day of _____ , 19___.

_____
Member

_____
Member

_____
Member

B.   THE OPERATING AGREEMENT

The limited liability company Operating Agreement governs the relationship of the limited liability company Members. A written agreement is not
required in all states, but it would be extremely poor practice not to provide one. Each state statute has numerous default provisions which govern in the absence of contrary provisions in the Articles of Organization or
the Operating Agreement. As with the Uniform Partnership Act, many of
these default provisions would not be what the Members would have
selected. Operating Agreements typically deal with issues involving management of the limited liability company, distributions, and assignment of
membership interests.

In preparing the Operating Agreement for a limited liability company not formed in a state with a "bullet proof" statute, great care must be
taken to avoid risking corporate tax liability for entities having more than
one of the attributes of centralized management, continuity of existence
and free transferability of interests.

Two factors make preparing a limited liability company organizing
agreement more difficult than preparing a partnership agreement. First,
the statutory provisions of the states that have enacted statutes are not
nearly as consistent as those of the Uniform Partnership Act. Second, if
under the relevant state law, more than two of the four corporate characteristics may be found, there is the significant risk of losing the flow-
through tax treatment that is generally the reason for choosing to do
business as a limited liability company.

An entity will have centralized management if any person (or group
not including all Members) has continuing exclusive authority to make
management decisions. *See* Treas. Regs. §301.7701-2(c)(1). There is no centralized management unless the Managers have the sole authority to make
decisions. *See* Treas. Regs. §301.7701-2(c)(4). In Delaware, in the absence of
a contrary provision, there is Member management with each Member
having voting rights in proportion to the Member's current percentage in
the limited liability company's profits, with majority rule of such Members' percentage interests controlling. In Delaware, the Operating Agreement may provide for management by hired Managers rather than by
Members. Managers need not be Members, and their right to manage is an
indication of centralized management.

An entity will lack continuity of life if death, insanity, bankruptcy,
retirement, resignation, or expulsion of any Member will cause dissolution. Treas. Regs. §301.7701-2(b)(1). When the state statute, like
Delaware's, provides that the death or withdrawal of any Member causes
a dissolution (§18-801), there is generally no continuity of life unless the
Operating Agreement provides that the business will be continued by the
remaining Members. Treas. Regs. §301.7701-2(b)(2). There is no continuity
of life if the Members merely have the right to elect to continue the business.

An entity will have free transferability of interests if each Member
has the power, without the consent of the other Members, to substitute a
non-member. There is no free transferability if a Member can assign only
the Member's right to share in profits but not the right to participate in

management. Treas. Regs. §301.7701-2(e)(1). The requirement of approval of a majority in percentage interest of the Members does not constitute free transferability. In Delaware, in the absence of a contrary provision in the Operating Agreement, unanimous approval is required.

The following form is especially interesting because it provides alternative provisions for centralized management, free transferability of interests, and continuity of life.

Form 6: Limited Liability Company Operating Agreement

**OPERATING AGREEMENT
FOR**

_____

LIMITED LIABILITY COMPANY (L.L.C. or L.C.)

A Michigan Limited Liability Company

THIS OPERATING AGREEMENT is made and entered into as of _____, 199__ by and among the _____ Limited Liability Company (or L.L.C. or L.C.), a Michigan Limited Liability Company (the "Company"), and the persons executing this Operating Agreement as members of the Company and all of those who shall hereafter be admitted as members (individually, a "Member" and collectively, the "Members") who agree as follows:

ARTICLE I
Organization

1.1 *Formation.* The Company has been organized as a Michigan Limited Liability Company under and pursuant to the Michigan Limited Liability Company Act, being Act No. 23, Public Acts of 1993 (the "Act"), by the filing of Articles of Organization ("Articles") with the Department of Commerce of the State of Michigan as required by the Act.

1.2 *Name.* The name of the Company shall be the _____ Limited Liability Company (or L.L.C. or L.C.). The Company may also conduct its business under one or more assumed names.

1.3 *Purposes.* The purposes of the Company are to engage in any activity for which Limited Liability Companies may be formed under the Act (including (insert specific purposes)). The Company shall have all the powers necessary or convenient to effect any purpose for which it is formed, including all powers granted by the Act.

Note: Footnotes from the original have been omitted, but some of this information has been included in the annotations.

Note: This is an excellent form but it is drafted for use in *Michigan*. The drafting exercises at the end of the chapter are set in *Delaware*. Study and compare the Michigan and Delaware statutes before attempting to complete the drafting exercises.

Note: Frequently, in practice, lawyers adapt forms from other jurisdictions and must therefore apply the appropriate law.

Note: Owners of the LLC are referred to as "Members."

Note: In Delaware, this is Chapter 18 Limited Liability Company Act.

Note: The Delaware statute does not require a particular form of Operating Agreement, but it may contain the items included in the statutory definition. (§18-101(6)).

Note: In Delaware the name must include "Limited Liability Company" or "L.L.C."

Q: In Delaware, can you use the name of a Member or Manager? Can it be called an "Association" or "Society"?

Q: What are good reasons to specify purposes or powers?

Q: What purposes are prohibited in Delaware?

Form 6: Limited Liability Company Operating Agreement
(continued)

Note: In Delaware, duration cannot exceed 30 years. In Article IX below, we will address the issue of continuity of existence.

Q: Must this be the same as the limited liability company's place of business?

Q: How can a LLC register as a foreign LLC in Delaware? *See* §18-902.

Q: What are the penalties for doing business without registering? *See* §18-907.

Note: This may be included because the agreement resembles a partnership agreement and the Members certainly do not want to be liable as partners.

Q: What legal effect will this provision probably have?

Q: When is a Member or Manager an agent of the LLC for purposes of its business?

Q: If the LLC is using a company like CT Corporation System to provide an address in Delaware, should books and records be kept there?

Q: Will the LLC have Managers or will it be managed by its Members? *See* Article VII below, in which we will address the issue of centralized management.

1.4 *Duration.* The Company shall continue in existence for the period fixed in the Articles for the duration of the Company or until the Company shall be sooner dissolved and its affairs wound up in accordance with the Act or this Operating Agreement.

1.5 *Registered Office and Resident Agent.* The Registered Office and Resident Agent of the Company shall be as designated in the initial Articles or any amendment thereof. The Registered Office and/or Resident Agent may be changed from time to time. Any such change shall be made in accordance with the Act. If the Resident Agent shall ever resign, the Company shall promptly appoint a successor.

1.6 *Intention for Company.* The Members have formed the Company as a Limited Liability Company under and pursuant to the Act. The Members specifically intend and agree that the Company not be a partnership (including a limited partnership) or any other venture, but a Limited Liability Company under and pursuant to the Act. No Member or Manager shall be construed to be a partner in the Company or a partner of any other Member, Manager or person and the Articles, this Operating Agreement and the relationships created thereby and arising therefrom shall not be construed to suggest otherwise.

ARTICLE II
Books, Records and Accounting

2.1 *Books and Records.* The Company shall maintain complete and accurate books and records of the Company's business and affairs as required by the Act and such books and records shall be kept at the Company's Registered Office.

2.2 *Fiscal Year; Accounting.* The Company's fiscal year shall be the calendar year. The particular accounting methods and principles to be followed by the Company shall be selected by the Managers from time to time.

2.3 *Reports.* The Managers shall provide reports concerning the financial condition and results of operation of the Company and the Capital Accounts of the Members to the Members in the time, manner and form as the Managers determine. Such reports shall be provided at least annually as soon as practicable after the end of each calendar year and shall include a statement of each Member's share of profits and other items of income, gain, loss, deduction and credit.

Form 6: Limited Liability Company Operating Agreement (continued)

2.4 *Member's Accounts.* Separate Capital Accounts for each Member shall be maintained by the Company. Each Member's Capital Account shall reflect the Member's capital contributions and increases for the Member's share of any net income or gain of the Company. Each Member's Capital Account shall also reflect decreases for distributions made to the Member and the Member's share of any losses and deductions of the Company.

ARTICLE III
Capital Contributions

3.1 *Initial Commitments and Contributions.* By the execution of this Operating Agreement, the initial Members hereby agree to make the capital contributions set forth in the attached Exhibit A. The interests of the respective Members in the total capital of the Company (their respective "Sharing Ratios," as adjusted from time to time to reflect changes in the Capital Accounts of the Members and the total capital in the Company) is also set forth in Exhibit A. Any additional Member (other than an assignee of a membership interest who has been admitted as a Member) shall make the capital contribution set forth in an Admission Agreement. No interest shall accrue on any capital contribution and no Member shall have any right to withdraw or to be repaid any capital contribution except as provided in this Operating Agreement.

Q: Are there any types of specific information required by the Members in this particular business?

Q: Should this be changed to provide for income as well as capital accounts as general partnership agreements often provide?

Note: For clarity, Exhibit A can list the names of initial Members, their respective commitments, initial capital contributions and proportionate percentage interests in profits. It can provide for additional capital contributions.

Note: If property rather than cash is contributed, it must be given a cash value.

Note: The respective Sharing Ratios are very important for determining allocations, distributions and voting.

Note: An admission agreement is a good way to provide that new Members will be bound by the Operating Agreement and will make required capital contributions.

Note: In the absence of agreement, voting rights will be governed by the state statute. Statutes may provide for voting in the same proportion as capital contributions, interest in profits or that each Member gets one vote.

Note: In Delaware, contributions may be in cash, property, services rendered, by promissory note, obligation to contribute cash or services. (§18-501).

Q: Could an ownership interest be issued in a Delaware company in exchange for a promise to provide future services?

Form 6: Limited Liability Company Operating Agreement (continued)

Note: This assumes the Company will be managed by Managers rather than by Members.

Note: In Delaware, unless otherwise provided in the Operating Agreement, each Member is obligated to perform any promise to contribute cash, property or services. If the Member fails to do so, the LLC has the option to force the Member to contribute the cash equivalent of his or her promised contribution. The Member's obligation to contribute may be compromised only by consent of all Members. The statute also has a "reasonable reliance" provision to protect third party creditors. The Operating Agreement could be drafted to subject the breaching Member to penalties, including: reducing or eliminating his or her LLC interest share; subordinating his or her LLC interest to non-defaulting Member LLC interests; forced sale of his or her LLC interest; forfeiture of his or her LLC interest; lending by other Members of the amount needed to meet his or her commitment; fixing of the value of his or her LLC interest by formula or appraisal and redemption or sale of his or her interest at such value; or any other penalty or consequence. (§18-502).

3.2 *Additional Contributions.* In addition to the initial capital contributions, the Managers may determine from time to time that additional capital contributions are needed to enable the Company to conduct its business and affairs. Upon making such a determination, notice thereof shall be given to all Members in writing at least ten (10) business days prior to the date on which such additional contributions are due. Such notice shall describe, in reasonable detail, the purposes and uses of such additional capital, the amounts of additional capital required, and the date by which payment of the additional capital is required. Each Member shall be obligated to make such additional capital contribution to the extent of any unfulfilled commitment. Any Member who has fulfilled that Member's commitment shall have the right, but not the obligation, to make the additional capital contributions needed according to that Member's Sharing Ratio.

3.3 *Failure to Contribute.* If any Member fails to make a capital contribution when required, the Company may, in addition to the other rights and remedies the Company may have under the Act or applicable law, take such enforcement action (including the commencement and prosecution of court proceedings) against such Member as the Managers consider appropriate. Moreover, the remaining Members may elect to contribute the amount of such required capital themselves according to their respective Sharing Ratios. In such an event, the remaining Members shall be entitled to treat such amounts as an extension of credit to such defaulting Member, payable upon demand, with interest accruing thereon at the rate of _____% per annum until paid, all of which shall be secured by such defaulting Member's interest in the Company, each Member who may hereafter default, hereby granting to each Member who may hereafter grant such an extension of credit, a security interest in such defaulting Member's interest in the Company.

Form 6: Limited Liability Company Operating Agreement (continued)

ARTICLE IV
Allocations and Distributions

4.1 *Allocations.* Except as may be required by the Internal Revenue Code of 1986 as amended or this Operating Agreement, net profits, net losses, and other items of income, gain, loss, deduction and credit of the Company shall be allocated among the Members in accordance with their Sharing Ratios.

4.2 *Distributions.* The Managers may make distributions to the Members from time to time. Distributions may be made only after the Managers determine, in their reasonable judgment, that the Company has sufficient cash on hand which exceeds the current and the anticipated needs of the Company to fulfill its business purposes (including, needs for operating expenses, debt service, acquisitions, reserves and mandatory distributions, if any). All distributions shall be made to the Members in accordance with their Sharing Ratios. Distributions shall be in cash or property or partially in both, as determined by the Managers. No distribution shall be declared or made if, after giving it effect, the Company would not be able to pay its debts as they become due in the usual course of business or the Company's total assets would be less than the sum of its total liabilities plus, the amount that would be needed if the Company were to be dissolved at the time of the distribution, to satisfy the preferential rights of other Members upon dissolution that are superior to the rights of the Members receiving the distribution.

ARTICLE V
Disposition of Membership Interests

5.1 *General.* Every sale, assignment, transfer, exchange, mortgage, pledge, grant, hypothecation or other disposition of any membership interest shall be made only upon compliance with this Article. No membership interest shall be disposed of if the disposition would cause a termination of the Company under the Internal Revenue Code of 1986, as amended; without compliance with any and all state and federal securities laws and regulations; and unless the assignee of the membership interest provides the Company with the information and agreements that the Managers may require in connection with such disposition. Any attempted disposition of a membership interest in violation of this Article is null and void *ab initio.*

Note: The Operating Agreement may, of course, provide that the Members could make these decisions.

Note: In Delaware, in the absence of an agreement to the contrary, the allocation of profits and losses, and the distribution of cash and other assets, is done on the basis of the agreed value of contributions made by each Member and reserved by the LLC (§§18-503, 18-504).

Q: Would it be a good idea to require mandatory distributions based upon certain criteria? If distributions are not made, would it be possible for a Member to be liable for taxes on profits not yet distributed to the Member?

Note: The provision has been drafted for a LLC for which there is centralized management. Accordingly, this Article has been drafted not to provide for free transferability of interests. Following this Article will be an Alternative Article V that will provide for free transferability of interests.

Q: What is the legal effect of agreeing that disposal of a Member's interest shall be void *ab initio*?

Note: In Delaware, in the absence of an agreement, a Member may withdraw upon six months' written notice. (§18-603).

Form 6: Limited Liability Company Operating Agreement (continued)

Note: The assignee of a Member's interest is only entitled to receive distributions and does not become a Member. This is similar to the rights of an assignee of a general partner's interest.

Q: In what situations would you provide that Members could not even assign their right to receive distributions?

Note: By requiring unanimous consent there can be no finding that interests are freely transferable.

Q: Would there be free transferability for tax purposes if Members provided in the Agreement that they would consent to the assignment of a Member's interest including management rights, but that failure to do so would only be subject to an action for damages but not for specific performance?

Q: Practically speaking, would there be much market for most LLC membership interests? Would it be a good idea to provide for buy-sell provisions similar to those used for partnerships and closely held corporations?

Q: Would a Member's interest in a LLC in which management is not vested in one or more Managers be a security for purposes of state or federal laws regulating the sale or exchange of securities?

Note: Voting will be in accordance with Sharing Ratios. The statute allows voting by Members on a per capita, number, financial interest, class, group or any other basis. (§18-302(b)).

5.2 *Permitted Dispositions.* Subject to the provisions of this Article, a Member may assign such Member's membership interest in the Company in whole or in part. The assignment of a membership interest does not itself entitle the assignee to participate in the management and affairs of the Company or to become a Member. Such assignee is only entitled to receive, to the extent assigned, the distributions the assigning Member would otherwise be entitled to.

5.3 *Admission of Substitute Members.* An assignee of a membership interest shall be admitted as a substitute Member and shall be entitled to all the rights and powers of the assignor only if the other Members unanimously consent. If admitted, the substitute Member has, to the extent assigned, all of the rights and powers, and is subject to all of the restrictions and liabilities, of a Member.

ALTERNATIVE ARTICLE V
Disposition of Membership Interests

A.5.1 *General.* Each Member or those Members owning substantially all of the interests in the Company shall have the power, without the consent of other Members, to substitute for themselves in the Company, a person who is not a Member of the Company thereby conferring upon the substituted Member, all the attributes of the transferring Member's interest in the Company. Such person shall be admitted as a substitute Member and shall be entitled to all the rights and powers of a Member. The substitute Member shall also thereafter be subject to all of the restrictions and liabilities of a Member.

ARTICLE VI
Meetings of Members

6.1 *Voting.* All Members shall be entitled to vote on any matter submitted to a vote of the Members. Notwithstanding the foregoing, the Members shall have the right to vote on all of the following: (a) the dissolution of the Company pursuant to Paragraph 9.1(c) of this Operating Agreement; (b) the merger of the Company; (c) a transaction involving an actual or potential conflict of interest between a Manager

Form 6: Limited Liability Company Operating Agreement (continued)

and the Company; (d) an amendment to the Articles; or (e) the sale, exchange, lease or other transfer of all or substantially all of the assets of the Company other than in the ordinary course of business.

6.2 *Required Vote.* Unless a greater vote is required by the Act or the Articles, the affirmative vote or consent of a majority of the Sharing Ratios of all the Members entitled to vote or consent on such matter shall be required.

6.3 *Meetings.* An annual meeting of Members, for the transaction of such business as may properly come before the Meeting, shall be held at such place, on such date and at such time as the Managers shall determine. Special meetings of Members for any proper purpose or purposes may be called at any time by the Managers or the holders of at least ten percent (10%) of the Sharing Ratios of all Members. The Company shall deliver or mail written notice stating the date, time, place and purposes of any meeting to each Member entitled to vote at the meeting. Such notice shall be given not less than ten (10) nor more than sixty (60) days before the date of the meeting. All meetings of Members shall be presided over by a Chairperson who shall be a Manager so designated by the Managers.

6.4 *Consent.* Any action required or permitted to be taken at an annual or special meeting of the Members may be taken without a meeting, without prior notice, and without a vote, if consents in writing, setting forth the action so taken, are signed by the Members having not less than the minimum number of votes that would be necessary to authorize or take such action at a meeting at which all membership interests entitled to vote on the action were present and voted. Every written consent shall bear the date and signature of each Member who signs the consent. Prompt notice of the taking of action without a meeting by less than unanimous written consent shall be given to all Members who have not consented in writing to such action.

ARTICLE VII
Management

7.1 *Management of Business.* The Company shall be managed by _____ persons ("Managers") who shall be designated by resolution by the Members. The terms, duties, compensation and benefits, if any, of the Managers shall be determined by the Members. The Managers shall serve at the will and pleasure of the Members.

Q: Should there be super majority voting requirements for certain actions? Will Members insist on veto power?

Note: There is no statutory requirement in Delaware that annual meetings be held.

Note: It is a good idea to provide for action by consent without a meeting.

Note: This Article provides for centralized management as the second corporate attribute of this LLC. If either the attribute of free transferability of interests or continuity of life is elected, this Article cannot be used. The following Alternative Article VII does not provide for centralized management.

Note: In the absence of an agreement to the contrary, the Delaware statute provides

Form 6: Limited Liability Company Operating Agreement
(continued)

that the LLC will be managed by its Members, with each Member having voting rights in proportion to the Member's current percentage in LLC profits, with majority rule of such percentage controlling.

Note: If the LLC Agreement provides for Manager management: (1) Members choose Manager(s) per the LLC agreement, and (2) Members set out Manager(s) duties in the LLC agreement. Under §18-602, a Manager may resign per the LLC agreement, but the LLC agreement may prohibit a Manager from resigning.

The Manager may still resign by giving written notice to Members and Managers, and if the Manager resigns in violation of the LLC agreement, the LLC may recover damages for breach of contract and offset any award against amounts distributable to the resigning Manager.

Q: Should the Operating Agreement provide that Managers be selected by majority vote of Members? Should there be any requirement as to qualification of Managers? Can a Member also be a Manager?

Note: In Delaware, in the absence of an agreement to the contrary, one or more Managers can be removed without cause.

Q: Should there be any limitation on the powers delegated to the Managers?

7.2 *General Powers of Managers.* Except as may otherwise be provided in this Operating Agreement, the ordinary and usual decisions concerning the business and affairs of the Company shall be made by the Managers.

Each Manager has the power, on behalf of the Company, to do all things necessary or convenient to carry out the business and affairs of the Company, including the power to: (a) purchase, lease or otherwise acquire any real or personal property; (b) sell, convey, mortgage, grant a security interest in, pledge, lease, exchange or otherwise dispose or encumber any real or personal property; (c) open one or more depository accounts and make deposits into and checks and withdrawals against such accounts; (d) borrow money, incur liabilities and other obligations; (e) enter into any and all agreements and execute any and all contracts, documents and instruments; (f) engage employees and agents, define their respective duties, and establish their compensation or remuneration; (g) establish pension plans, trusts, profit sharing plans and other benefit and incentive plans for Members, employees and agents of the Company; (h) obtain insurance covering the business and affairs of the Company and its property and on the lives and well being of its Members, employees and agents; (i) commence, prosecute or defend any proceeding in the Company's name; and (j) participate with others in partnerships, joint ventures and other associations and strategic alliances.

7.3 *Limitations.* Notwithstanding the foregoing and any other provision contained in this Operating Agreement to the contrary, no act shall be taken, sum expended, decision made, obligation incurred or power exercised by any Manager on behalf of the Company except by the unanimous consent of all Members with respect to (a) any significant and material purchase, receipt, lease, exchange or other

Form 6: Limited Liability Company Operating Agreement (continued)

acquisition of any real or personal property or business; (b) the sale of all or substantially all of the assets and property of the Company; (c) any mortgage, grant of security interest, pledge or encumbrance upon all or substantially all of the assets and property of the Company; (d) any merger; (e) any amendment or restatement of the Articles or this Operating Agreement; (f) any matter which could result in a change in the amount or character of the Company's capital; (g) any change in the character of the business and affairs of the Company; (h) the commission of any act which would make it impossible for the Company to carry on its ordinary business and affairs; or (i) any act that would contravene any provision of the Articles or this Operating Agreement or the Act.

7.4 *Standard of Care; Liability.* Every Manager shall discharge his or her duties as a manager in good faith, with the care an ordinarily prudent person in a like position would exercise under similar circumstances, and in a manner he or she reasonably believes to be in the best interests of the Company. A Manager shall not be liable for any monetary damages to the Company for any breach of such duties except for receipt of a financial benefit to which the Manager is not entitled; voting for or assenting to a distribution to Members in violation of this Operating Agreement or the Act; or a knowing violation of the law.

Note: This language eliminates most monetary liabilities of a Manager. The Delaware statute allows the Operating Agreement to provide that (1) a Manager who fails to perform in accordance with, or to comply with the terms and conditions of, the limited liability company agreement shall be subject to specified penalties or specified consequences; and (2) at the time or upon the happening of events specified in the agreement, a Manager shall be subject to specified penalties or specified consequences. (§18-405).

ALTERNATIVE ARTICLE VII
Management

A.7.1 *Management Vested with Members.* The business and affairs of the Company shall be managed by the Members in proportion to their capital contributions, as adjusted from time to time to reflect any additional contributions to or withdrawals from the capital of the Company by the Members. Each Member has the power, on behalf of the Company, to do all things necessary or convenient to carry out the business and affairs of the Company, including the power to: (a) purchase, lease or otherwise acquire any real or personal property; (b) sell, convey, mortgage, grant a security interest in, pledge, lease, exchange or otherwise dispose or encumber any real or personal property; (c) open one or more depository accounts and make deposits into and checks and withdrawals against such accounts; (d) borrow money, incur liabilities and other obligations; (e) enter into any and all agreements and execute any and all contracts,

Note: This Alternative Article provides for a LLC without centralized management. If there are to be no Managers, all references to Managers in this form should be deleted.

Note: This conservatively drafted provision gives the Members the power to manage in accordance with their capital contributions and gives each Member the power to act on behalf of the LLC. Any limitation on these powers could increase the likelihood that the corporate attribute of centralized management could be found.

Form 6: Limited Liability Company Operating Agreement
(continued)

Note: Section 301.7701-2(c)(4) of the Treasury Regulations provides that there is no centralization of management unless Managers have sole authority to make the decisions.

Note: If all Members have the power to manage, there is no requirement that they actually use their power.

documents and instruments; (f) engage employees and agents, define their respective duties, and establish their compensation or remuneration; (g) establish pension plans, trusts, profit sharing plans and other benefit and incentive plans for Members, employees and agents of the Company; (h) obtain insurance covering the business and affairs of the Company and its property and on the lives and well being of its Members, employees and agents; (i) commence, prosecute or defend any proceeding in the Company's name; and (j) participate with others in partnerships, joint ventures and other associations and strategic alliances.

A.7.2 *Standard of Care; Liability.* Every Member shall discharge his or her duties as a manager in good faith, with the care an ordinarily prudent person in a like position would exercise under similar circumstances, and in a manner he or she reasonably believes to be in the best interests of the Company. A Member shall not be liable for monetary damages to the Company for any breach of any such management duties except for receipt of a financial benefit to which the Member is not entitled; voting for or assenting to a distribution to Members in violation of this Operating Agreement or the Act; or a knowing violation of the law.

A.7.3 *Reimbursement.* Members shall be entitled to reimbursement from the Company of all expenses of the Company reasonably incurred and paid for by such Member on behalf of the Company.

This provision is the *raison d'être* for using the LLC business entity.

ARTICLE VIII
Exculpation of Liability; Indemnification

8.1 *Exculpation of Liability.* Unless otherwise provided by law or expressly assumed, a person who is a Member or Manager, or both, shall not be liable for the acts, debts or liabilities of the Company.

Note: The Delaware statute allows for sweeping indemnification. Subject to any standards or restrictions in the Operating Agreement, the LLC may indemnify and hold harmless any Member, Manager or other person from or against any and all claims and demands whatsoever. *See* §18-108.

Q: What is the difference between indemnifying and holding harmless? How are these rights different than the right to contribution?

8.2 *Indemnification.* Except as otherwise provided in this Article, the Company shall indemnify any Manager and may indemnify any employee or agent of the Company who was or is a party or is threatened to be made a party to a threatened, pending or completed action, suit or proceeding, whether civil, criminal, administrative, or investigative, and whether formal or informal, other than an action by or in the right of the Company, by reason of the fact that such person is or was a Manager, employee or agent of the Company against expenses, including attorneys fees, judgments, penalties, fines and amounts paid in settlement actually and reasonably incurred by such person in connection with the action, suit or proceeding, if the person acted in good faith, with the care an ordinarily prudent person in a like position would exercise under similar circumstances, and in a manner that such person reasonably believed to be in the best

Form 6: Limited Liability Company Operating Agreement (continued)

interests of the Company and with respect to a criminal action or proceeding, if such person had no reasonable cause to believe such person's conduct was unlawful. To the extent that a Member, employee or agent of the Company has been successful on the merits or otherwise in defense of an action, suit or proceeding or in defense of any claim, issue or other matter in the action, suit or proceeding, such person shall be indemnified against actual and reasonable expenses, including attorneys fees incurred by such person in connection with the action, suit or proceeding and any action, suit or proceeding brought to enforce the mandatory indemnification provided herein. Any indemnification permitted under this Article, unless ordered by a court, shall be made by the Company only as authorized in the specific case upon a determination that the indemnification is proper under the circumstances because the person to be indemnified has met the applicable standard of conduct and upon an evaluation of the reasonableness of expenses and amounts paid in settlement. This determination and evaluation shall be made by a majority vote of the Members who are not parties or threatened to be made parties to the action, suit or proceeding. Notwithstanding the foregoing to the contrary, no indemnification shall be provided to any Manager, employee or agent of the Company for or in connection with the receipt of a financial benefit to which such person is not entitled, voting for or assenting to a distribution to Members in violation of this Operating Agreement or the Act or a knowing violation of law.

ARTICLE IX
Dissolution and Winding Up

9.1 *Dissolution.* The Company shall dissolve and its affairs shall be wound up on the first to occur of the following events: (a) at any time specified in the Articles or this Operating Agreement; (b) upon the happening of any event specified in the Articles or this Operating Agreement; (c) by the unanimous consent of all of the Members; (d) upon the death, withdrawal, expulsion, bankruptcy, or dissolution of a Member or the occurrence of any other event that terminates the continued membership of a Member in the Company unless within ninety (90) days after the disassociation of membership as so provided in subparagraph (d), a majority of the remaining Members consent to continue the business of the Company and to the admission of one or more Members as necessary.

Q: Should the agreement provide for the advancement of expenses and indemnification in derivative actions?

Note: This Article does not provide for the corporate attribute of continuity of life. Alternative Article IX which follows this Article provides for a LLC with continuity of life.

Note: Under the Delaware statute, in the absence of a contrary provision in the Operating Agreement, a LLC dissolves upon the first to occur of the following: existence for 30 years since formation; the happening of any event specified in the Operating Agreement; the written consent of all Members; any event of Member withdrawal unless the business is continued either by the consent of all remaining Members within 90 days after the event of with-

Form 6: Limited Liability Company Operating Agreement
(continued)

drawal, or a right to continue as stated in the Operating Agreement; death, retirement, resignation, expulsion, bankruptcy, dissolution or any other event terminating membership of a Member dissolves the LLC (§18-801).

Note: If consent by a majority of the remaining Members can continue the LLC's life, the IRS has said there is not continuity of life.

Q: Could Members lose their share of the going concern value of a LLC if a minority of Members could force its dissolution?

Q: What is the difference between dissolution of a LLC and its winding up? See §18-801.

Note: In Delaware, in the absence of a contrary provision in the Operating Agreement, if a LLC is managed by its Members, the following have the right to wind up: Members; or person(s) authorized by Members; or if more than one class of Members, then by Members owning greater than 50 percent of the then current percentage of profits in the LLC owned by all Members or by the Members in each class. If Manager managed: the Manager who has not wrongfully dissolved the LLC may wind up; but, any Member or Manager (or his or her legal representative or assignee) may obtain winding up by a Court of Chancery for cause. (§18-803).

Upon dissolution, in the absence of contrary provisions in the Operating Agreement, assets are distributed first to creditors (including Member creditors), then to Members/former Members

9.2 *Winding Up.* Upon dissolution, the Company shall cease carrying on its business and affairs and shall commence the winding up of the Company's business and affairs and complete the winding up as soon as practicable. Upon the winding up of the Company, the assets of the Company shall be distributed first to creditors to the extent permitted by law, in satisfaction of Company debts, liabilities and obligations and then to Members and former Members first, in satisfaction of liabilities for distributions and then, in accordance with their Sharing Ratios. Such proceeds shall be paid to such Members within ninety (90) days after the date of winding up.

Form 6: Limited Liability Company Operating Agreement (continued)

to satisfy liability for distributions under §18-601 (Interim Distributions) or §18-604 (Resignation), then to Members first for return of their contributions then respecting their LLC interests in the proportions in which the Members share in distributions. (§18-804).

Note: In Delaware upon dissolution of a limited liability company, a Certificate of Cancellation must be filed with the Secretary of State. Under §18-203, a Certificate of Cancellation is required: when dissolution and winding up is completed; any time where there are less than two Members; upon failure to designate a new registered agent pursuant to §18-104(d); or where the LLC is not a surviving entity of a merger or consolidation.

Delaware statute §18-803 governs the procedure upon dissolution so that the persons winding up may: prosecute and defend suits; settle and close the LLC business; dispose of and convey LLC property; discharge debts or make provision to do so; and/or distribute any remaining assets to Members.

Pursuant to §18-802, upon application by a Member or Manager, the Chancery Court may order dissolution whenever it is not reasonably practicable to carry on the LLC business in conformity with the LLC agreement.

Form 6: Limited Liability Company Operating Agreement
(continued)

ALTERNATIVE ARTICLE IX
Dissolution and Winding Up;
Continuation of Business

A.9.1 *Dissolution.* The Company shall dissolve and its affairs shall be wound up on the first to occur of the following events: (a) at any time specified in the Articles or this Operating Agreement; (b) upon the happening of any event specified in the Articles or this Operating Agreement; or (c) by the unanimous consent of all of the Members.

A.9.2 *Winding Up.* Upon dissolution, the Company shall cease carrying on its business and affairs and shall commence the winding up of the Company's business and affairs and complete the winding up as soon as practicable. Upon the winding up of the Company, the assets of the Company shall be distributed first to creditors to the extent permitted by law, in satisfaction of Company debts, liabilities and obligations and then to Members and former Members first, in satisfaction of liabilities for distributions and then, in accordance with their Sharing Ratios. Such proceeds shall be paid to such Members within ninety (90) days after the date of winding up.

A.9.3 *Continuation of Company After Disassociation.* Notwithstanding the death, withdrawal, expulsion, bankruptcy or dissolution of a Member or the occurrence of any other event that terminates the continued membership of a Member in the Company, the business and affairs of the Company shall continue. Upon any such event, the Company shall purchase and the holder thereof shall sell, the disassociating Member's interest in the Company at its book value, determined in accordance with generally accepted accounting principles, consistently applied. Such sale and purchase shall be completed within ninety (90) days of any such event.

ARTICLE X
Miscellaneous Provisions

10.1 *Terms.* Nouns and pronouns will be deemed to refer to the masculine, feminine, neuter, singular and plural, as the identity of the person or persons, firm or corporation may in the context require.

10.2 *Article Headings.* The Article headings contained in this Operating Agreement have been inserted only as a matter of convenience and for reference, and in no way shall be construed to define, limit or describe the scope or intent of any provision of this Operating Agreement.

10.3 *Counterparts.* This Operating Agreement may be executed in several counterparts, each of which will be deemed an original but all of which will constitute one and the same.

Q: Would it be possible to provide a buy-out of a withdrawing Member's interest in the manner of a corporate stock redemption agreement? Can one be certain that the LLC would have funds to do this?

Q: Would this provision be enforceable by a decree of specific performance?

Form 6: Limited Liability Company Operating Agreement
(continued)

10.4 *Entire Agreement.* This Operating Agreement constitutes the entire agreement among the parties hereto and contains all of the agreements among said parties with respect to the subject matter hereof. This Operating Agreement supersedes any and all other agreements, either oral or written, between said parties with respect to the subject matter hereof.

10.5 *Severability.* The invalidity or unenforceability of any particular provision of this Operating Agreement shall not affect the other provisions hereof, and this Operating Agreement shall be construed in all respects as if such invalid or unenforceable provisions were omitted.

10.6 *Amendment.* This Operating Agreement may be amended or revoked at any time by a written agreement executed by all of the parties to this Operating Agreement. No change or modification to this Operating Agreement shall be valid unless in writing and signed by all of the parties to this Operating Agreement.

10.7 *Notices.* Any notice permitted or required under this Operating Agreement shall be conveyed to the party at the address reflected in this Operating Agreement and will be deemed to have been given when deposited in the United States mail, postage paid, or when delivered in person, or by courier or by facsimile transmission.

10.8 *Binding Effect.* Subject to the provisions of this Operating Agreement relating to transferability, this Operating Agreement will be binding upon and shall inure to the benefit of the parties, and their respective distributees, heirs, successors and assigns.

10.9 *Governing Law.* This Operating Agreement is being executed and delivered in the State of Michigan and shall be governed by, construed and enforced in accordance with the laws of the State of Michigan.

IN WITNESS WHEREOF, the parties hereto make and execute this Operating Agreement on the dates set below their names, to be effective on the date first above written.

WITNESSETH: THE COMPANY

By: _____

Its: _____

Date: _____

Note: Delaware law would generally be selected for a Delaware LLC.

Q: What are the concerns about doing business in a state that does not have an LLC Act and which does not recognize LLC's?

Q: Must signatures be verified or acknowledged?

Form 6: Limited Liability Company Operating Agreement
(continued)

MEMBERS:

_____
                                                    Date

_____
                                                    Date

_____
                                                    Date

                              EXHIBIT A
Initial Capital Interest in
_____Limited Liability Company

$ _____   _____ %

$ _____   _____ %

$ _____   _____ %

Drafting Exercise 7:

Prepare Articles of Organization and Operating Agreement for a Limited Liability Company

Kent Clothing Company, L.L.C.

An entire cottage industry has arisen in converting general partnerships to limited liability companies. *See, e.g.,* Mo. Stat. §347.125.

Formulate a plan for converting the Kent Clothing Company, the general partnership formed in Drafting Exercise 2, to a Delaware L.L.C. Prepare the Certificate of Formation and the Operating Agreement.

In addition to limited liability, which corporate attribute should be included? Continuity of life? Centralized management? Free transferability of interests?

Do we want Linda and Donna to act as Managers, or give all Members the right to manage, recognizing as a practical matter that Linda and Donna will actually do all the day to day work, and that approval of a "supermajority" in interest of Members should be necessary for some actions?

Drafting Exercise 8:

Prepare Articles of Organization and Operating Agreement for Adrenaline Addiction, L.L.C.

Adrenaline Addiction, L.L.C.

James Jones, a client of our firm, is interested in starting a new business enterprise. Jones is a former astronaut, and he would like to form Adrenaline Addiction, L.L.C., a Delaware limited liability company that will conduct bungee-jumping operations. The company name is available, and we have filed to reserve it.

Jones and his wife Laura will invest $500,000. His brother John, and Laura's father, George Adams, will each invest $150,000. The four investors will be Members, and profits, losses and voting will be in proportion to their initial investment. The company will be managed by one professional manager who will not be a Member.

The Members hope to own the company for five years and then sell it for a profit to a new group of investors.

Practical Pointers

1. There was some concern that the Internal Revenue Service might try to oppose the rapidly expanding use of limited liability companies. By issuing Rev. Proc. 95-10 in early 1995, the IRS appears to be accepting this rapidly growing new entity. The entity was also given greater status by the adoption of the Uniform Limited Liability Act in 1994. *See* Michael Bamberger & Arthur J. Jacobson, Editors, *State Limited Liability Company Laws Practice Guide* (Prentice Hall), a very useful treatise.

2. Needless to say, check the statute in the jurisdiction in which you will be organizing the LLC very carefully and keep up to date with all IRS developments.

3. It will be easier to work with LLCs once there is a body of case law interpreting them. Use of the entity is less risky now that it has been adopted in all but three states, and nearly all states allow foreign LLCs to qualify to do business. Nevertheless, check local statutes carefully.

4. As Rev. Proc. 95-10 has made even more clear, it may be helpful to think of member-managers as akin to general partners for analysis purposes.

5. When requiring a vote by members, be careful to define whether it is by percentage ownership of both capital and profit interests, if they are not the same.

6. Some states allow one-member LLCs. Be careful when you form one because it is not clear that the IRS will give it partnership tax

treatment. Also be careful if the second member owns less than a one-percent interest.

7.   Before forming an LLC make sure that it can qualify, and use its name, in each jurisdiction in which it will be doing business.

8.   An LLC will be deemed to have centralized management unless management rights are reserved to members.

9.   Generally speaking, most LLCs should lack free transferability of interest and continuity of life. Free transferability of interest occurs when a member can assign rights to profits and management without consent and no continuity of life occurs when dissociation of a member will dissolve the entity unless the remaining members consent to its continuity.

10.   LLCs are more flexible than S corporations because there are not limitations on the number and types of members, and there can be more than one class of ownership interest.

11.   Generally, the LLC is more stable than a general partnership because it is harder to dissolve. A general partner can dissolve a partnership under the UPA, even if it is a breach of contract. In some states, LLC members may not be able to do this. If the operating agreement prohibits members from readily dissolving the entity be careful in planning to avoid minority oppression problems.

12.   It may be possible in some states to limit the fiduciary duties of managers.

13.   In drafting operating agreements, be careful to provide a remedy for failure of a member to make required contributions.

14.   Be careful to comply with all statutory formalities to avoid potential "piercing the corporate veil" problems.

15.   Before forming an LLC, check to see whether use of state forms is mandatory. Note that in most cases, the effective date will be the date of filing, and not the date of the operating agreement.

Chapter 6

Setting Up a Closely Held Corporation

A.   INTRODUCTION

There are two basic types of corporations: closely held and public. Public corporations generally have a class of equity securities held by 500 share-holders and assets of $1 million. They are always C corporations. Many securities law issues for public companies are discussed in Chapter 8.

Closely held corporations may be either C corporations or, if they qualify, shareholders may elect Subchapter S status and flow-through tax treatment. The election of Subchapter S status by shareholders is a federal tax election that has nothing to do with state law.[1]

B.   PRACTICAL ADVANTAGES OF THE CORPORATE FORM

1.   Limited Liability

The benefits of limited liability for shareholders of a small corporation are often exaggerated. Lenders will probably require personal guarantees from shareholders to cover the corporation's contract liability.

Also, as a practical matter much of the wealth of the shareholders may be tied up in the corporation even if the shareholder's liability were limited to the amount of their investment in the corporation. Neverthe-less, limited liability is still very valuable for tort liability which could be catastrophic.

One good way to protect valuable assets is to keep them in a separate entity from the operating corporation. For example, valuable fixed assets like real estate can be kept in one corporation and leased to the operating corporation. Be careful to comply with all corporate formalities to avoid piercing the corporate veil. Also, if assets are likely to appreciate in value, keep them out of C corporations to avoid double taxation on the appreciation.[2]

2. Centralized Management

The corporate form offers the advantage of centralized management, but in a small closely held corporation all owners will often be involved in management. Having to maintain the three-tiered structure of shareholders, officers and directors may be somewhat costly and cumbersome.

3. Ease of Raising Capital

The corporate form is excellent for raising capital because investors are only liable to the extent of their investment. The ability to offer flexible investments like convertible debt or participating preferred stock is limited to C corporations and is not available in S corporations which can have only one class of stock.

4. Continuity of Life

Corporations have continuity of life. The ability to survive death, disability or retirement of an owner means that the going concern value will not be lost. As a practical matter for smaller corporations, this continuity is often exaggerated since the services of the owner may be essential for the business to continue.

On the other hand, the problem of the absence of continuity of life for a partnership is often exaggerated and can be cured with a properly drafted partnership agreement. It is not difficult to provide for the enterprise to continue despite the technical dissolution of the old partnership.

5. Free Transferability

Another attractive feature of corporations is the free transferability of ownership interests. This is of tremendous importance for publicly traded companies but is really of very little importance for closely held corporations. First, as a practical matter, there is generally very little market for a minority interest in a closely held company. Second, there are almost invariably restrictions on the transfer of shares. Shareholder agreements typically allow the remaining shareholders to control the disposition of shares upon the occurrence of events like death, disability and retirement.

C.   CORPORATE TAX CONCERNS FOR C CORPORATIONS

There are often significant tax disadvantages imposed on doing business as a C corporation. These disadvantages increased after the 1986 amendments to the federal income tax code. For this reason, it is important that corporations elect to be treated as S corporations whenever possible. S corporation election allows flow-through tax treatment and avoids many of the disadvantages of C corporation tax treatment, while being treated like C corporations in all other respects. Unfortunately, an S election is not available for many corporations.

C corporations are subject to double taxation. First, the entity must pay corporate income tax on its profits, and the shareholders must then pay federal income tax on their corporate dividends. Payment of dividends is not tax deductible for the corporation. Also, shareholders may not deduct corporate losses from their own tax liability.

Typically, many small C corporations have been able to avoid this double tax problem by "zeroing out" corporate earnings. The Internal Revenue Code and relevant case law allow the corporation to deduct reasonable salaries, rent payments and interest payments made by the corporation to its shareholders. The shareholders must pay tax on these distributions, but they do not receive dividends if the corporation is able to distribute all its "profits" in this manner. Obviously, it is not possible for all corporations to make its distributions to shareholders in this manner, and accordingly dividends are subject to double taxation.

These tax problems for C corporations were exacerbated by the 1986 changes in the federal income tax laws. For the first time, the corporate income tax rates for all but the very smallest C corporations were higher than the rate for some individual shareholders. This was true for a short time after 1986. Currently, the highest individual income tax rate is 39.6 percent (including the surtax) while the highest corporate rate is 35 percent.

In 1986, preferential capital gain tax treatment was reduced, although the 1993 amendments have again made capital gain treatment more significant. Congress also repealed the *General Utilities* doctrine in 1986, which basically allowed C corporations to make liquidating sales of assets or liquidating distributions of property to shareholders without the recognition of gain at the corporate level. The repeal of this doctrine made liquidation of a C corporation a taxable event at both the corporate and shareholder levels. Generally, therefore, it is no longer a good idea to use a C corporation to hold assets which will appreciate in value except for big companies (with many shareholders) or where it is desirable to accumulate earnings (subject to personal holding and accumulated earnings tax problems).

D. S CORPORATION ADVANTAGES

The income or loss to an S corporation flows through to the shareholders. Accordingly, an S corporation provides the advantages of the corporate form without double taxation. Whenever possible, assets that will appreciate in value should be held by an S corporation. The complete liquidation of an S corporation will result in gain or loss recognition to the S corporation, just as for a C corporation.

However, because the gain or loss is allocated directly to the shareholders, there is a basis adjustment to their shares which prevents the gain or loss from being recognized for a second time.

When doing business as an S corporation, it is not necessary to "zero out" profits, and shareholders can take direct advantage of corporate losses subject to the limitations on at risk and passive loss rules.

S corporations are tax flow-through entities like partnerships, but there are several important differences. For an S corporation, the loss pass-through for a shareholder generally will not include a share of the corporation's debts. For a partnership, a share of the partnership's debts is generally included in a partner's basis. For planning purposes, allocations of partnership income, loss, deductions, or credits are also more flexible for a partnership.

The allocations for an S corporation must be made pro rata based upon stock ownership and are not flexible. If losses are anticipated for the first years of a business venture, it is best to use a partnership or S corporation. This is also true for the entity that will own assets likely to appreciate in value. If an S corporation is not available, it may be possible to avoid the unlimited liability of a partnership by purchasing appropriate insurance.

E. DIFFICULTY OF QUALIFYING FOR S CORPORATION STATUS

There are many restrictions that prevent corporations from being able to elect S corporation status. Currently, an S corporation may not have more than 35 shareholders—although the 1995 S Corporation Revision bill pending in Congress would increase this number.

An S corporation can only issue one class of stock, although its stock may be separated into "voting" and "non-voting" sections without thereby creating a second class.

The only qualified shareholders are individuals (not including non-resident aliens, estates and some trusts). Corporations and partnerships cannot be shareholders, and restrictions on trusts as shareholders can frustrate the use of S corporations for estate planning purposes. Also, an S corporation cannot be a member of some affiliated groups of corporations. The requirements are continuous, and liability for a non-qualifying event can be substantial.

F.   CORPORATE CHARTER DOCUMENTS

Corporate formation is accomplished by means of generally simple but vital procedures that vary slightly from state to state, depending upon the local statute. Common characteristics of these procedures include defining the nature of the enterprise, capitalization, and filing the articles of incorporation (also known as "charter" or sometimes as "certificate of incorporation") with the secretary of state. Some states also require publication of intent to incorporate and of the articles of incorporation.

Much can be learned by close reading of sample incorporation documents. Examples given below include a Delaware Certificate of Incorporation, By-Laws, Unanimous Written Consent of Incorporators, Waiver of Notice of First Meeting, Minutes of First Meeting of Board of Directors.

1.   Articles of Incorporation

The articles of incorporation are filed with the secretary of state, and contain basic information about the corporation, including its name and the address of its registered office, the identity of the corporation's registered agent and incorporators, the purpose of the business, its authorized capital structure, and so forth. This information is made available to the public and should be drafted with that in mind. Proprietary information is reserved for the corporate by-laws.

2.   By-Laws

By-laws of a corporation are a contract among the shareholders that establish the internal rules for the management of the corporation. The by-laws are contained in a private document that is not available for public inspection. Lawyers usually rely upon a standard form specifically tailored for the state of incorporation, and spend very little time and client money customizing the document.

There are certain provisions in each state that must be included in the articles, and others that may be set forth in either the articles or the by-laws. For convenience, materials which must be in the articles may also be repeated in the more detailed by-laws.

When drafting, it is important to be consistent. If there is any inconsistency between the articles and the by-laws, the articles will rule. If the state statute requires that a provision be in the articles, placing it in the by-laws will be a nullity. Moreover, mandatory provisions of the state statute take precedence over both articles and by-laws.

Note that certain provisions may only be contained in a by-law provision adopted by the shareholders, and not by the board of directors.

Remember that by-law provisions adopted by the incorporators before subscription for shares had been accepted are deemed to be adopted by the shareholders.

The form that follows is a standard form of by-laws for a Delaware corporation provided by C.T. Corporation, one of the corporate service companies that lawyers use. This is a useful and generally well-drafted standard form. You might consider making some stylistic changes for clarity and consistency. For example, the first time the corporation is mentioned, it should be defined (hereinafter the "Corporation"). It should then be capitalized each time it is used. The Board of Directors (hereinafter the "Board") and the stockholders of the Corporation (hereinafter the "Stockholders") should also be defined. The Corporation's stock (hereinafter the "Stock") should be defined and the term used thereafter consistently. Elegant variation like "stock," "shares," "stockholders," "owner of shares," and "holder of stock," should be avoided.[3]

The form keeps referring to directors and officers as "he" and actions as being "his." This sexist language can be easily avoided by speaking of the person by title (for example, "the president may, if in the president's judgment . . .") and by avoiding the masculine third person pronoun and its possessive.[4]

Form 7: Delaware Certificate (Articles) of Incorporation

CERTIFICATE OF INCORPORATION
OF

_____

_____

1. The name of the corporation is

_____

2. The address of its registered office in the State of Delaware is

_____

in the City of _____

County of_____

The name of its registered agent at such address is

_____

_____

3. The nature of the business or purposes to be conducted or promoted is:

To engage in any lawful act or activity for which corporations may be organized under the General Corporation Law of Delaware.

To manufacture, purchase or otherwise acquire, invest in, own, mortgage, pledge, sell, assign and transfer or otherwise dispose of, trade, deal in and deal with goods, wares and merchandise and personal property of every class and description.

Note: In Delaware, the Articles of Incorporation are called the Certificate of Incorporation. This is also true in New York.

Note: In Delaware, the name of the corporation must include "association," "company," "corporation," "club," "foundation," "fund," "incorporated," "institute," "society," "union," "syndicate," "limited" or such abbreviations as "Co.," "Corp.," "Inc." or "Ltd." (Delaware §102).

Note: The corporate name can be reserved in advance for 30 days.

_Q._ In New York, under the Business Corporation Law, can a corporation merely be identified as "company" in its official name?

Note: For a fee, service companies like CT Corporation System will supply an address in Delaware, which a corporation can use as its registered office, and they will also act as registered agent.

Note: Very broad language is now permitted in many states, including Delaware. It is not necessary to list the powers that the Delaware statute grants to corporations.

Note: While very general language is allowed for corporate purpose, some states like New York require the express statement that the corporation "is not formed to engage in any act or activity requir-

Form 7: Delaware Certificate of Incorporation (continued)

ing the consent or approval of any state official, department, board, agency, or other body without such consent or approval first being obtained." N.Y. B.C.L. §402.

To acquire, and pay for in cash, stock or bonds of this corporation or otherwise, the good will, rights, assets and property, and to undertake or assume the whole or any part of the obligations or liabilities of any person, firm, association or corporation.

To acquire, hold, use, sell, assign, lease, grant licenses in respect of, mortgage or otherwise dispose of letters patent of the United States or any foreign country, patent rights, licenses and privileges, inventions, improvements and processes, copyrights, trademarks and trade names, relating to or useful in connection with any business of this corporation.

To acquire by purchase, subscription or otherwise, and to receive, hold, own, guarantee, sell, assign, exchange, transfer, mortgage, pledge or otherwise dispose of or deal in and with any of the shares of the capital stock, or any voting trust certificates in respect of the shares of capital stock, scrip, warrants, rights, bonds, debentures, notes, trust receipts, and other securities, obligations, choses in action and evidences of indebtedness or interest issued or created by any corporations, joint stock companies, syndicates, associations, firms, trusts or persons, public or private, or by the government of the United States of America, or by any foreign government, or by any state, territory, province, municipality or other political subdivision or by any governmental agency, and as owner thereof to possess and exercise all the rights, powers and privileges of ownership, including the right to execute consents and vote thereon, and to do any and all acts and things necessary or advisable for the preservation, protection, improvement and enhancement in value thereof.

To borrow or raise money for any of the purposes of the corporation and, from time to time without limit as to amount, to draw, make, accept, endorse, execute and issue promissory notes, drafts, bills of exchange, warrants, bonds, debentures and other negotiable or non-negotiable instruments and evidences of indebtedness, and to secure the payment of any thereof and of the interest thereon by mortgage upon or pledge, conveyance or assignment in trust of the whole or any part of the property of the corporation. whether at the time owned or thereafter acquired, and to sell, pledge or otherwise dispose of such bonds or other obligations of the corporation for its corporate purposes.

To purchase, receive, take by grant, gift, devise, bequest or otherwise, lease, or otherwise acquire, own, hold, improve, employ, use and otherwise deal in and with real or personal property, or any interest therein, wherever situated, and to sell, convey, lease, exchange, transfer or otherwise dispose of, or mortgage or pledge, all or any of the corporation's property and assets, or any interest therein, wherever situated.

Form 7: Delaware Certificate of Incorporation (continued)

In general, to possess and exercise all the powers and privileges granted by the General Corporation Law of Delaware or by any other law of Delaware or by this Certificate of Incorporation together with any powers incidental thereto, so far as such powers and privileges are necessary or convenient to the conduct, promotion or attainment of the business or purposes of the corporation.

The business and purposes specified in the foregoing clauses shall, except where otherwise expressed, be in nowise limited or restricted by reference to, or inference from, the terms of any other clause in this Certificate of Incorporation, but the business and purposes specified in each of the foregoing clauses of this article shall be regarded as independent business and purposes.

4. The total number of shares of stock which the corporation shall have authority to issue is _____ (_____) and the par value of each of such shares is _____ Dollars ($_____) amounting in the aggregate to _____Dollars ($_____).

Note: The kind of stock which the corporation is authorized to issue must be set forth in the Articles. It must state the categories of stock that are authorized. Note that only one category of stock can be authorized for an S corporation, but there can be both voting and non-voting common stock.

Note: It is generally a good idea to follow very simple arrangements when first forming a corporation. If all stock is common stock each share will have ordinary rights including: one vote per share; participating equally in dividends; upon liquidation receiving value based upon proportional share of total stock owned. The Articles must also set forth the number of shares authorized and the par value. Par value has nothing to do with the market value of the stock, but stock cannot be issued for less than par value. This is one reason why par value should be kept low.

Form 7: Delaware Certificate of Incorporation (continued)

Note: The use of voting and nonvoting common stock can be a useful control mechanism.

Note: If there is to be more than one class of stock this needs to be set out in the articles of incorporation.

Note: Preferred stock may have a preference as to dividends which can make it a more conservative investment. It also typically has a liquidation preference. This makes it something of a hybrid between an equity investment and debt. Preferred stock is a safer investment than common stock, but holders of common stock will do better if there is an upswing in corporate profitability. Preferred stock can also be issued in series.

Note: It is possible to customize securities to be issued and lawyers and investment bankers can show great ingenuity. For example, participating preferred stock has a set dividend but also has a right to receive additional dividends if the company is profitable. Debt securities, like bonds and debentures, which pay interest can also be convertible into common stock at the option of the investor upon the occurrence of certain circumstances so that holders of debt can also participate in increased profits. Corporations may also be authorized to issue warrants and options convertible into stock.

Note: The franchise tax payable upon incorporating will also depend on the total par value of all the authorized shares of stock. One drawback of issuing stock without par value is some states treat it as a par value of $100/share in calculating franchise taxes.

(Alternative paragraph 4-a:)

4/a. The total number of shares of stock which the corporation shall have authority to issue is _____ (____) of which stock _____ (____) shares of the par value of _____ Dollars ($____) each, amounting in the aggregate to _____ Dollars ($____) shall be _____ stock and of which (____) shares of the par value of _____ Dollars ($____) each, amounting in the aggregate to _____ Dollars ($____) shall be_____ stock.

The designations and the powers, preferences and rights, and the qualifications, limitations or restrictions thereof are as follows:

_____

_____

_____

(Alternative paragraph 4-b:)

4/b. The total number of shares of stock which the corporation shall have authority to issue is _____ (____); all of such shares shall be without par value.

Form 7: Delaware Certificate of Incorporation (continued)

(Alternative paragraph 4-c:)

4/c. The total number of shares of stock which the corporation shall have authority to issue is _____ (_____); all of such shares shall be without par value, and _____ (_____) shares thereof shall be _____ stock and _____ (_____) shares thereof shall be _____ stock.

The designations and the powers, preferences and rights, and the qualifications, limitations or restrictions thereof are as follows:

_____

_____

(Alternative paragraph 4-d:)

4/d. The total number of shares of stock which the corporation shall have authority to issue is _____ (_____), of which _____ (_____) shares of the par value of _____ Dollars ($_____) each, amounting in the aggregate to _____ Dollars ($_____) shall be _____ stock and of which _____ (_____) shares without par value shall be _____ stock.

The designations and the powers, preferences and rights, and the qualifications, limitations or restrictions thereof are as follows:

_____

_____

At all elections of directors of the corporation, each stockholder shall be entitled to as many votes as shall equal the number of votes which (except for such provision as to cumulative voting) he would be entitled to cast for the election of directors with respect to his shares of stock multiplied by the number of directors to be elected by him, and he may cast all of such votes for a single director or may distribute them among the number to be voted for, or for any two or more of them as he may see fit.

Note: The corporation may have one or more classes of stock with or without par value. The stock may have such voting power and such designations, preferences and relative, participating, optional or other special rights and qualifications, limitations or restrictions as provided in the certificate. The certificate may also provide for one or more series of stock within any class.

Note: In Delaware, consideration for the issuance of stock must be for money paid, labor done, personal property, real estate, or leases of real property actually acquired by the corporation.

Note: Par value or the consideration for issuing stock without par value shall be fixed by the directors, or by the shareholders if the certificate of incorporation so provides.

Note: If expressly authorized in the certificate of incorporation, the directors can be granted the power by resolution to issue one or more classes of stock, with or without par value, and may issue one or more series of stock within any class, and to establish voting power and such designations, preferences and relative, participating, optional or other special rights, and qualifications, limitations or restrictions.

Note: An express provision like this authorizes cumulative voting. (§214). Cumulative voting must be authorized in the articles of incorporation. With straight voting, the majority of shareholders could elect every director.

Form 7: Delaware Certificate of Incorporation (continued)

Note: Shareholders will only have pre-emptive rights if the articles of incorporation contains this provision.

The holders of _____ shall, upon the issuance or sale of shares of stock of any class (whether now or hereafter authorized) or any securities convertible into such stock, have the right, during such period of time and on such conditions as the board of directors shall prescribe, to subscribe to and purchase such shares or securities in proportion to their respective holdings of _____ at such price or prices as the board of directors may from time to time fix and as may be permitted by law.

Q: In Delaware, how many incorporators must there be, and what are their qualifications?

5. The name and mailing address of each incorporator is as follows:

NAME   MAILING ADDRESS

_____

_____

(Alternative paragraph 5-a)
5/a. The name and mailing address of each person who is to serve as a director until the first annual meeting of the stockholders or until a successor is elected and qualified, is as follows:

Note: The initial board of directors can be established in the articles of incorporation before subscriptions are taken for any shares of stock and before any stock is issued.

NAME   MAILING ADDRESS

_____

_____

Note: This provision only needs to be included if the corporation is not to have perpetual existence. Not providing for perpetual existence, without a good reason, could be malpractice.

6. The corporation is to have perpetual existence.

Note: Directors only have this power over the bylaws if expressly provided in the certificate of incorporation.

7. In furtherance and not in limitation of the powers conferred by statute, the board of directors is expressly authorized:

Q: Is there any difference between by-laws adopted by the shareholders and by-laws adopted by the directors? Can the directors repeal a by-law provision adopted by the shareholders?

To make, alter or repeal the by-laws of the corporation.

To authorize and cause to be executed mortgages and liens upon the real and personal property of the corporation.

To set apart out of any of the funds of the corporation available for dividends a reserve or reserves for any proper purpose and to abolish any such reserve in the manner in which it was created.

Form 7: Delaware Certificate of Incorporation (continued)

By a majority of the whole board, to designate one or more committees, each committee to consist of one or more of the directors of the corporation. The board may designate one or more directors as alternate members of any committee, who may replace any absent or disqualified member at any meeting of the committee. The by-laws may provide that in the absence or disqualification of a member of a committee, the member or members thereof present at any meeting and not disqualified from voting, whether or not he or they constitute a quorum, may unanimously appoint another member of the board of directors to act at the meeting in the place of any such absent or disqualified member.

Note: This requires a majority of the whole board and not just of a quorum at a meeting.

Any such committee, to the extent provided in the resolution of the board of directors, or in the by-laws of the corporation, shall have and may exercise all the powers and authority of the board of directors in the management of the business and affairs of the corporation, and may authorize the seal of the corporation to be affixed to all papers which may require it; but no such committee shall have the power or authority in reference to amending the Certificate of Incorporation, adopting an agreement of merger or consolidation, recommending to the stockholders the sale, lease or exchange of all or substantially all of the corporation's property and assets, recommending to the stockholders a dissolution of the corporation or a revocation of a dissolution, or amending the by-laws of the corporation; and, unless the resolution or by-laws expressly so provide, no such committee shall have the power or authority to declare a dividend or to authorize the issuance of stock.

When and as authorized by the stockholders in accordance with law, to sell, lease or exchange all or substantially all of the property and assets of the corporation, including its good will and its corporate franchises, upon such terms and conditions and for such consideration, which may consist in whole or in part of money or property including shares of stock in, and/or other securities of, any other corporation or corporations, as its board of directors shall deem expedient and for the best interests of the corporation.

Note: There must be approval by a resolution adopted by holders of a majority of the outstanding stock of the corporation entitled to vote. Meetings must be called on at least 20 days' notice and must state that such a resolution will be considered.

8. Elections of directors need not be by written ballot if the certificate of the corporation shall so provide.

Meetings of stockholders may be held within or without the State of Delaware, as the by-laws may provide. The books of the corporation may be kept (subject to any provision contained in the statutes) outside the State of Delaware at such place or places as may be designated from time to time by the board of directors or in the by-laws of the corporation.

Note: This provision in the certificate of incorporation should exactly track the language of §211.

Whenever a compromise or arrangement is proposed between this corporation and its creditors or any class of them and/or between this corporation and its stockholders

Form 7: Delaware Certificate of Incorporation (continued)

Q: Must supermajority provisions for quorums at meetings and for action to be taken by shareholders and directors be included in the articles or by-laws? Would the same be true in New York?

or any class of them, any court of equitable jurisdiction within the State of Delaware may, on the application in a summary way of this corporation or of any creditor or stockholder thereof or on the application of any receiver or receivers appointed for this corporation under the provisions of Section 291 of Title 8 of the Delaware Code or on the application of trustees in dissolution or of any receiver or receivers appointed for this corporation under the provisions of Section 279 of Title 8 of the Delaware Code order a meeting of the creditors or class of creditors, and/or of the stockholders or class of stockholders of this corporation, as the case may be, to be summoned in such manner as the said court directs. If a majority in number representing three-fourths in value of the creditors or class of creditors, and/or of the stockholders or class of stockholders of this corporation, as the case may be, agree to any compromise or arrangement and to any reorganization of this corporation as consequence of such compromise or arrangement, the said compromise or arrangement and the said reorganization shall, if sanctioned by the court to which the said application has been made, be binding on all the creditors or class of creditors, and/or on all the stockholders or class of stockholders, of this corporation, as the case may be, and also on this corporation.

9. The corporation reserves the right to amend, alter, change or repeal any provision contained in this Certificate of Incorporation, in the manner now or hereafter prescribed by statute, and all rights conferred upon stockholders herein are granted subject to this reservation.

Note: This requirement that directors will not be liable under certain circumstances must be contained in the articles of incorporation. §102(b)(7).

10. A director of the corporation shall not be personally liable to the corporation or its stockholders for monetary damages for breach of fiduciary duty as a director except for liability (i) for any breach of the director's duty of loyalty to the corporation or its stockholders, (ii) for acts or omissions not in good faith or which involve intentional misconduct or a knowing violation of law, (iii) under Section 174 of the Delaware General Corporation Law, or (iv) for any transaction from which the director derived any improper personal benefit.

Q: Must the signature be verified, acknowledged or affirmed? What are the statutory requirements to be an incorporator?

Note: In most states one incorporator is sufficient

Note: "/s" means that the document was manually signed and that this is a "conformed" copy.

WE, THE UNDERSIGNED, being each of the incorporators hereinbefore named, for the purpose of forming a corporation pursuant to the General Corporation Law of the State of Delaware, do make this Certificate, hereby declaring and certifying that this is our act and deed and the facts herein stated are true, and accordingly have hereunto set our hands this _____ day of _____, 19___.

/s_____
    INCORPORATOR

/s_____
    INCORPORATOR

Form 8: By-Laws for a Delaware Corporation

BY-LAWS

ARTICLE I
Offices

Section 1.
The registered office shall be in the City of _____, County of _____, State of Delaware.

Section 2.
The corporation may also have offices at such other places both within and without the State of Delaware as the board of directors may from time to time determine or the business of the corporation may require.

ARTICLE II

Section 1.
All meetings of the stockholders for the election of directors shall be held in the City of _____, State of _____, at such place as may be fixed from time to time by the board of directors, or at such other place either within or without the State of Delaware as shall be designated from time to time by the board of directors and stated in the notice of the meeting. Meetings of stockholders for any other purpose may be held at such time and place, within or without the State of Delaware, as shall be stated in the notice of the meeting or in a duly executed waiver of notice thereof.

Section 2.
Annual meetings of stockholders, commencing with the year 19___ shall be held on the _____ if not a legal holiday, and if a legal holiday, then on the next secular day following, at ___, or at such other date and time as shall be designated from time to time by the board of directors and stated in the notice of the meeting, at which they shall elect by a plurality vote a board of directors, and transact such other business as may properly be brought before the meeting.

Section 3.
Written notice of the annual meeting stating the place, date and hour of the meeting shall be given to each stockholder entitled to vote at such meeting not less than _____ nor more than _____ days before the date of the meeting.

Section 4.
The officer who has charge of the stock ledger of the corporation shall prepare and make, at least ten days before every meeting of stockholders, a complete list of the stockholders entitled to vote at the meeting, arranged in alphabetical order, and showing the address of each stockholder

---

Note: The registered office must be in Delaware. The office address of a company like CT Corporation System may be used.

Q: What is the rule in New York? *See* N.Y.B.C.L. §402(a)(3).

Q: Must these meetings take place within the State of Delaware?

Note: It is less likely that the corporate veil will be pierced if formalities such as meetings are strictly observed.

Note: It is probably a good idea to pick a date by which the Corporation's accountants will be able to provide accurate year end figures.
Of course, one cannot use this simple plurality language if there is to be cumulative voting or if classes of directors are to be elected by different groups of shareholders.

Q: How much notice is required in Delaware?

Form 8: By-Laws for a Delaware Corporation (continued)

Q: In Delaware, does the statute require that the notice state the purpose of the proposed meeting?

Note: This calls for a request by Stockholders owning a majority of all Stock issued, outstanding and entitled to vote. This may be a much larger number than just Stockholders that would attend the meeting.

Q: What does the Delaware statute require?

Note: Sections 8 and 9 govern Stockholder quorum and voting requirements.

Q: In Delaware, could the By-laws alone, and not the Articles, provide for a quorum to be more than a majority of the holders of outstanding Stock? What about less than a majority? Less than one-third?

and the number of shares registered in the name of each stockholder. Such list shall be open to the examination of any stockholder, for any purpose germane to the meeting, during ordinary business hours, for a period of at least ten days prior to the meeting, either at a place within the city where the meeting is to be held, which place shall be specified in the notice of the meeting, or, if not so specified, at the place where the meeting is to be held. The list shall also be produced and kept at the time and place of the meeting during the whole time thereof, and may be inspected by any stockholder who is present.

Section 5.
Special meetings of the stockholders, for any purpose or purposes, unless otherwise prescribed by statute or by the certificate of incorporation, may be called by the president and shall be called by the president or secretary at the request in writing of a majority of the board of directors, or at the request in writing of stockholders owning a majority in amount of the entire capital stock of the corporation issued and outstanding and entitled to vote. Such request shall state the purpose or purposes of the proposed meeting.

Section 6.
Written notice of a special meeting stating the place, date and hour of the meeting and the purpose or purposes for which the meeting is called, shall be given not less than nor more than _____ days before the date of the meeting, to each stockholder entitled to vote at such meeting.

Section 7.
Business transacted at any special meeting of stockholders shall be limited to the purposes stated in the notice. Sections 8 and 9 govern Stockholder quorum and voting requirements.

Section 8.
The holders of _____ of the stock issued and outstanding and entitled to vote thereat, present in person or represented by proxy, shall constitute a quorum at all meetings of the stockholders for the transaction of business except as otherwise provided by statute or by the certificate of incorporation. If, however, such quorum shall not be present or represented at any meeting of the stockholders, the stockholders entitled to vote thereat, present in person or represented by proxy, shall have power to adjourn the meeting from time to time, without notice other than announcement at the meeting, until a quorum shall be present or represented. At such adjourned meeting at which a quorum shall be present or represented any business may be transacted which might have been transacted at the meeting as originally notified. If the adjournment is for more than thirty days, or if after the adjournment a new record date is fixed for the adjourned meeting, a notice of the adjourned meeting shall be given to each stockholder of record entitled to vote at the meeting.

Form 8: By-Laws for a Delaware Corporation (continued)

Section 9.
When a quorum is present at any meeting, the vote of the holders of a majority of the stock having voting power present in person or represented by proxy shall decide any question brought before such meeting, unless the question is one upon which by express provision of the statutes or of the certificate of incorporation, a different vote is required in which case such express provision shall govern and control the decision of such question.

Section 10.
Unless otherwise provided in the certificate of incorporation each stockholder shall at every meeting of the stockholders be entitled to one vote in person or by proxy for each share of the capital stock having voting power held by such stockholder, but no proxy shall be voted on after three years from its date, unless the proxy provides for a longer period.

Alternative Provision 10.A
At all elections of directors of the corporation each stockholder having voting power shall be entitled to exercise the right of cumulative voting as provided in the certificate of incorporation.

Section 11.
Unless otherwise provided in the certificate of incorporation, any action required to be taken at any annual or special meeting of stockholders of the corporation, or any action which may be taken at any annual or special meeting of

Q: When is a different vote required under the Delaware statute?

Q: Must provisions requiring super-majority votes (i.e., more than 50 percent) by Stockholders be set forth in the Articles or may they just be in these By-laws?

Note: In New York, the statute requires the vote of two-thirds of the outstanding shares to: amend the articles of incorporation to add or delete provisions for a greater requirement as to quorum or vote of directors, or to delete control of board of directors from articles, unless the articles require more than a two-thirds vote, and for dissolution, guarantees not in furtherance of corporate purpose, merger or consolidation, or sale, lease, exchange or other disposition of assets not in usual or regular course of business.

Q: In Delaware, must the Articles provide for cumulative voting or may it just be set forth in the By-laws?

Note: Cumulative voting is defined as the Stockholder's "[r]ight to vote in an election of directors as many votes as equal the number of votes which a shareholder would be entitled to cast for the election of directors with respect to his shares multiplied by the number of directors to be elected, all of such votes being permitted to be cast for a single director or distributed as the shareholder sees fit." Fogelman, West's McKinney's Forms, Business Corporation Law at LXXIV.

Form 8: By-Laws for a Delaware Corporation (continued)

Q: In Delaware, is there any requirement that consent without notice, or without a meeting, must be unanimous?

Note: Often, it is a good idea to have an odd number of directors.

Q: Who can increase or decrease the number of directors? Under the Delaware statute, can this be done by simple majority of directors? Of Stockholders? How can we protect against Stockholders owning more than 50 percent of the Stock from packing the Board? When can directors remove a director for cause? Does it matter if a director was elected by the directors pursuant to power given to the directors in the articles or a by-law adopted by the Shareholders? Compare to New York.

Q: In Delaware, does it matter if a director vacancy was the result of removal with or without cause?

Q: Is simple majority of directors at a meeting at which a quorum is present sufficient for corporate action? How could we provide for a super-majority to be required?

such stockholders, may be taken without a meeting, without prior notice and without a vote, if a consent in writing, setting forth the action so taken, shall be signed by the holders of outstanding stock having not less than the minimum number of votes that would be necessary to authorize or take such action at a meeting at which all shares entitled to vote thereon were present and voted. Prompt notice of the taking of the corporate action without a meeting by less than unanimous written consent shall be given to those stockholders who have not consented in writing.

ARTICLE III
Directors

Section 1.
The number of directors which shall constitute the whole board shall be _____. The directors shall be elected at the annual meeting of the stockholders, except as provided in Section 2 of this Article, and each director elected shall hold office until his successor is elected and qualified. Directors need not be stockholders.

Section 2.
Vacancies and newly created directorships resulting from any increase in the authorized number of directors may be filled by a majority of the directors then in office, though less than a quorum, or by a sole remaining director, and the directors so chosen shall hold office until the next annual election and until their successors are duly elected and shall qualify, unless sooner displaced. If there are no directors in office, then an election of directors may be held in the manner provided by statute. If, at the time of filling any vacancy or any newly created directorship, the directors then in office shall constitute less than a majority of the whole board (as constituted immediately prior to any such increase), the Court of Chancery may, upon application of any stockholder or stockholders holding at least ten percent of the total number of the shares at the time outstanding having the right to vote for such directors, summarily order an election to be held to fill any such vacancies or newly created directorships, or to replace the directors chosen by the directors then in office.

Section 3.
The business of the corporation shall be managed by or under the direction of its board of directors which may exercise all such powers of the corporation and do all such lawful acts and things as are not by statute or by the certificate of incorporation or by these by-laws directed or required to be exercised or done by the stockholders.

Form 8: By-Laws for a Delaware Corporation (continued)

Meetings of the Board of Directors

Section 4.
The board of directors of the corporation may hold meetings, both regular and special, either within or without the State of Delaware.

Q: Is there a statutory requirement as to how often meetings must be held?

Section 5.
The first meeting of each newly elected board of directors shall be held at such time and place as shall be fixed by the vote of the stockholders at the annual meeting and no notice of such meeting shall be necessary to the newly elected directors in order legally to constitute the meeting, provided a quorum shall be present. In the event of the failure of the stockholders to fix the time and place of such first meeting of the newly elected board of directors, or in the event such meeting is not held at the time or place so fixed by the stockholders, the meeting may be held at such time and place as shall be specified in a notice given as hereinafter provided for special meetings of the board of directors, or as shall be specified in a written waiver signed by all of the directors.

Section 6.
Regular meetings of the board of directors may be held without notice at such time and at such place as shall from time to time be determined by the board.

Section 7.
Special meetings of the board of directors may be called by the president on _____ days' notice to each director, either personally or by mail or by telegram; special meetings shall be called by the president or secretary in like manner and on like notice on the written request of two directors unless the board consists of only one director; in which case special meetings shall be called by the president or secretary in like manner and on like notice on the written request of the sole director.

Q: Is it risky to allow meetings to be held without notice? Could a majority of the quorum needed to vote act without giving the other directors an opportunity to oppose their action?

Section 8.
At all meetings of the board _____ directors shall constitute a quorum for the transaction of business and the act of a majority of the directors present at any meeting at which there is a quorum shall be the act of the board of directors, except as may be otherwise specifically provided by statute or by the certificate of incorporation. If a quorum shall not be present at any meeting of the board of directors the directors present thereat may adjourn the meeting from time to time, without notice other than announcement at the meeting, until a quorum shall be present.

Q: In Delaware, must a requirement that a quorum consist of more than a majority of directors be in the Articles? May it be only in the By-laws? Can the directors rather than the Stockholders determine what a quorum may be, or change the quorum requirement?

Section 9.
Unless otherwise restricted by the certificate of incorporation or these by-laws, any action required or permitted to be taken at any meeting of the board of directors or of any

Note: All action without a meeting must be unanimous.

Form 8: By-Laws for a Delaware Corporation (continued)

committee thereof may be taken without a meeting, if all members of the board or committee, as the case may be, consent thereto in writing, and the writing or writings are filed with the minutes of proceedings of the board or committee.

Section 10.
Unless otherwise restricted by the certificate of incorporation or these by-laws, members of the board of directors, or any committee designated by the board of directors, may participate in a meeting of the board of directors, or any committee, by means of conference telephone or similar communications equipment by means of which all persons participating in the meeting can hear each other, and such participation in a meeting shall constitute presence in person at the meeting.

COMMITTEES OF DIRECTORS

Section 11.
The board of directors may, by resolution passed by a majority of the whole board, designate one or more committees, each committee to consist of one or more of the directors of the corporation. The board may designate one or more directors as alternate members of any committee, who may replace any absent or disqualified member at any meeting of the committee.

In the absence or disqualification of a member of a committee, the member or members thereof present at any meeting and not disqualified from voting, whether or not he or they constitute a quorum, may unanimously appoint another member of the board of directors to act at the meeting in the place of any such absent or disqualified member.

Any such committee, to the extent provided in the resolution of the board of directors, shall have and may exercise all the powers and authority of the board of directors in the management of the business and affairs of the corporation, and may authorize the seal of the corporation to be affixed to all papers which may require it; but no such committee shall have the power or authority in reference to amending the certificate of incorporation, (except that a committee may, to the extent authorized in the resolution or resolutions providing for the issuance of shares of stock adopted by the board of directors as provided in Section 151(a) fix any of the preferences or rights of such shares relating to dividends, redemption, dissolution, any distribution of assets of the corporation or the conversion into, or the exchange of such shares for, shares of any other class or classes or any other series of the same or any other class or classes of stock of the corporation) adopting an agreement of merger or consolidation, recommending to the stockholders the sale, lease or exchange of all or substantially all of the corporation's property and assets, recommending to the stockholders a disso-

Note: The use of telephone conference meetings is becoming more frequent and is very useful when directors travel a great deal.

Q: In Delaware, how small may a committee of directors be? In New York, committees must have at least three members.

Note: There are corporate actions that cannot be authorized without the approval of the entire Board.

Form 8: By-Laws for a Delaware Corporation (continued)

lution of the corporation or a revocation of a dissolution, or amending the by-laws of the corporation; and, unless the resolution or the certificate of incorporation expressly so provide, no such committee shall have the power or authority to declare a dividend or to authorize the issuance of stock or to adopt a certificate of ownership and merger. Such Committee or committees shall have such name or names as may be determined from time to time by resolution adopted by the board of directors.

Section 12.
Each committee shall keep regular minutes of its meetings and report the same to the board of directors when required.

Compensation of Directors

Section 13.
Unless otherwise restricted by the certificate of incorporation or these by-laws, the board of directors shall have the authority to fix the compensation of directors. The directors may be paid their expenses, if any, of attendance at each meeting of the board of directors and may be paid a fixed sum for attendance at each meeting of the board of directors or a stated salary as director. No such payment shall preclude any director from serving the corporation in any other capacity and receiving compensation therefor. Members of special or standing committees may be allowed like compensation for attending committee meetings.

Removal of Directors

Section 14.
Unless otherwise restricted by the certificate of incorporation or by law, any director or the entire board of directors may be removed, with or without cause, by the holders of a majority of shares entitled to vote at an election of directors.

Note: Minutes for these meetings, as for regular and special meetings of the Board of Directors, should be prepared by legal counsel.

Q: Should we provide in the Articles or By-laws that the Stockholders shall fix the compensation for directors?

Note: For many small companies, the Stockholders and directors will be the same people.

Q: Are the fiduciary duties of loyalty and care owed to the Corporation by directors and officers the same.

Q: In order to attract the best directors, should the By-laws expressly permit contracts and other transactions between the company and directors?

Note: The phrase "by law" is ambiguous. Does it mean "by-law" or by the Delaware Corporation Law?

Note: As drafted, a majority vote of the Stockholders can remove any director with or without cause unless there is cumulative voting by Stockholders or the election of classes of directors by different groups of Stockholders.

Q: Is it a good idea to allow this to be done without cause?

Form 8: By-Laws for a Delaware Corporation (continued)

Q: In Delaware, may Articles or By-laws permit a vote of directors to remove a director with cause? Without cause? What is the comparable provision in New York?

Q: In Delaware, is there any difference between removing a director, with or without cause, who was elected by directors rather than by Stockholders?

Q: In New York, can a provision only in the By-laws set forth the vote necessary to remove a director without cause?

Q: In Delaware, may one person hold more than one office?

Note: In New York, if a company has more than one officer, one person cannot serve both as president and secretary.

ARTICLE IV
Notices

Section 1.
Whenever, under the provisions of the statutes or of the certificate of incorporation or of these by-laws, notice is required to be given to any director or stockholder, it shall not be construed to mean personal notice, but such notice may be given in writing, by mail, addressed to such director or stockholder, at his address as it appears on the records of the corporation, with postage thereon prepaid, and such notice shall be deemed to be given at the time when the same shall be deposited in the United States mail. Notice to directors may also be given by telegram.

Section 2.
Whenever any notice is required to be given under the provisions of the statutes or of the certificate of incorporation or of these by-laws, a waiver thereof in writing, signed by the person or persons entitled to said notice, whether before or after the time stated therein, shall be deemed equivalent thereto.

ARTICLE V
Officers

Section 1.
The officers of the corporation shall be chosen by the board of directors and shall be a president, a vice-president, a secretary and a treasurer. The board of directors may also choose additional vice-presidents, and one or more assistant secretaries and assistant treasurers. Any number of offices may be held by the same person, unless the certificate of incorporation or these by-laws otherwise provide.

Form 8: By-Laws for a Delaware Corporation (continued)

Section 2.
The board of directors at its first meeting after each annual meeting of stockholders shall choose a president, one or more vice-presidents, a secretary and a treasurer.

Section 3.
The board of directors may appoint such other officers and agents as it shall deem necessary who shall hold their offices for such terms and shall exercise such powers and perform such duties as shall be determined from time to time by the board.

Section 4.
The salaries of all officers and agents of the corporation shall be fixed by the board of directors.

Section 5.
The officers of the corporation shall hold office until their successors are chosen and qualify. Any officer elected or appointed by the board of directors may be removed at any time by the affirmative vote of a majority of the board of directors. Any vacancy occurring in any office of the corporation shall be filled by the board of directors.

Q: Do we want to specify in the By-laws who will serve in each capacity? Would it be possible to provide in the By-laws to rotate positions? For example, could one person serve as president/treasurer in even numbered years and vice-president/secretary in odd numbered years?

Note: This language leaves the Board with the flexibility of changing officer's responsibilities as necessary.

Q: Would it be possible for a bare majority of the Board to reduce an officer's salary and effectively force a resignation?

Q: Should a super-majority vote of Stockholders be necessary to remove an officer, especially without cause? Must such a provision be in the Certificate or may it just be in the By-laws?
Should a simple majority of directors be able to fire officers for cause? Without cause?

Q: In Delaware, may the Certificate or By-laws provide for officers to be elected by Stockholders? Should directors be able to fire such officers for cause? Without cause?

Note: In New York, an officer elected by the Stockholders can only be removed by a vote of the Stockholders, with or without cause, but the Board has the power to suspend the officer's authority to act for cause. See West's McKinney's Forms, Business Corporation Law §3:85 at 409.

Form 8: By-Laws for a Delaware Corporation (continued)

The President

Section 6.
The president shall be the chief executive officer of the corporation, shall preside at all meetings of the stockholders and the board of directors, shall have general and active management of the business of the corporation and shall see that all orders and resolutions of the board of directors are carried into effect.

Q: Should Board approval be necessary for certain actions like borrowing money in excess of a certain amount, and for making loans to directors, officers, and employees?

Section 7.
He shall execute bonds, mortgages and other contracts requiring a seal, under the seal of the corporation, except where required or permitted by law to be otherwise signed and executed and except where the signing and execution thereof shall be expressly delegated by the board of directors to some other officer or agent of the corporation.

The Vice-Presidents

Q: Should there be a requirement that checks in excess of a certain amount be signed by more than one officer?

Section 8.
In the absence of the president or in the event of his inability or refusal to act, the vice-president (or in the event there be more than one vice-president, the vice-presidents in the order designated by the directors, or in the absence of any designation, then in the order of their election) shall perform the duties of the president, and when so acting, shall have all the powers of and be subject to all the restrictions upon the president. The vice-presidents shall perform such other duties and have such other powers as the board of directors may from time to time prescribe.

Q: What does "absence of the president" mean? Will third parties hesitate to accept an action taken by the vice president when the president is absent?

The Secretary and Assistant Secretary

Section 9.
The secretary shall attend all meetings of the board of directors and all meetings of the stockholders and record all the proceedings of the meetings of the corporation and of the board of directors in a book to be kept for that purpose and shall perform like duties for the standing committees when required. He shall give, or cause to be given, notice of all meetings of the stockholders and special meetings of the board of directors, and shall perform such other duties as may be prescribed by the board of directors or president, under whose supervision he shall be. He shall have custody of the corporate seal of the corporation and he, or an assistant secretary, shall have authority to affix the same to any instrument requiring it and when so affixed, it may be attested by his signature or by the signature of such assistant secretary. The board of directors may give general authority to any other officer to affix the seal of the corporation and to attest the affixing by his signature.

Q: For convenience, should a lawyer in your firm be elected an assistant secretary of the Corporation? Would this expose the firm to significant liability?

Form 8: By-Laws for a Delaware Corporation (continued)

Section 10.

The assistant secretary, or if there be more than one, the assistant secretaries in the order determined by the board of directors (or if there be no such determination, then in the order of their election) shall, in the absence of the secretary or in the event of his inability or refusal to act, perform the duties and exercise the powers of the secretary and shall perform such other duties and have such other powers as the board of directors may from time to time prescribe.

The Treasurer and Assistant Treasurers

Section 11.

The treasurer shall have the custody of the corporate funds and securities and shall keep full and accurate accounts of receipts and disbursements in books belonging to the corporation and shall deposit all moneys and other valuable effects in the name and to the credit of the corporation in such depositories as may be designated by the board of directors.

Section 12.

He shall disburse the funds of the corporation as may be ordered by the board of directors, taking proper vouchers for such disbursements, and shall render to the president and the board of directors, at its regular meetings, or when the board of directors so requires, an account of all his transactions as treasurer and of the financial condition of the corporation.

Section 13.

If required by the board of directors, he shall give the corporation a bond (which shall be renewed every six years) in such sum and with such surety or sureties as shall be satisfactory to the board of directors for the faithful performance of the duties of his office and for the restoration to the corporation, in case of his death, resignation, retirement or removal from office, of all books, papers, vouchers, money and other property of whatever kind in his possession or under his control belonging to the corporation.

Section 14.

The assistant treasurer, or if there shall be more than one, the assistant treasurers in the order determined by the board of directors (or if there be no such determination, then in the order of their election) shall, in the absence of the treasurer or in the event of his inability or refusal to act, perform the duties and exercise the powers of the treasurer and shall perform such other duties and have such other powers as the board of directors may from time to time prescribe.

Form 8: By-Laws for a Delaware Corporation (continued)

ARTICLE VI
Certificates for Shares

Note: The form of the stock certificates will be approved at the first meeting of the Board of Directors. All certificates shall bear a legend explaining the strict limits on transferability.

Note: This will be done by the lawyer or corporate secretary if there is no Transfer Agent.

Note: If there are a large number of Stockholders, the Corporation should hire a Transfer Agent. If the number is few, the Corporation's lawyers or secretary should retain possession of the stock ledger book.

Section 1.
The shares of the corporation shall be represented by a certificate or shall be uncertificated. Certificates shall be signed by, or in the name of the corporation by, the chairman or vice-chairman of the board of directors, or the president or a vice-president, and by the treasurer or an assistant treasurer, or the secretary or an assistant secretary of the corporation.

Upon the face or back of each stock certificate issued to represent any partly paid shares, or upon the books and records of the corporation in the case of uncertificated partly paid shares, shall be set forth the total amount of the consideration to be paid therefor and the amount paid thereon shall be stated.

If the corporation shall be authorized to issue more than one class of stock or more than one series of any class, the powers, designations, preferences and relative, participating, optional or other special rights of each class of stock or series thereof and the qualification, limitations or restrictions of such preferences and/or rights shall be set forth in full or summarized on the face or back of the certificate which the corporation shall issue to represent such class or series of stock, provided that, except as otherwise provided in section 202 of the General Corporation Law of Delaware, in lieu of the foregoing requirements, there may be set forth on the face or back of the certificate which the corporation shall issue to represent such class or series of stock, a statement that the corporation will furnish without charge to each stockholder who so requests the powers, designations, preferences and relative, participating, optional or other special rights of each class of stock or series thereof and the qualifications, limitations or restrictions of such preferences and/or rights.

Within a reasonable time after the issuance or transfer of uncertificated stock, the corporation shall send to the registered owner thereof a written notice containing the information required to be set forth or stated on certificates pursuant to Sections 151, 156, 202(a) or 218(a) or a statement that the corporation will furnish without charge to each stockholder who so requests the powers, designations, preferences and relative participating, optional or other special rights of each class of stock or series thereof and the qualifications, limitations or restrictions of such preferences and/or rights.

Section 2.
Any of or all the signatures on a certificate may be facsimile. In case any officer, transfer agent or registrar who has signed or whose facsimile signature has been placed upon

Form 8: By-Laws for a Delaware Corporation (continued)

a certificate shall have ceased to be such officer, transfer agent or registrar before such certificate is issued, it may be issued by the corporation with the same effect as if he were such officer, transfer agent or registrar at the date of issue.

Lost Certificates

Section 3.

The board of directors may direct a new certificate or certificates or uncertificated shares to be issued in place of any certificate or certificates theretofore issued by the corporation alleged to have been lost, stolen or destroyed, upon the making of an affidavit of that fact by the person claiming the certificate of stock to be lost, stolen or destroyed. When authorizing such issue of a new certificate or certificates or uncertificated shares, the board of directors may, in its discretion and as a condition precedent to the issuance thereof, require the owner of such lost, stolen or destroyed certificate or certificates, or his legal representative, to advertise the same in such manner as it shall require and/or to give the corporation a bond in such sum as it may direct as indemnity against any claim that may be made against the corporation with respect to the certificate alleged to have been lost, stolen or destroyed.

Transfer of Stock

Section 4.

Upon surrender to the corporation or the transfer agent of the corporation of a certificate for shares duly endorsed or accompanied by proper evidence of succession, assignation or authority to transfer, it shall be the duty of the corporation to issue a new certificate to the person entitled thereto, cancel the old certificate and record the transaction upon its books. Upon receipt of proper transfer instructions from the registered owner of uncertificated shares such uncertificated shares shall be cancelled and issuance of new equivalent uncertificated shares or certificated shares shall be made to the person entitled thereto and the transaction shall be recorded upon the books of the corporation.

Note: This will be done by the lawyer or corporate secretary if there is no Transfer Agent.

Fixing Record Date

Section 5.

In order that the corporation may determine the stockholders entitled to notice of or to vote at any meeting of stockholders or any adjournment thereof, or to express consent to corporate action in writing without a meeting, or entitled to receive payment of any dividend or other distribution or allotment of any rights, or entitled to exercise any rights in respect of any change, conversion or exchange of stock or for the purpose of any other lawful action, the board of directors may fix, in advance, a record date, which shall not be more than sixty nor less than ten days before the date of

Form 8: By-Laws for a Delaware Corporation (continued)

such meeting, nor more than sixty days prior to any other action. A determination of stockholders of record entitled to notice of or to vote at a meeting of stockholders shall apply to any adjournment of the meeting: provided, however, that the board of directors may fix a new record date for the adjourned meeting.

Registered Stockholders

Section 6.
The corporation shall be entitled to recognize the exclusive right of a person registered on its books as the owner of shares to receive dividends, and to vote as such owner, and to hold liable for calls and assessments a person registered on its books as the owner of shares, and shall not be bound to recognize any equitable or other claim to or interest in such share or shares on the part of any other person, whether or not it shall have express or other notice thereof, except as otherwise provided by the laws of Delaware.

ARTICLE VII
General Provisions

Dividends

Section 1.
Dividends upon the capital stock of the corporation, subject to the provisions of the certificate of incorporation, if any, may be declared by the board of directors at any regular or special meeting, pursuant to law. Dividends may be paid in cash, in property, or in shares of the capital stock, subject to the provisions of the certificate of incorporation.

Section 2.
Before payment of any dividend, there may be set aside out of any funds of the corporation available for dividends such sum or sums as the directors from time to time, in their absolute discretion, think proper as a reserve or reserves to meet contingencies, or for equalizing dividends, or for repairing or maintaining any property of the corporation, or for such other purpose as the directors shall think conducive to the interest of the corporation, and the directors may modify or abolish any such reserve in the manner in which it was created.

Annual Statement

Section 3.
The board of directors shall present at each annual meeting, and at any special meeting of the stockholders when called for by vote of the stockholders, a full and clear statement of the business and condition of the corporation.

Q: Under what circumstances, if any, should Stockholders be able to cause directors to pay dividends?

Note: For many small C corporations, few, if any, dividends are paid to Stockholders, and the Stockholders, who are usually employees of the company, receive distributions as salaries, rental payments, and interest on loans to the company. All of these distributions, if reasonable, are tax deductible by the company, and double income tax payment is avoided.

Form 8: By-Laws for a Delaware Corporation (continued)

Checks

Section 4.
All checks or demands for money and notes of the corporation shall be signed by such officer or officers or such other person or persons as the board of directors may from time to time designate.

Fiscal Year

Section 5.
The fiscal year of the corporation shall be fixed by resolution of the board of directors.

Seal

Section 6.
The corporate seal shall have inscribed thereon the name of the corporation, the year of its organization and the words "Corporate Seal, Delaware." The seal may be used by causing it or a facsimile thereof to be impressed or affixed or reproduced or otherwise.

Indemnification

Section 7.
The corporation shall indemnify its officers, directors, employees and agents to the extent permitted by the General Corporation Law of Delaware.

ARTICLE VIII
Amendments

Section 1.
These by-laws may be altered, amended or repealed or new by-laws may be adopted by the stockholders or by the board of directors, when such power is conferred upon the board of directors by the certificate of incorporation at any regular meeting of the stockholders or of the board of directors or at any special meeting of the stockholders or of the board of directors if notice of such alteration, amendment, repeal or adoption of new by-laws be contained in the notice of such special meeting. If the power to adopt, amend or repeal by-laws is conferred upon the board of directors by the certificate of incorporation it shall not divest or limit the power of the stockholders to adopt, amend or repeal by-laws.

Note: Signatures by more than one officer for checks above a certain amount is often a good idea.

Note: This should be established at the first meeting of the Board of Directors after consultation with the Corporation's accountants.

Note: The seal should be ordered by the lawyers before the first meeting of the Board of Directors as part of the company's "corporate kit" (seal, minute book, stock ledger book and stock certificates). Its use will be approved at that meeting by the Board.

Q: Is it a good idea to provide greater detail here or in the articles? What about director's and officer's liability insurance?

Note: As a way of preserving control, there may be a requirement for super-majority approval by Stockholders of any changes. If, for example, a By-law required a 90 percent vote by the Stockholders for a particular action but a simple majority could amend the By-laws, the 90-percent By-law could be repealed.

Q: In Delaware, can the articles or the By-laws require unanimous approval of any amendment to the By-laws?

Q: What is the law in New York?

Drafting Exercise 9:

> **Prepare Articles of Incorporation and By-Laws for Kent Clothing Company, Ltd.**
>
> Prepare articles of incorporation and by-laws for Kent Clothing Company, Ltd. using the same general information provided in Drafting Exercise 2 for the Kent General Partnership.
>
> 1. The Company will be a Delaware corporation.
>
> 2. The lawyers will act as incorporators. Use the simplest capitalization structure.
>
> 3. Which of the standard by-laws, if any, would you customize for this company?
>
> Note: We will be looking at additional, more complex provisions of articles of incorporation and by-laws in Chapter 7, when we deal with various control issues.

G. HOUSEKEEPING TASKS: SETTING UP THE CORPORATION

At the time that the lawyer arranges to have a corporate service company, like CT Corporation System, actually file the articles of incorporation, the lawyer will prepare the other necessary documents. The lawyer will also order a corporate "kit" which includes a minute book, stock ledger book, blank stock certificates and a corporate seal from a stationery company. These will all be needed at the organizational meeting.

The incorporators or sole incorporator, either at a meeting or by unanimous consent, will adopt the by-laws and elect the board of directors.

The lawyer will also prepare the draft minutes for the first meeting of the board of directors. By preparing the minutes in advance, they can be used as a script to insure that the board takes all required action, and that nothing is forgotten. Because there is a notice requirement for board meetings, the lawyer also prepares a Waiver of Notice to be executed by the directors before the meeting. All these documents will be kept in the corporate minute book.

Form 9: Unanimous Written Consent of the
                Incorporator(s)

UNANIMOUS WRITTEN CONSENT OF
THE INCORPORATOR(S) OF
_____ CORPORATION

I (We), the undersigned, being the Incorporator(s) of
_____ Corporation, a Missouri corporation (the "Corporation"), do by this Unanimous Written Consent designate
the following actions for the purpose of organizing the Corporation:

1. By-laws for the regulation of the affairs of the Corporation
are adopted by the undersigned and shall be inserted in
the minute book of the Corporation.

2. The following persons are designated as Directors to hold
office until the first annual meeting of Shareholders or until
their respective successors are elected and qualified:

(insert names)

IN WITNESS WHEREOF, the undersigned Incorporator(s) has
(have) executed this Unanimous Written Consent as of the
_____ day of _____, 19___.

s/_____
INCORPORATOR

s/_____
INCORPORATOR

Q. In Delaware is there any
statutory requirement that
there be more than one incorporator? Who may serve as
an incorporator?

Note: Incorporators in Delaware may act at a meeting or
by unanimous consent.

Note: If the persons to constitute the first Board of Directors of the Corporation are
not named in the Articles of
Incorporation of the Corporation, the incorporators by
unanimous vote at a meeting
or by unanimous written consent, may adopt the original
by-laws of the Corporation
and name the persons who
shall constitute the first Board
of Directors of the Corporation.

Form 10: Waiver of Notice for the First Meeting of the
Board of Directors

**WAIVER OF NOTICE
FIRST MEETING OF
THE BOARD OF DIRECTORS**

We, the undersigned, being all the directors of _____ do hereby call and waive notice of the time, place and purpose of the first meeting of the board of directors of said corporation.

We call and designate the _____ day of _____, 19_____, at _____ m., as the time, and _____ as the place of said meeting, the purpose thereof being to elect officers, authorize the issue of the capital stock, complete the organization of said corporation, and to transact such other business as may be necessary or advisable.

Dated, _____, 19 _____ .

s/_____
DIRECTOR

s/_____
DIRECTOR

s/_____
DIRECTOR

Note: Use this language if by-laws have already been adopted by Incorporators. If by-laws have not yet been adopted, add their adoption to the agenda for this meeting.

Note: When Incorporators adopt the by-laws, they will be considered to have been adopted by shareholders (if no stock subscriptions had previously been accepted) and this can be significant.

Form 11: Minutes of the First Board Meeting

MINUTES OF FIRST MEETING OF
BOARD OF DIRECTORS OF

_____

A DELAWARE CORPORATION

The first meeting of the board of directors _____ of _____ was called and held at _____ on the _____ day of _____, 19___ at _____ . ___m. Note that all directors are present.

Note: Note that all directors are present. The directors may have been appointed in the Certificate of Incorporation, or more commonly, elected by the incorporators.

Note: In New York, directors must meet at the organizational meeting in person and not by proxy. *See* N.Y. B.C.L. §708. The Board can, however, act by unanimous consent.

Present: _____ constituting _____ of the board.

_____ was chosen temporary chairman and _____ was chosen temporary secretary of the meeting.

Q: What is the rule in Delaware?

The secretary presented and read a waiver of notice of the meeting, signed by all the directors, which was ordered filed with the minutes of the meeting.

Q: In Delaware, must all directors waive notice?

(The following three paragraphs may be omitted if directors are not named in the Certificate of Incorporation.)

The chairman reported that the Certificate of Incorporation was filed in the office of the Secretary of State of Delaware, on _____, and that a certified copy thereof was recorded on _____, in the office of the Recorder of New Castle County, Delaware and the secretary was instructed to cause a copy of such Certificate of Incorporation to be inserted in the minute book adopted by the shareholders.

Q: How does one determine which county in Delaware to file in?

The secretary presented a form of by-laws for the regulation of the affairs of the corporation, which was read, section by section.

Upon motion, duly made, seconded and carried, it was RESOLVED, that the by-laws submitted at and read to this meeting be and the same hereby are adopted as and for the by-laws of this corporation, and that the secretary be and he hereby is instructed to cause the same to be inserted in the minute book immediately following the copy of the Certificate of Incorporation.

Note: It is good practice to have incorporators adopt By-laws, which have, of course, been prepared in advance by the lawyers. Under certain circumstances in some states By-laws adopted by shareholders are treated differently than those adopted, where permitted, by the Board of Directors.

Form 11: Minutes of the First Board Meeting (continued)

Note: If By-laws were adopted by incorporators, the directors in this provision should "ratify" the adoption of By-laws by the incorporators. The directors should expressly ratify the actions taken at the incorporators meeting or in the Statement of Incorporators in lieu of a meeting.

Q: Can the board ratify acts made before the corporation existed, or merely adopt them?

Q: For the purpose of sharing control, would it be possible to rotate the presidency between two individuals?

The following persons were nominated for officers of the corporation to serve until their respective successors are chosen and qualify:

_____ President

_____ Vice-President

_____ Secretary

_____ Treasurer

All the directors present having voted, the chairman announced that the aforesaid persons had been unanimously elected to the offices set before their respective names.

The president and the secretary thereupon entered upon the discharge of their duties.

(Any desired resolutions fixing salaries of officers may be inserted here.)

Q: In fixing salaries for officers, how can you prevent the Board from later reducing salaries to force out an officer?

Note: It may be a good idea for the Board to adopt a resolution authorizing employment agreements with key officers, which should be prepared in advance by counsel.

Note: The directors may set their own compensation unless this power is left to the Stockholders in the articles of incorporation or By-laws.

Q: When would you suggest that a bond be posted by the Treasurer? Would payment for the bond be expensive for the Corporation? Would this be offensive to the Treasurer?

(If it is desired that the treasurer give a bond, insert here necessary provision therefor.)

Form 11: Minutes of the First Board Meeting (continued)

Upon motion, duly made, seconded and carried, it was RESOLVED, That there shall be an executive committee of _____ members of the board of directors which shall have authority to exercise all the powers of the board, except such powers prohibited by law, in the current business of the corporation while the board is not in session and the executive committee may authorize the seal of the corporation to be affixed to all papers, which may require it.

FURTHER RESOLVED, That _____, _____, and _____ be and they are hereby designated as members of the executive committee and _____ to be chairman thereof and that _____ and _____ be and they are designated as alternate members of the executive committee who may replace any absent or disqualified member at any meeting of the committee.

Upon motion, duly made, seconded and carried, it was RESOLVED, That the form of stock certificate presented and read be and it is hereby approved and adopted, and the secretary is instructed to insert a specimen thereof in the minute book.

Upon motion, duly made, seconded and carried, it was RESOLVED, That the seal, an impression of which is hereto affixed, be and it is hereby adopted as the corporate seal of the corporation.

The secretary was authorized and directed to procure the proper corporate books.

Note: Appointing a committee to do much of the Board's work could be comparable to electing managing partners for a general partnership. For convvenience, inside directors are more likely to serve on this committee.

Q: In Delaware, are there limits on the size of committees? Are there limits on what committees may do?

Note: The stock certificate will be provided in the "corporate kit" ordered by the lawyers from a legal stationery company.

Note: Each certificate should contain a restrictive legend on the back which should provide that "These are restricted securities which are subject to the terms of a Shareholders' Agreement, dated _____, and which are not registered with the Securities and Exchange Commission and which may not be resold without such registration or exemption from registration and without the approval of the Corporation's counsel. All sales must also comply with the terms of the Shareholders' Agreement."

Note: As part of your practice of preventive lawyering, no certificates without a restrictive legend should ever leave your office.

Note: The seal and blank minute book are part of the corporate kit purchased from a legal stationery company. An impression, using the seal, as adopted, should be placed in the corporate minute book.

Form 11: Minutes of the First Board Meeting (continued)

Note. Never commingle funds from one corporation to another even if the shareholders are the same. This will help prevent piercing the corporate veil.

Note: Because different banks require slightly different corporate resolutions, obtain one from the bank the Corporation intends to use and adopt it at this meeting. One original should be annexed to these minutes and another provided to the bank.

Q: Who may sign checks written on the corporate account? Should there be a requirement for signature by more than one officer for checks above a certain dollar amount?

Note: This provision should be set forth in the By-laws. It is a good idea to provide for telephonic board of directors meetings where allowed by statute.

Note: This form covers four alternative situations for the issuance of stock.

Note: Only the Board of Directors can authorize the issuance of the Corporation's stock. The Minutes must set forth the name of the purchaser, the number of shares purchased, and the price paid which must be more than the par value of the shares. To avoid potential problems, the purchase price should always be substantially higher than the par value.

Upon motion, duly made, seconded and carried, it was RESOLVED, That the treasurer be and he is hereby authorized to open a bank account in behalf of the corporation with the Bank.

FURTHER RESOLVED, That until otherwise ordered, said bank be and hereby is authorized to make payments from the funds of this corporation on deposit with it upon and according to the check of this corporation signed by _____.

Upon motion, duly made, seconded and carried, it was RESOLVED, That an office of the corporation be established and maintained at _____, in the City of _____, State of _____, and that meetings of the board of directors from time to time may be held either at the registered office in Wilmington, Delaware, or at such office in the City of _____ or elsewhere, as the board of directors shall from time to time order.

FURTHER RESOLVED, That, until otherwise ordered, regular meetings of the board of directors be held at said office in the City of _____, State of _____, on the _____ day of each month at _____ ___.m.

(For use when par value shares are issued for cash)

The president stated that the corporation had received subscriptions to _____ shares of _____ stock of this corporation having a par value of _____ Dollars ($_____) per share at _____ Dollars ($_____) per share.

The treasurer thereupon stated that the subscribers had tendered to the corporation the sum of _____ Dollars ($_____) in full payment at par for the _____ stock subscribed.

Upon motion, duly made, seconded and carried, the president and the _____ were authorized to issue to the said subscribers or their nominees certificates representing full paid and non-assessable _____ stock of this corporation to the amount of their respective subscriptions.

Form 11: Minutes of the First Board Meeting (continued)

(For use when par value shares are issued for property.)

The president stated that an offer had been made to the corporation to transfer to it certain property in consideration of the issuance of stock. Said offer, of which the following is a copy, was presented and read to the meeting:

> To:
>
> I hereby offer to transfer to _____ complete title in fact and of record free from lien or incumbrance, to the following described real (or personal) property, to wit:
>
> *(insert description)*
> in consideration of the issuance to me of _____ shares of _____ stock, the total par value of which is _____ Dollars ($_____).
>
> It is understood that if this offer is accepted, the above mentioned shares of _____ stock are to be issued to me or my nominees upon the delivery to your corporation of the proper instruments of transfer and conveyance of the above mentioned property.
>
> Dated at _____, 19_____.

Upon motion, duly made, seconded and carried, the following preambles and resolutions were adopted:

WHEREAS, _____ has offered to transfer to this corporation in full payment for _____ shares of the _____ stock of this corporation, to be issued to him or his nominees, property as follows: *(insert description)*
    and
WHEREAS, In the judgment of this board said property is necessary for the business of this corporation and is of a value at least equal to the aggregate par value of the stock demanded therefor;

Now, therefore, be it RESOLVED, That the offer of said _____ to transfer to this corporation the property hereinbefore described, which said property the board of directors does hereby adjudge and declare to be the value of at least _____ Dollars ($_____), and necessary for the business of this corporation, be and it is hereby accepted and that the _____ and _____ of this corporation be and they hereby are authorized and directed to execute and deliver, in the name and on behalf of this corporation and under its corporate seal, such agreement or agreements as may be necessary for the acquisition of said property in accordance with said offer and that the officers of this corporation be and they hereby are further authorized and directed to issue to the order of said _____ or his nominees, certificates of full paid and non-assessable stock of this corporation for the shares provided to be issued by the foregoing resolutions upon transfer of said property to this corporation.

Note: In New York, shares cannot be purchased with a promissory note.

Q: What is the rule in Delaware?

Note: This is a rebuttable presumption in favor of the value that the board establishes for property. In some cases, it would be a good idea for the board to get a formal appraisal.

Form 11: Minutes of the First Board Meeting (continued)

Note: The Board of Directors must clearly establish how to account for the payment on the Corporation's books. They will determine how much is to go to stated capital, and how much to capital surplus.

(For use when shares without par value are issued for cash.)

Upon motion, duly made, seconded and carried, it was RESOLVED, That _____ Dollars ($_____) per share be fixed as the amount of consideration to be received by this corporation for _____ shares of _____ stock without par value.

The president thereupon stated that the corporation had received subscriptions to _____ shares of _____ stock of this corporation without par value at _____ Dollars ($_____) per share.

The treasurer thereupon stated that the subscribers had tendered to the corporation the sum of _____ Dollars ($_____) in full payment for the foregoing shares without par value and, upon motion, duly made, seconded and carried, the officers of the corporation were authorized to issue to said subscribers or their nominees certificates representing full paid and non-assessable _____ stock to the amount of their respective subscriptions.

Upon motion, duly made, seconded and carried, it was RESOLVED, That the sum of _____ Dollars ($_____) received in payment for the foregoing share be declared part of the capital of this corporation.

(For use when shares without par value are issued for property.)

The president stated that an offer had been made to the corporation to transfer to it certain property in consideration of the issuance of stock. Said offer, of which the following is a copy, was presented and read to the meeting:

To: _____

I hereby offer to transfer to _____ complete title in fact and of record free from lien or incumbrance to the following described real (or personal) property, to wit: *(insert description)* _____ in consideration of the issuance to me of _____ shares of the _____ stock of said corporation without par value.

It is understood that if this offer is accepted, the above mentioned shares of _____ stock are to be issued to me or my nominees upon the delivery to your corporation of the proper instruments of transfer and conveyance of the above mentioned property.

Dated at _____, 19_____.

Upon motion, duly made, seconded and carried, the following preambles and resolutions were adopted:

WHEREAS, _____ has offered to transfer to this corporation in consideration of the issuance to him or his nominees

Form 11: Minutes of the First Board Meeting (continued)

of _____ shares of _____ stock of this corporation without par value, the following described property: *(insert description)* and

WHEREAS, In the judgment of this board of directors such property is necessary for the business of this corporation and a proper consideration for the issue of shares of stock of this corporation without par value;

Now, therefore, be it RESOLVED, That this corporation accept the offer of said _____ to transfer the above described property, which said property the board of directors hereby declares to be necessary for the business of this corporation and a proper consideration for the issue of _____ shares of stock without par value.

FURTHER RESOLVED, That the officers of this corporation be and they hereby are authorized and directed to execute in the name and on behalf of this corporation and under its corporate seal such agreement or agreements as may be necessary for the acquisition of said property in accordance with said offer and that the officers of this corporation be and they hereby are authorized to issue to the said _____ or his nominees certificate representing full paid and non-assessable _____ stock of this corporation for the shares provided to be issued by the foregoing resolutions upon transfer of said property to this corporation.

Upon motion, duly made, seconded and carried, it was RESOLVED, That the consideration received for the foregoing shares of stock without par value be declared part of the capital of this corporation, and the board of directors does hereby adjudge and declare the said property to be of the value of at least _____ Dollars ($____) for all purposes where a valuation must be given or set forth.

Upon motion, duly made, seconded and carried, it was RESOLVED, That for the purpose of authorizing the corporation to do business in any state, territory or dependency of the United States or any foreign country in which it is necessary or expedient for this corporation to transact business, the proper officers of this corporation are hereby authorized to appoint and substitute all necessary agents or attorneys for service of process, to designate and change the location of all necessary statutory offices and, under the corporate seal, to make and file all necessary certificates, reports, powers of attorney and other instruments as may be required by the laws of such state, territory, dependency or country to authorize the corporation to transact business therein and whenever it is expedient for the corporation to cease doing business therein and withdraw therefrom, to revoke any appointment or surrender of authority as may be necessary to terminate the authority of the corporation to do business in any such state, territory, dependency or country.

Note: If an allocation of part of the consideration is to be made to surplus, this language must be modified.

Note: If you intend to qualify the Corporation to do business in other states, you must determine that the Corporation's name is not deceptively similar to other corporations in that state.

Note: Research will be necessary to determine what acts constitute doing business in each state. Companies like CT Corporation System can be retained to assist with filings and serving as registered agent and registered office in other states.

Form 11: Minutes of the First Board Meeting (continued)

> Upon motion, duly made, seconded and carried, it was RESOLVED, That the fiscal year of the corporation shall begin the first day of _____ in each year.
>
> Upon motion, duly made, seconded and carried, it was RESOLVED, That the treasurer be and he hereby is authorized to pay all fees and expenses incident to and necessary for the organization of the corporation.
>
> Upon motion, duly made, seconded and carried, the meeting thereupon adjourned.
>
> s/_____
>   SECRETARY
> (SEAL)

Drafting Exercise 10:

Prepare Draft Minutes for the Organizational Meeting of the Kent Clothing Company, Ltd. Board of Directors

1.   Donna Kent will be president and treasurer. Linda Chen will be vice president and secretary.

2.   The shareholders will buy the following amounts of common stock:

Henry Kent	$100,000.00
Donna Kent	$50,000.00
Linda Chen	$50,000.00
Otto Chen	$50,000.00
Hugo Chen	$50,000.00

3.   The Company will give Henry Kent a promissory note for $150,000 with a reasonable rate of interest and a security interest in the Company's inventory, equipment, and accounts receivable.

4.   Your law firm will be retained as counsel to the Company.

Practical Pointers

1. *First Meeting of the Board of Directors.* All corporate formalities should be strictly adhered to in order to avert any threat of piercing the corporate veil. All action taken by the Board should follow the format so that the Minutes indicate what action has been resolved, voted upon, and approved. A good corporate lawyer always prepares a draft of the Minutes prior to the meeting, in addition to an agenda.

Before the meeting, the lawyer for the corporation should order a "corporate kit" from a commercial supplier. This will consist of a corporate seal in the company's name, a minute book for shareholder and director meetings and consents, a stock ledger book and blank stock certificates. It is also important to obtain the text of the corporate resolution authorizing Corporate banking from the Corporation's bank. Since different banks use slightly different forms and language, it is quicker, cheaper and easier to use the bank's form of resolution for the Board to adopt.

2. *Minutes of the First Meeting of the Board of Directors.* While the example provided is quite serviceable, it is a good idea to use it as a checklist and build on it with provisions that apply to your client's situation. You may also identify helpful provisions to include by examining other forms. Examples of additional useful resolutions:

a. appointing lawyers and accountants for the Corporation

b. authorizing the election of S Corporation status

c. authorizing lease or rental of office space

d. appointing a transfer agent if there is a sufficiently large number of stockholders

e. authorizing the Corporation to be a party to a Shareholder Agreement, an important control mechanism discussed in Chapter 7

f. authorizing the Corporation to borrow funds from a Stockholder by executing a promissory note and security agreement, and authorizing the terms and conditions for these instruments

If you opt to adapt form provisions from another state, double-check the corporate statute of your state of incorporation to be certain that the language you use is in full compliance with the relevant law.

Notes

1. Excellent reference works for students to consult include: Hern & Alexander, Corporations (3d ed. 1983); Robert C. Clark, Corporate Law (1986); Larry D. Soderquist & A.A. Sommer, Jr., Understanding Corporation Law (Practising Law Inst., 1990); and the three-volume treatise, Cox, Hazen & O'Neal, Corporations (1995).

2. Edwin T. Hood & John J. Mylan, Federal Taxation of Close Corporations (1991). Chapter One on choice of entity has an excellent general discussion of corporate tax issues.

3. *See generally* Scott Burnham, Drafting Contracts (2d ed. 1993), especially Chapter 17, *The Language of Drafting.*

4. Id.

Chapter 7

Control Issues for Closely Held Corporations

A statement attributed to J.P. Morgan is that if you need to ask how much a yacht costs, you cannot afford to buy it. Somewhat similarly, if you need to draft a corporate control provision to solve an existing problem, it is almost certainly too late to help. When first setting up a corporation, a good corporate lawyer, practicing prospective and preventive law, uses imagination and shrewdness to predict potential disputes and problems. The lawyer then makes an informed selection from among a multitude of control mechanisms. These include: (a) shareholder class voting provisions for Articles of Incorporation; (b) cumulative voting provisions; (c) supermajority voting provision for shareholder or board of director action; (d) employment agreements; (e) Voting Trust Agreements; and (f) shareholder agreements containing pooled voting provisions, and (g) shareholder agreements with buy-sell provisions.

A.   CLASS VOTING BY SHAREHOLDERS

There are certain extraordinary transactions that must be approved by a majority of holders of particular classes of stock. These are statutory requirements that vary somewhat among the corporation statutes of different states. Where they exist, they are mandatory and cannot be superceded by placing a contrary provision in a corporate charter. Note that class voting often occurs when there will be an increase or decrease in the number of shares in a class, a change in par value or a change in the rights or preferences of a class.

The careful planner may wish to provide additional protection by inserting class voting provisions in the corporate charter.

Form 12: Class Voting Provision for Articles of Incorporation

West's McKinney's Forms, New York Business Corporation Law, 4:69

Q: What exactly is a series of a class of preferred stock?

Note: Generally, preferred shareholders do not vote to elect directors. Frequently, however, they get to elect one or more directors if dividends are not paid for a specified time period.

CLASS VOTING PROVISION FOR ARTICLES OF INCORPORATION

The holders of record of (specify classes, e.g., Class A preferred shares, Class B preferred shares, and Class C preferred shares) (or of any series thereof) of this corporation shall vote as a class in connection with the (specify business, e.g., the election of directors) at a meeting of the shareholders by the following proportionate vote, to wit: (specify proportions, e.g.)

Holders of Class A preferred shares shall elect three directors by the affirmative vote of (ninety) (90%) percent of the holders entitled to vote thereon.

Holders of Class B preferred shares shall elect two directors by the affirmative vote of (seventy-five) (75%) percent of the holders entitled to vote thereon.

Holders of Class C preferred shares shall elect one director by the affirmative vote of (fifty-five) (55%) percent of the holders entitled to vote thereon.

B.   CUMULATIVE VOTING BY SHAREHOLDERS

Cumulative voting by shareholders is generally optional but there are a few states in which it is mandatory. There are also states in which cumulative voting is automatic unless the corporate charter provides otherwise.

Cumulative voting can make it possible for a minority of shareholders to be assured of electing one or more directors, whereas if there were straight voting, shareholders owning a simple majority of shares would be able to elect all directors.

Cumulative voting does not necessarily guarantee that minority shareholders will be able to elect any directors. Moreover, if the number of directors is reduced, a minority group might be unable to elect as many (or any) directors. Sometimes instead of reducing the total number of directors, the board is staggered and elected for different terms, or in different years. This has the same effect.

A formula and problem may serve to make clear how cumulative voting works. This will be the only mathematical formula in this book.

$$X = \frac{(N)(S)}{D+1} + 1$$

X = number of shares needed to elect
N = number of directors attempting to elect
S = total number of shares to be noted
D = total number of directors to be elected

Sample Problem: XYZ Corporation has 50,000 shares of common stock authorized and 40,000 issued and outstanding. At a duly called shareholders meeting, 30,000 shares are represented in person or by proxy. The Board of Directors is comprised of fifteen directors who have staggered terms of three years each. At this meeting a shareholder (or cooperating group of shareholders) must be able to vote a minimum of how many shares in order to be certain of electing two directors?

$$X = \frac{(2)(30,000)}{5+1} + 1$$

so, X = 10,001 shares

If there were straight rather than cumulative voting, holders of 15,001 shares could elect all directors.

Form 13: Cumulative Voting Provision for Articles of
            Incorporation

West's McKinney's Forms, New York Business Corporation Law, 4:71

Q: Would it be possible for a number of shareholders who could not prevent a director from being elected (because of cumulative voting) to remove such a director without cause? Would a supermajority requirement be a good way to prevent this from happening?

Note: In certain states (including Pennsylvania and Illinois), provisions relating to cumulative voting are contained in the state constitution.

CUMULATIVE VOTING PROVISION FOR ARTICLES OF INCORPORATION

In all elections of directors of this corporation, each shareholder of record shall be entitled to as many votes as shall equal the number of votes which, except for this provision as to cumulative voting, he would be entitled to cast for the election of directors with respect to his shares multiplied by the number of directors to be elected, and he may cast all of such votes for a single director or may distribute them among the number to be voted for, or any two or more of them, as he may see fit.

C.   SUPERMAJORITY PROVISIONS

Supermajority provisions requiring the vote of more than a simple majority of shareholders or directors can be an excellent method for protecting the minority. The provisions can apply to all shareholders or director action, or just to certain especially important actions that would be applicable to certain companies or situations. Note that these provisions can give a single shareholder or director or a minority of shareholders or directors a veto power. Accordingly, it is necessary to balance the need for these provisions against the likelihood and danger of deadlocks. Some courts have refused to enforce provisions requiring a unanimous vote, but less than unanimous supermajority provisions will generally be enforced, and can have the same effect.

When drafting, be very careful not to confuse shareholder votes with board of director votes and not to confuse voting with quorum requirements.

Be very careful to check the corporation statute of the state of incorporation to determine whether supermajority provisions must be set forth in the Articles of Incorporation, or whether they may instead be included in the by-laws. Provisions in the incorrect place will be a nullity.

It is easy to "shoot yourself in the foot" while drafting supermajority provisions which result in little or no protection. For example, if the Articles of Incorporation provide that a director can only be removed without cause by the vote of 75 percent of the shareholders, 51 percent of the shareholders could vote to amend the Articles and delete this provision, unless a similar supermajority provision also applied to amending the Articles.

Requirements for larger quorums are fairly similar to supermajority voting requirements. Note that it is not a good idea to require that all shareholders or directors be present to constitute a quorum, since this is cumbersome and may not be enforced by courts. Also, in calculating whether a quorum is present for a board of directors meeting, the requirement is the percentage of the full board (i.e., the total number authorized in the charter) and not just the number of directors actually in the office.

Form 14: Supermajority Provision for Shareholder Action

Note: If there were three directors, the supermajority requirement of 75 percent would give each shareholder (having 33 percent) a veto power, just as if a unanimous vote was required.

SUPERMAJORITY PROVISION FOR SHAREHOLDER ACTION

Notwithstanding any provision of law to the contrary, the affirmative vote of at least 3/4 of all of the votes entitled to be cast on the following matters may be required to approve and authorize the following acts of the Corporation:

(a) the consolidation of the Corporation with one or more corporations to form a new consolidated corporation;

(b) the merger of the Corporation into another corporation or the merger of one or more other corporations into the Corporation;

(c) the sale, lease, exchange or other transfer of all, or substantially all, of the property and assets of the Corporation, including its goodwill and franchises;

(d) the voluntary or involuntary liquidation, dissolution or winding up of the Corporation.

Form 15: Supermajority Provision for Board of Directors Action

Note: These are important transactions that would require a supermajority vote.

SUPERMAJORITY PROVISION FOR BOARD OF DIRECTORS ACTION

In addition to any shareholder approval that may be required, the following corporate actions must be approved by the affirmative vote of at least three-fourths (75 percent) of the directors of the corporation in office: amending the articles of incorporation; amending the bylaws; dissolving the corporation; merging or consolidating the corporation; selling, leasing, mortgaging, or transferring all or substantially all of the corporation's assets; issuing stock; purchasing, redeeming or retiring the corporation's stock.

D. EMPLOYMENT AGREEMENTS

One method used to protect the position of a corporate officer is with an employment agreement. Use of such agreements is helpful but they are not foolproof. For one thing, courts are very unlikely to enforce them with specific performance so that the only remedy available to a wronged employee is money damages.

Moreover, even if an employee is guaranteed a particular title, the job description may change. The employee may also be made to feel uncomfortable in an effort to force a resignation. Therefore, it is a good idea to provide some specific description of responsibilities and perquisites. Also, some formula for salary increases should be included so that the employee's salary does not remain stagnant until the employee is obliged to quit.

One area of particular concern in drafting is the use of non-compete provisions. When drafting these, it is important to research the statutory and case law in the relevant jurisdiction. Most states will only enforce non-competition agreements that are reasonable as to scope, time and location, but there is great variation as to what each jurisdiction believes to be reasonable. Moreover, in some jurisdictions if the agreement has unreasonable provisions, courts will only enforce them to the degree that they would find reasonable (i.e., reducing five years to one year), while in others the entire agreement would be unenforceable. Accordingly, by providing for too much, a lawyer could get nothing for the client and a malpractice suit for himself.

Form 16: Employment Agreement

Note: Tone is important. It is always a good idea to be polite.

Q. If you are representing the employee, would you want to describe powers and duties more fully? Would you want to provide that they could not change without generous severance pay?

Q: What does "eleemosynary" mean?

Q. What is the longest term to which you could bind an employee? Does the 13th Amendment (abolishing slavery) establish a limit?

Q. If you were representing the employee, would there be a way to assure that the employee's salary would at least keep pace with inflation?

EMPLOYMENT AGREEMENT

(COMPANY LETTERHEAD)

_____, 19_____

Dear (EMPLOYEE NAME):

I am delighted that you are going to be with us and am pleased to confirm our agreement with you.

1. *Employment.* _____, Inc. (the "Company") hereby agrees that the Company will employ you upon the terms and conditions set forth to perform such executive duties as may be determined and assigned to you from time to time by or upon the authority of the Board of Directors of the Company. It is intended that initially you will be the President and Chief Executive Officer of the Company. You hereby accept such employment and agree to devote all of your time and efforts with undivided loyalty to the performance of such duties. During the period of your employment hereunder you shall not, without the consent of the Board of Directors of the Company (a) be engaged, directly or indirectly, in any active work (other than the services herein provided for) for which you receive compensation, (b) be a director of any corporation or firm (other than eleemosynary) or (c) have any interest or relationship (other than social), direct or indirect, financial or otherwise, in any firm, corporation or other entity or any person doing business, directly or indirectly with the Company or any of the Subsidiaries, except through ownership of less than 5% of the outstanding securities of any such firm, corporation or entity of a class which are traded on a national securities exchange or would be eligible for continued listing on the list of OTC Margin Stocks promulgated by the Federal Reserve Board.

2. *Term.* The term of your employment hereunder shall be for a minimum period commencing as of the date of this Agreement and ending _____, 19_____ and shall continue thereafter until terminated by either party by at least _____ month's written notice given at any time during or after such minimum period; provided, however, that the Company may by written notice immediately terminate this Agreement at any time after you have been unable by reason of illness, physical or mental incapacity or other disability to perform your duties hereunder for a period of _____ consecutive months.

3. *Compensation.* The Company agrees to pay to you during the term of your employment, and you agree to accept, in full payment for the services to be performed by you hereunder, a salary payable in equal installments not less often than monthly at the rate of $_____ per annum through _____, 19_____ and at the rate of $_____ thereafter. In

Form 16: Employment Agreement (continued)

the event of your death during the term of your employment, your legal representatives shall be entitled to receive the salary due you through the last day of the calendar month in which your death shall have occurred. The Company will review your salary arrangements annually and may at its discretion increase the salary hereunder, the first adjustment to be effective _____, 19_____.

4. *Expenses.* The Company shall reimburse you for travel, hotel, entertainment and other expenses actually and reasonably incurred by you in connection with and in the course of your employment hereunder.

5. *Other Benefits.* You will also be entitled to participate on a non-contributory basis in the Company's (i) retirement plan, (ii) Major Medical Plan (family coverage) and (iii) Blue Cross insurance plan, in each case, in accordance with its terms.

    The Company will purchase, and will maintain so long as this Agreement remains in force, a life insurance policy or life insurance policies on your life with a total face amount equal to at least $_____.

    You will be entitled to four weeks of paid vacation per year. Any vacation which remains unutilized on December 31 of the year in which such vacation is accrued shall be forfeited. Upon the termination of your employment under this Agreement, you will receive an amount equal to one week's compensation for each week of accrued but unused vacation at the time of such termination. For purposes of the foregoing, vacation will accrue at the rate of one week per calendar quarter.

6. *Non-Competition.* You agree that, for a period commencing with the date hereof and continuing until one year after the termination of this Agreement, you will not, except pursuant to this Agreement, directly or indirectly, on your own behalf or as a partner, officer, director, trustee, employee, agent, consultant or member of any person, firm or corporation, or otherwise, (a) in any state in which the business of the Company or any of the Company's subsidiaries or affiliates was conducted during the term of your employment hereunder, in competition with the Company, or any of the Company's subsidiaries or any affiliates of the Company engaged in the business of the Company or any of the Company's subsidiaries, enter into the employ of, render any service to or engage in any business or activity which is the same as, similar to or competitive with any business or activity (other than investment and reinvestment in securities permissible under paragraph 1(c) of this Agreement and in real estate) conducted by the Company or any of the Company's subsidiaries during the term of your employment hereunder and (b) use or disclose to any person, firm or corporation (other than the Company or any of the Company's subsidiaries or affiliates) or otherwise employ your knowledge of the products and business of, or any trade

Q. Do these non-competition provisions seem reasonable? You must check the statutory and case law in the relevant jurisdiction before hazarding an opinion.

Q. Is it possible to protect the employee from the Company's assignment of its right to employ the employee? The employee could always quit, but might lose all accrued benefits.

Form 16: Employment Agreement (continued)

Q: Is this provision potentially dangerous to the employee?

Note: It is always a good idea to include an integration clause. If you do not include such a standard provision, it may be assumed that you intentionally left it out.

Note: Correct execution by the corporation would be:

XYZ Corp.
by John Doe, President
Attest: Jane Roe, Secretary

secrets or other confidential information as to, the Company's or any of the Company's subsidiaries' or affiliates' processes, operations, products or customers.

7. *Assignment.* The rights and benefits of the Company under this Agreement shall be transferable and all covenants and agreements hereunder shall inure to the benefit of, and be enforceable by, its successors and assigns.

8. *Entire Agreement.* This Agreement incorporates the entire understanding between the parties in regard to your employment by the Company and supersedes all prior agreements with the Company. No modifications or additions to this Agreement, or waiver or cancellation of any provision hereof, shall be valid except by written notice by the party to be charged therewith.

If the above terms and conditions are acceptable to you, will you please so indicate by signing and returning to the Company the enclosed copy of this letter.

Yours sincerely,
(COMPANY)

By _____ Date_____

Accepted:

_____ Date_____
(EMPLOYEE)

E.   VOTING TRUSTS

The voting trust is one of the oldest corporate control mechanisms. It is little used now because it is cumbersome, expensive to set up, and requires that legal ownership of the shares must actually vest in trustees who act as independent fiduciaries on behalf of the shareholders. Nevertheless, it is still a useful mechanism to use for shareholders who are hostile and who will find a way to disagree destructively if less draconian control measures are used.

Voting trusts were allowed at a time when other types of agreements were not enforced because courts which were generally conservative could rely on the comfort of hundreds of years of trust law as precedent.

In a voting trust, the shares of stock are transferred to the trust. The shareholders now own shares in the voting trust and will be issued voting trust certificates. It may even be possible to market voting trust certificates. The trustees now vote the shares. In Delaware, a voting trust cannot be for longer than ten years. Trustees may be elected for the entire term of the voting trust, or they may be elected each year.

If you establish a voting trust, it is necessary to comply strictly with the statute or the agreement will be treated as void. This is largely because courts wish to avoid the possibility of secret, uncontrolled coalitions among shareholders, and public notice of the formation of a trust is therefore required in most states.

Form 17: Voting Trust Agreement

VOTING TRUST AGREEMENT

VOTING TRUST AGREEMENT dated _____, 19_____, among the persons signed below as shareholders (hereafter individually and jointly referred to as the "Shareholders"), and CARL CHARLEY (the "Trustee") whose address is _____.

WHEREAS, XYZ, Inc., a Missouri corporation (the "Company"), is authorized to issue 30,000 shares of common capital stock, par value $1.00 per share, of which on the date hereof 10,000 shares are issued and outstanding (the "Common Stock"); and

The Shareholders are, on the date of execution, the owners of an aggregate of 10,000 shares of Common Stock (the "Shares") of the exact number of shares owned by each Shareholder being set forth opposite his name on the signature page hereof.

In order to ensure the safe and competent management of the Company, the parties hereto desire to create an irrevocable trust for the voting of the Shares.

In consideration of the premises and the covenants, agreements, representation, and warranties hereinafter set forth, the parties hereto agree as follows:

1. (a) Each Shareholder assigns and transfers the number of Shares set forth opposite his name on the signature page hereof to the Trustees and, in furtherance thereof, is simultaneously herewith delivering to the Trustee the certificate representing the Shares.

(b) The Trustee shall surrender to the proper officers of the Company for cancellation the certificates representing the Shares and shall receive new certificates for the Shares to be issued to the Trustee under this Agreement.

(c) The Trustee shall hold the Shares in trust on the terms and conditions herein set forth. Except as otherwise expressly provided herein, the Trustee shall possess the legal title to the Shares and be entitled to exercise all rights of every kind and nature with respect thereto, except that the Trustee shall distribute any cash dividends or other distributions in respect of the Shares other than securities having any direct or contingent voting power to elect directors of the Company, pro rata among the Voting Trust Certificates issued to and held by each of them.

2. The Trustee shall issue to each Stockholder a Voting Trust Certificate or Certificates for the Shares, each of which Certificate(s) shall indicate the number of Shares represented thereby. The Trustee shall maintain a record of all Voting Trust

Note: In many states, there may be a limit on the duration of the trust. In Delaware, to be enforceable it cannot be for more than ten years. See Section 16 of this Agreement.

Note: The original shareholders are now called holders of Voting Trust Certificates.

Form 17: Voting Trust Agreement (continued)

Certificates issued or transferred on his books, which record shall contain the name and address of the holder of each Voting Trust Certificate, the number of shares represented by each such Voting Trust Certificate and the date when the owner became the record owner thereof. Such list and record shall be open to the inspection of the holder of Voting Trust Certificates, the Company and all other shareholders of the Company at all reasonable times upon reasonable notice in advance. Upon transfer on the books of the Trustee of any Voting Trust Certificate in accordance with and as permitted by this Agreement, the transferee shall succeed to all of the rights and become subject to all of the obligations hereunder of the transferor.

3. At all meetings of the stockholders of the Company, the Trustee shall have full power and authority and he is hereby fully empowered and authorized to vote the Shares in person or by proxy, as he in his discretion may deem proper, as fully as any stockholder of the Company might do. The Trustee may consent to any action requiring the consent of stockholders without a meeting of stockholders of the Company, or waive notice of any meeting to the same extent as any other stockholder of the Company.

4. In case the Trustee shall receive any certificate or certificates for Shares or other securities having any direct or contingent voting power to elect directors of the Company as a dividend or distribution upon the Shares, or as a split-up or combination of the Shares, he shall hold the certificate or certificates for such securities subject to the terms of this Agreement.

5. For and during the period in which the irrevocable voting trust created by this Agreement is effective and remains in force, neither the stockholders nor the Trustee shall have the power to sell, transfer, exchange, pledge or otherwise dispose of or encumber Shares deposited hereunder except pursuant to any merger, consolidation, reorganization, or other transaction of similar nature requiring the approval of stockholders; provided, however, that each Voting Trust Certificate shall be transferable except that, to the extent the Shares are subject to restrictions on transfer by any provision of the Articles of Incorporation or By-laws of the Company, the transfer of Voting Trust Certificates shall be similarly restricted as if subject to the same restriction. Each Voting Trust Certificate shall bear a legend setting forth any such restriction. Every purchaser or transferee of a Voting Trust Certificate hereunder, shall, by the acceptance of such Voting Trust Certificate, become a party to this Agreement and be bound by the provisions hereof with the same force and effect as if he had subscribed his name hereto.

Note: It would be possible just to have the trustees elect directors, or to have all powers that shareholders would have.

Form 17: Voting Trust Agreement (continued)

Note: Trustees in this case would only be liable for gross negligent or willful misconduct. It may also be possible to provide that the Trustees are empowered to construe the agreement and their construction shall be final, conclusive and binding on all holders of Voting Trust Certificates.

6. The Trustee shall not incur any liability for any action taken by him or for his omissions or failures to act, or otherwise, except for his individual willful malfeasance. In no circumstance shall failure to act, vote or respond to the demand of any person be deemed malfeasance. The Trustee shall not be required to give bond or security for the discharge of his duties as Trustee. The Trustee shall be entitled to $_____ as compensation for his services as Trustee. The Shareholders shall jointly and severally indemnify the Trustee and hold him harmless from and against any expenses and disbursements reasonably incurred by the Trustee in connection with any litigation which may arise in respect of this Agreement or in respect of the Company, to which the Trustee in any way becomes a party, and any other expenses reasonably and actually incurred by the Trustee in carrying out the terms of this Agreement, including, without limitation, the compensation of agents and attorneys employed by him incident to the performance of his duties hereunder.

7. If at any time the Trustee should die, resign (by giving at least five days prior written notice thereof to the holders of Voting Trust Certificates), become incapacitated or for any reason whatsoever or be unable or unwilling to act hereunder, then thereafter Shareholders holding Voting Trust Certificates representing a majority of the Shares deposited hereunder, shall appoint an individual to act as the successor Trustee hereunder, with all of the powers of the Trustee, or if the Shareholder shall fail so to do within 45 days, then _____ shall act as the successor Trustee hereunder, with all of the powers of the Trustee. Under no circumstances shall the Trustee be under any obligation to perform his duties with respect to this Agreement during the five day period subsequent to his giving notice of resignation, nor shall the timing of the Trustee's resignation in any way create any liability on his part with respect to this Agreement.

8. Unless otherwise terminated as provided in Section 16 hereof, this Agreement, and the irrevocable voting trust created hereby, shall terminate upon the earlier of (i) ten years from the date hereof or (ii) such time as the Trustee holds no securities of the Company having any direct or contingent power to vote for the election of directors.

9. Notwithstanding the termination of this Agreement, the Trustee shall thereafter have the power to take or cause to be taken such further and other action to conclude the duties imposed upon him by this Agreement, provided that after the termination of this Agreement the Trustee shall have no authority to vote any Shares deposited with him hereunder.

Form 17: Voting Trust Agreement (continued)

10. All notices to be given hereunder to the holders of Voting Trust Certificates or the Trustee shall be sent, postage prepaid, by certified or registered mail to the holder of a Voting Trust Certificate, at the latest address furnished by (him/her) in writing to the Trustee, and to the Trustee at the address set forth on the first page of this Agreement, or at such other address as may be designated by notice given in the manner provided in this paragraph.

11. Each Shareholder shall pay all stamp taxes and other governmental charges incident to the transfer of the Shares from such Shareholder to the Trustee.

12. In case the Shares shall be reclassified or changed, the Trustee shall receive and hold under this Agreement any securities having direct or contingent power to vote for directors of the Company received by him on account of the Shares. Any Voting Trust Certificates issued and outstanding under this Agreement at the time of any such reclassification or change may remain outstanding, but Trustee may, in his discretion, substitute for such Voting Trust Certificates new Voting Trust Certificates in appropriate form.

13. This Agreement may be executed in several counterparts, each of which when so executed shall be deemed to be original, and such counterparts shall together constitute one and the same instrument.

14. Wherever necessary, the Trustee may issue a Voting Trust Certificate for fractional shares.

15. The validity of this Agreement, or any part hereof, and of the Voting Trust Certificates, and the interpretation of all provisions hereof and thereof, shall be governed by the laws of the State of Missouri.

16. The term of this Agreement and the irrevocable Voting Trust hereby created may be terminated at any time by the unanimous written consent thereto of the holders of all Voting Trust Certificates. This Agreement may be altered or amended only by the unanimous written consent thereto of the holders of all Voting Trust Certificates and the Trustee, if such amendment is adverse to the Trustee.

17. The invalidity of any term or provision of this Agreement shall not affect the validity of the remainder of this Agreement.

Note: Unanimity is required to terminate or amend.

Form 17: Voting Trust Agreement (continued)

18. This Agreement shall bind and benefit the parties hereto and their respective heirs, administrators, executors, successors and assigns.

IN WITNESS WHEREOF, the parties hereto have executed this Agreement as of the date and year first above written.

Name and Address	Number of Shares	Signature
Albert Able	5,000	_____
Barbara Baker	5,000	_____

F.   SHAREHOLDER AGREEMENTS

It is difficult to imagine a closely held corporation for which counsel should not prepare a shareholder agreement at the time of formation. At the organizational meeting, the board of directors should authorize the corporation to execute the shareholder agreement, thereby becoming a party to it, and all of the shareholders should also simultaneously sign it.

Just about all corporate control problems can be solved, at least in theory, by drafting an appropriate sharesholder's agreement. In the earlier development of corporate law, shareholders had limited power to direct corporate affairs and many states eventually passed Close Corporation Acts to give shareholders greater power. Now that most states enforce shareholders' agreements, it is unnecessary to form a corporation under these special acts, which are often cumbersome and confusing. Lenders and other third parties often have problems dealing with statutory close corporations and the results can be needlessly expensive. For example, when the local bank asks for a certified board of directors resolution authorizing an action, they are perplexed to learn that the borrower is a statutory close corporation without a board of directors. For that reason, I have ignored this business entity in this book. (Form 18 deals with shareholder voting issues.)

The most important aspects of most shareholder agreements involve shareholder voting and buy-sell provisions (with related price valuation formulae). These agreements allow for almost infinite variety, but are comprised of certain basic components. Drafting shareholder agreements is among the most challenging and satisfying tasks for the corporate lawyer. The next section deals with these issues.

G.   BUY-SELL AGREEMENTS AND THE PROBLEM OF VALUATION OF STOCK

There are many reasons to have a shareholder buy-sell agreement. If a company is being managed by its shareholders, it would prevent the stock from going into the hands of inactive successors. In a C corporation, in which profits were zeroed out as salaries to working shareholders, problems could arise if later shareholders were inactive and demanded dividends. In S corporations, buy-sell restrictions could prevent the stock from being transferred to ineligible persons or entities. Such transfer would result in the loss of S corporation status and could precipitate catastrophic tax liability for all shareholders.

Buy-sell provisions may protect minority shareholders from the majority and may also serve to preserve proportionate ownership for surviving shareholders. For corporations that are managed by all their shareholders, buy-sell provisions assure that those shareholders who remain active (and thereby retain ownership of their shares) will obtain the benefits of future growth. Because shares in a closely held corporation are usually not liquid, the use of optional or mandatory buy-sell provisions may be the only way to create a market that will enable shares to be sold.

Buy-sell provisions that are triggered by the death of a shareholder, often funded by term life insurance policies, provide liquidity to a decedent shareholder's estate and financial security for the decedent's family.

There are two generic types of buy-sell agreements: redemption and cross-purchase. In a redemption, the corporation buys the transferring shareholder's shares, while in a cross-purchase, some or all of the remaining shareholders make the purchase. While tax concerns are often important in determining which to select (especially for S corporations), generally speaking the most important concern should be whether the corporation or the remaining shareholders are more likely to be in a better position to fund the obligations created by the agreement. This will be less important, however, if the buy-out triggering event is death and the payment is to be funded by insurance. Nevertheless, it is essential to establish a mechanism to make certain that the corporation (in a redemption agreement) or the other shareholders (in a cross-purchase agreement) actually buy the insurance and pay the premiums to keep it in effect.

In a redemption agreement, the remaining shareholders do not acquire any additional stock, but the percentage ownership interest in the corporation increases. In a cross-purchase agreement, the remaining shareholders acquire the shares of the transferring shareholders. In an S corporation, this yields a tax advantage since their tax basis in the stock generally increases.

Redemption agreements are easier to monitor than cross-purchase agreements. Also, cross-purchase agreements may be overly cumbersome where numerous shareholders are going to participate. For example, in a cross-purchase agreement with three shareholders, where life insurance is going to fund a buy-out, each shareholder would have to insure the other two, for a total of six policies. Obviously this could be difficult to monitor.

Combinations of cross-purchase and redemption may be used in which there is cross-purchase for the first to die and redemption thereafter.

In drafting a buy-sell provision, there are many conditions to be considered. Will the buy out be mandatory or optional? What will trigger it? Death, disability (clearly defined), retirement, resignation? Are transfers among family members to be permitted? Remember, if you leave loopholes as to lifetime transfers, it will prevent the buy-sell provisions from being effective.

An option to purchase over the objection of the other party is called a "call" and protects the buyer. An option to sell over the objection of the other party is called a "put" and protects the seller.

A crucial aspect of buy-sell provisions is valuation or how the purchase price is to be determined. This may vary depending upon what triggers the sale. All valuation methods have drawbacks and sometimes a hybrid or combination is best.

Methods for valuing stock include:

1. *Fixed Price.* Agreements may provide that the shareholders will keep adjusting the price, and will turn to another method if they cannot agree.

2. *Book Value.* This may yield a low figure if it does not include goodwill. The method of accounting used will have an enormous effect if this method is used.

3. *Right of First Refusal.* The corporation or other shareholders may have the right to match an offer made by a third party. The drawbacks include the difficulty of getting a third party to bid on an illiquid, often minority interest on one hand, and bogus or collusive offers on the other.

4. *Appraisal or Arbitration.* It is important to specify a method for selection of an appraiser or arbitrator. Also, clearly specify valuation criteria for setting a price on the stock.

5. *Capitalization of Earnings.* It is necessary to establish the multiplier in the agreement. There is always the danger that one or more atypical good or bad years may unrealistically skew a valuation.

6. *Earn Out.* Often used by parties that do not trust each other. The transferring shareholder gets a percentage of profits for a period of time following the sale. This method provides an opportunity for unfair manipulation by management while also potentially limiting management's freedom to run the corporation.

7. *Shotgun (a.k.a. Russian Roulette).* One side sets the price, the other decides whether it will buy or sell at that price. Like small children dividing a cookie (one breaks it, the other chooses), this can yield a very fair result. The major problem is that both sides need to have the resources and potential desire to buy, or one side will have the capacity to overreach.

If the sale is not to be for cash, the credit and security terms need to be clearly identified.

Form 18: Shareholder Agreement for Pooled Voting
West's McKinney's Forms, New York Business Corporation Law, 7:08

Note: The "party of the first part," "party of the second part," and "party of the third part" language is archaic and could be deleted without harm.

Note: A shareholder agreement is, of course, more likely to be enforced when it has been signed by all shareholders. Accordingly, counsel might advise a minority shareholder not to sign a shareholder agreement unless the shareholder was receiving a substantial benefit.

Note: Courts generally will enforce shareholder voting agreements for close corporations that do not prejudice minority shareholders or third parties (like creditors). The fact that a shareholder willingly signed the agreement is some evidence that it was not prejudicial to the shareholder.

Q. Is it against public policy for the shareholders to dictate how the directors must vote in managing the business? Check the case law in the relevant jurisdiction.

AGREEMENT AMONG SHAREHOLDERS AS TO VOTING

THIS AGREEMENT, made this _____ day of _____, 19_____, between and among _____, residing at _____, the party of the first part, _____, residing at _____, the party of the second part, and _____, residing at _____, the party of the third part,

WITNESSETH:

WHEREAS each of the parties hereto are respectively in control of a (one-third) (1/3) interest in all of the shares of the (name of corporation), and

WHEREAS the parties hereto desire to make provision for the harmonious operation of (name of corporation) with the aim of making said corporation prosper and grow and with the intention of protecting the investments of the respective parties hereto in the corporation;

NOW THEREFORE, it is agreed by and among the parties, in consideration of the premises, the mutual undertakings herein provided, and other good and valuable consideration, as follows:

1. That as shareholders the parties will vote, or cause their designees to vote, all of their shares (for the election of each of the other shareholders as directors of (name of corporation), or) for the election of the following directors: (specify names of directors); and will at all times during the term of this agreement vote all their shares for the election as directors of (two) persons designated by the party of the first part; and (two) persons designated by the party of the second part; and (two) persons designated by the party of the third part; and that this equal division of directors as between the parties will be maintained in the case of vacancies, death, disability, or other event.

2. That as directors of the corporation, the parties will vote, or cause their designees to vote, for the election of the following officers or positions:

Office	Name
Chairman of the Board	_____
President	_____
Vice-President	_____
Treasurer	_____
Assistant Treasurer	_____
Secretary	_____

and will at all times during the term of this agreement vote, or cause their designees to vote, as directors, for the election

Form 18: Shareholder Agreement for Pooled Voting
   (continued)

of such person or persons as Chairman of the Board or President as may be designated by the party of the first part; and for the election of such person or persons as Vice-President or Treasurer as may be designated by the party of the second part; and for the election of such person or persons as Assistant Treasurer or Secretary as may be designated by the party of the third part.

Note: This provision would not be used in an agreement executed at the time of corporate formation, but rather to change an existing corporation.

3. That the by-laws of the corporation shall be amended in the following respects:
   (a) by creating the office of _____.
   (b) by deleting from Article ___ the words:

   _____.

Note: This is only included, of course, when it is necessary to amend the by-laws.

4. That as directors of the corporation the parties will vote for a resolution continuing _____, so long as he holds the office of Treasurer, in the same general duties as heretofore, except insofar as same are modified by this agreement.

5. That the annual salaries of the officers or holders of other positions shall be as follows:

Note: This could be used instead of, or in addition to, an employment agreement.

Chairman of the Board $ _____
President $ _____
Vice-President $ _____
Treasurer $ _____
Assistant Treasurer $ _____
Secretary $ _____

6. That this agreement shall be operative forthwith and the several provisions thereof requiring corporate action and sanction shall be effected by appropriate procedure as soon as practicable.

7. That this agreement does not undertake to cover all matters incident to the operation of the corporation.

8. The duration of this agreement shall run to the ___ day _____, 19____, unless sooner terminated or amended by mutual agreement of (specify parties) or their respective heirs, legal representatives and assigns.

(Signature) _____

(Signature) _____

(Signature) _____

Form 19: Cross-Purchase Agreement with Buy-Sell Provisions

Q: Are these all the share-holders of the corporation?

Note: This is a mandatory agreement funded by insur-ance and triggered only by death.

Note: Each shareholder is insuring the life of the other.

CROSS-PURCHASE AGREEMENT

THIS CROSS-PURCHASE AGREEMENT, made and entered into this _____ day of _____, 199___ by and between _____ (hereinafter called "_____") and _____ (hereinafter called "_____").

WITNESSETH:

WHEREAS, the parties own all of the stock of _____, a Missouri corporation (hereinafter called the "Corporation"); and

WHEREAS, as of this date, _____ owns _____ shares of said stock; and

WHEREAS, the parties desire to provide certain terms and conditions upon which the shares of Corporation's stock owned by a deceased party will be acquired by the surviv-ing party; and

WHEREAS, the parties wish to provide the funds necessary for the purchase of such shares of common stock owned by _____ through insurance insuring the life of _____;

NOW, THEREFORE, in consideration of the premises and of the mutual agreements contained herein, the parties hereto agree as follows:

1. *Shares Subject to Agreement.* The terms and conditions of this Cross-Purchase Agreement shall apply to all shares of the Corporation's stock owned by either party hereto, and to all other shares of such stock which may, from time to time, be issued in respect to any of such shares, including, without limitation, all such shares issued as a stock dividend or pursuant to any plan of reorganization, recapitalization, merger, consolidation or otherwise (all such shares here-inafter collectively are referred to as the "Shares").

2. *Purchase and Sale.* Upon the death of either party, the sur-viving party shall purchase, and the personal representative of the estate of such deceased party shall sell, all of the Shares owned by such estate at the time of such party's death. Payment shall be made in cash or cash equivalent in the manner and amount set forth below.

3. *Closing Date.* The closing of the purchase and sale pur-suant to this Cross-Purchase Agreement shall take place at the principal offices of the Corporation, within ninety (90) days after the appointment of the personal representative of such estate, but not later than one hundred eighty (180) days after such death. At the closing of the transaction con-templated hereby, the personal representative of such estate shall deliver to the purchaser the certificate(s) repre-senting all of the Shares owned by the estate, duly endorsed

Form 19: Cross-Purchase Agreement (continued)

for transfer, together with any other document or documents which may be reasonably required to effectuate the transfer of title thereto.

4. *Purchase Price.* The total purchase price for the Shares purchased hereunder shall be the price set forth in Exhibit A attached hereto, and by this reference made a part hereof, as such exhibit exists as of the date of such shareholder's death. Such purchase price shall be fixed on the date of this Agreement and may be modified by the parties at the beginning of each fiscal year commencing after such date.

Note: The valuation method being used is Fixed Price.

Q: Does the absence of restriction on lifetime transfers make the agreement easy to avoid prior to death?

5. *Insurance.* _____ and the Corporation shall purchase insurance on the life of _____, naming _____ as beneficiary, in an amount substantially equal to the purchase price for all Shares owned by _____, as set forth in Exhibit A. All policies, from time to time purchased, shall be listed on Exhibit B, attached hereto and incorporated herein, and shall be subject to the terms of this Agreement, and the Split-Dollar Agreement and the Assignment of Life Insurance Policy as Collateral, both dated this date, attached hereto as Exhibit C and incorporated herein by reference. Such policies shall be used for the purchase herein described, and shall be kept at the offices of the Corporation. The Corporation shall pay all the premiums due on such policies and shall be entitled to the repayment of all such premiums upon the death of _____, or upon the cancellation, transfer or surrender of said policies, in the manner set forth in the Split-Dollar Agreement. Any death proceeds due to _____ under such policies, shall be paid on behalf of _____ directly to _____ personal representative, in order to satisfy _____ purchase obligation hereunder.

Note: These documents would have to be included as Exhibit C.

Note: The corporation is initially paying the premiums.

If _____ predeceases _____ (except under the circumstances described in Section 6) or if this Agreement is terminated for any reason, _____ (hereinafter called "_____") shall thereupon have the right to purchase the policy or policies of insurance insuring _____ life acquired pursuant hereto from _____ or his personal representative for the cash value of each such policy, as of the date of such death or termination, less any existing indebtedness against such policy, plus that portion of the premium or premiums on such policy payable prior to the date of such purchase which premium or premiums cover the period beyond such date. Said right shall terminate if it is not exercised within one hundred eighty (180) days of the date of _____ death or the termination of this Agreement, and in such event, _____ or his personal representative shall be free to designate any person or persons as beneficiary of such policy or policies and such beneficiary shall be entitled to the use of the policy proceeds free from the purchase restrictions herein contained.

If _____ exercises said right, _____ or his personal representative shall simultaneously execute and deliver to _____ any and all documents reasonably required

Form 19: Cross-Purchase Agreement (continued)

to transfer ownership of such policy or policies to _____, and she shall have the right to name herself or any other person or persons as beneficiary, free from the purchase restrictions herein contained.

6. *Simultaneous or Nearly Simultaneous Death.* In the event that _____ and _____ die simultaneously, or within a period of thirty (30) days (regardless of the order of death), _____ shall be deemed to have survived _____ and his personal representative shall be obligated to purchase _____ Shares in the manner herein set forth.

7. *Termination.* Unless sooner terminated by the mutual consent of the parties hereto, this Agreement shall terminate, without notice, upon the occurrence of any of the following events: (a) the cessation of the Corporation's business; (b) the bankruptcy, receivership or complete dissolution of the Corporation or bankruptcy or insolvency of either party; or (c) transfer or sale of all Shares owned by either party during such party's lifetime.

Note: If this were a redemption, rather than a cross-purchase agreement, the Corporation, as well as the shareholders, should sign as a party. This would, of course, require board of director approval.

8. *Transfer of Shares.* Each party shall have the right to sell or otherwise transfer any or all of his Shares during his lifetime, free from the restrictions herein contained and in such event, the terms of this Agreement shall apply to all Shares still owned by such party at his death, provided, however, that if such party retains no Shares, this Agreement shall terminate, as set forth in Section 7.

9. *Endorsement of Certificate.* Upon the execution of this Agreement, each certificate representing shares now held by a party shall be endorsed as follows:

NOTICE
The shares evidenced by this certificate are subject to the restriction stated in, and are transferable at death only upon compliance with, the provisions of a Cross-Purchase Agreement dated the _____ day of _____, 199_____, between the shareholders thereof (the provisions of which are incorporated herein by reference). A copy of this aforesaid Agreement is on file in the office of the Secretary of this Corporation.

Note: It is a good idea to agree on the applicable remedy.

10. *Specific Performance.* The capital stock of the Corporation cannot be readily purchased or sold in the open market, and, for that reason, among others, the parties hereto will be irreparably damaged in the event this Cross-Purchase Agreement is not specifically enforced. In the event of any controversy concerning the purchase or sale of any Shares hereunder, the same shall be enforceable in a court of equity, by a decree of specific performance; provided, however, that such remedy shall be cumulative and not exclusive, it shall be in addition to any other remedy or remedies which either of the parties hereto may have.

Form 19: Cross-Purchase Agreement (continued)

11. *Binding Effect.* This Agreement shall be binding upon the parties, their heirs, legal representatives, successors, and assigns, and each party in furtherance thereof shall execute a will directing his executor to perform this Agreement and to execute all documents necessary to effectuate the purposes of this Agreement, but the failure to execute such will shall not affect the rights of any party or the obligation of any estate, as provided in this Agreement.

12. *Necessary Documents.* The parties hereto and their successors and assigns shall execute and deliver all documents necessary to implement the transactions contained and contemplated herein.

13. *Governing Law; Paragraph Titles.* This instrument shall be construed, administered and governed in accordance with the laws of the State of Missouri. The titles to the various paragraphs are for convenience only and neither limit nor amplify the provisions of this Agreement.

14. *Prior Agreement.* This Agreement supersedes all prior agreements made by the parties and the Corporation affecting the stock of the Corporation an all such prior agreements are hereby terminated.

15. *Invalid Provision.* The invalidity or unenforceability of any particular provision of this Agreement shall not affect the other provisions hereof, and the Agreement shall be construed in all respects as if such invalid or unenforceable provision were omitted.

16. *Entire Agreement.* This Cross-Purchase Agreement constitutes the entire agreement of the parties hereto with regard to the subject matter hereof, and may not be altered or amended except by written instrument signed by the parties hereto or their respective successors in interest.

17. *Notices.* Any notice permitted to be given under this Cross-Purchase Agreement may be given either by delivering the same to the other party hereto personally or by mailing the same by United States certified mail, postage prepaid, to such other party at the address set forth below. The date of such mailing shall be deemed the date of such notice.

IN WITNESS WHEREOF, the parties hereto have executed this Cross-Purchase Agreement, in triplicate, as of the day and year first above written.

_____

_____

Q: Is there any reason for the corporation to be a party to the agreement? What if it was a Redemption Agreement?

Form 19: Cross-Purchase Agreement (continued)

CROSS-PURCHASE AGREEMENT

EXHIBIT A

Purchase Price for Shares

Shareholder	Number of Shares Owned	Price per Share	Total Price

Dated: _____

CROSS-PURCHASE AGREEMENT

EXHIBIT B

Insurance Policies Insuring Life of _____

Insurer	Policy Number	Issue Date	Face Amount

Dated: _____

Note: Exhibit B is a good mechanism to insure that the necessary insurance policies are actually purchased. How can the shareholders insure that all premium payments will be made to keep them in force?

Drafting Exercise 11

Cumulative Voting

Prepare a provision for the Articles of Incorporation so that Otto Chen can elect at least one of five directors.

Drafting Exercise 12

Supermajority Voting Provisions

Prepare supermajority voting provisions that would give either Henry Kent, or Otto and Hugo Chen (voting together) a veto power over extraordinary corporate action. Use as your guide for what would be "extraordinary" the language provided above in Form 2, the General Partnership Agreement.

Drafting Exercise 13

Voting Trust Agreement

Prepare a Voting Trust Agreement for Kent Clothing Company, Ltd. in Delaware for a ten-year period. Have the Kent group elect two trustees and the Chen group elect two trustees, and provide that the four trustees are to elect a fifth, impartial trustee.

Drafting Exercise 14

Letter to Shareholders Concerning Buy-Sell and Valuation Issues

Prepare a letter to the Kents and Chens explaining why they need a shareholder's agreement with buy-sell and valuation provisions. Explain their options, the pros and cons and your recommendations. Advise each group that they should probably retain independent counsel to review the agreement, but as counsel to the corporation, discuss what an agreement that was fair to all parties would contain.

Drafting Exercise 15

Cross-Purchase Agreement

Prepare a cross purchase buy-sell agreement for Kent Clothing Company, Ltd. and its shareholders.

Practical Pointers

1.   There are serious ethical problems when the lawyer for the corporation drafts an employment agreement. While the corporate entity is the client, a senior corporate officer for whom the agreement is being prepared (and who may well have hired the lawyer and may sign his paychecks) could believe that the lawyer represents her. If it is not feasible to have the employee retain separate counsel, corporate counsel should disclose this inherent conflict in writing, get written permission from all parties and then endeavor to draft an agreement comparable to one that would result from arm's length negotiations by both sides with a full written explanation of the pros and cons of each provision for each party.

2.   When drafting any type of shareholder voting agreement, be careful that you do not inadvertently form a voting trust. If you accidently create a voting trust, the whole agreement may be treated as void unless you have somehow managed to comply with the relevant statutory provisions.

3.   Where there are numerous shareholders, or groups of shareholders, it may be necessary to utilize a voting trust agreement rather than a less formal vote pooling agreement.

4.   When drafting a shareholder agreement, be careful with buy-sell provisions. Chart the possible transfers to make sure that there cannot be an inadvertent and unwanted change in control.

5.   There are difficult ethical issues when counsel for the corporate entity drafts a buy-sell agreement. The different shareholders will always have divergent interests. If you cannot prevail upon the shareholders to retain separate counsel, clearly disclose your conflict of interest in writing, get written consents from each of the shareholders, and fully disclose, in writing, the effects to each shareholder, pro and con, of each provision.

6.   In drafting cross-purchase agreements, always specify the exact percentage of stock each remaining shareholder is to purchase. It is easy to make mistakes in arithmetic.

PART THREE

THE PUBLIC CORPORATION

Chapter 8

Securities Law Practice

A.   INTRODUCTION

Securities law can be very technical, but every corporate lawyer needs to have at least a basic understanding of its broad reach. Every high school student learns Santayana's maxim that those who do not learn history are doomed to repeat it. Similarly, corporate lawyers who do not learn securities law are doomed to violate it.

At its most basic, students need some familiarity with the Federal Securities Act of 1933 and the Securities Exchange Act of 1934.[1] Each state also has securities laws, called Blue Sky Acts, which are relevant to securities law practice.

The Securities Act of 1933 was adopted in response to the 1929 stock market crash. In general, it regulates a company's initial offer and sale of securities. The following year, Congress passed the Securities Exchange Act of 1934, which generally regulates trading of securities that are already owned by the public. It places reporting requirements on public companies to assure that appropriate information continues to reach the public market and also regulates securities exchanges, proxy solicitation and tender offers.

The Securities Act of 1933 requires that companies selling their securities (Issuers) must register them with the Securities and Exchange Commission (SEC) and provide each offerer with an offering disclosure document called a prospectus. The prospectus is a major part of the registration statement filed with the SEC and is detached from the rest of the registration statement for separate printing and distribution. Registering securities with the SEC, a very complex and expensive process called making a public offering, is required in all cases unless an exemption from the registration requirement of the 1933 Act applies. Because registration is so costly, issuers try assiduously to find exemptions but must proceed with great caution because there is tremendous liability if an exemption does not apply, and the securities are sold in violation of section 5 of the 1933 Act.[2] Liability is discussed in section D of this chapter.

The most important exemptions involve private placements, small offerings, and intrastate offerings. When no exemption is available, the issuer, generally along with a syndicate of underwriters (the investment bankers who sell the securities), registers the securities with the SEC as required by the 1933 Act. The process of making a public offering is both time-consuming and fascinating for the securities lawyer. It can be highly profitable for the issuer, the underwriters, lawyers for the issuer and lead underwriters, and even the specialized financial printers (who sometimes, horror of horrors, make more money than the lawyers). Public offerings are only conducted by law firms that specialize in securities law, and should not be attempted by the novice. (Note: Don't try this at home!) This book provides samples of many of the steps lawyers take and the documents they would prepare to conduct a small public offering of equity securities by a high tech company.

The theory behind the federal securities laws is that if issuers are forced to make timely and accurate disclosure of all material information, the investing public will be protected. The federal regulator is not opining about the value or merit of an investment, just about the completeness of disclosure. In this way, the federal statutes differ from many state Blue Sky statutes which do purport to evaluate the merit of an offering.

Prior to the 1980s, there was cumbersome duplication between requirements of the 1933 and 1934 Acts. This has been mitigated somewhat since 1982 by the integrated disclosure requirements of Regulation S-K, as promulgated and adopted by the SEC. Accordingly, as discussed below in connection with 1934 Act reporting requirements, much of the information required in an annual report on Form 10-K is similar to what would be required in a Registration Statement prepared pursuant to the 1933 Act.

The law of securities regulation may seem counter-intuitive at first. Once learned it does make sense, but securities law can have an "Alice in Wonderland" quality in which nothing is quite what it seems. Moreover, many common words like offer, sale, issuer, dealer, and underwriter have special meanings that could never be fathomed from merely reading the statutes. In fact, the term "securities" is broadly defined and includes all investments of money in a common enterprise with profits to come "solely" from the efforts of others. *SEC v. W.J. Howey Co.*, 328 U.S. 293 (1946).

B. EXEMPTIONS FROM REGISTRATION

By far the most important exemption is for "transactions by an issuer not involving a public offering." (Section 4(2) of the 1933 Act.) These are called "private placements." Other important exemptions include intrastate offerings (§3(a)(11)) and offerings which do not require registration "for the protection of investors by reason of the small amount involved or the limited character of the public offering." (Section 3(b) applies to certain offerings valued under $5,000,000 in the aggregate.)

Securities worth vast sums of money are routinely offered and sold without registration because sales are made to extremely knowledgeable investors who do not require the protection of the disclosures mandated in the registration process. These are "private placements," which are "transactions by an issuer not involving a public offering." (Section 4(2)). Two typical examples are: when institutional investors like insurance companies invest in major corporations; and when small groups of wealthy investors promote business ventures.

Traditionally the test for whether an offering is or is not "public" has been the offerees' level of sophistication and access to material information (this includes all offerees — not just those who accepted the offer and actually purchased the securities but also all the others who declined). Thus, an offer to just one inappropriate offeree could be a public offering in violation of the registration requirements of Section 5 of the 1933 Act.

While it is still possible to rely on the statutory exemption for private placements, it is safer for issuers to rely on the safe harbor provisions of Regulation D, promulgated by the SEC in 1982 pursuant to Sections 4(2) and 3(b) of the 1933 Act. Regulation D provides objective rules for offerings pursuant to Rules 504, 505 and 506. There are no requirements for filing a registration statement and for circulating a formal printed prospectus.

Regulation D allows offers to unlimited numbers of "accredited investors" (a carefully defined term generally referring to wealthy and sophisticated investors who do not need the protection of the registration process). Great care must be exercised because the mistaken offer to an investor who is not in fact "accredited" can lose the exemption for the entire offering, not just for that one investor. The resulting civil liability can be enormous, as discussed below in connection with Section 12(1) of the 1933 Act.

In making a private placement, counsel for the issuers must be very careful about the qualifications of the offerees. The SEC is concerned that the initial offerees are purchasing securities for investment puruposes and do not intend to resell them. Accordingly, purchasers must sign an investment letter stating that they understand that the offering is a private placement; they are buying for investment purposes; and they cannot resell the stock for a period of time. A legend should be placed on all stock certificates stating that the stock is restricted and cannot be sold without SEC registration, or an opinion of counsel that an exemption from registration is available.[3] A "Stop Transfer Order" should be sent to the stock transfer agent to prevent transfer of shares without the issuer's approval. Finally, the stock should be issued in certificates for large numbers of shares to make transfer more difficult.

Stock sold pursuant to most exemptions from registration is "restricted" as to resale. As discussed below, "restricted" stock can be sold publicly under certain circumstances, after two or three years, pursuant to SEC Rule 144. A Rule 144 sale is set forth below in connection with Form 39.

Form 20 is an example of a Private Placement Memorandum. Compare this form to the much longer and more complex registration statement for a public offering, Form 25.

Form 20: Private Placement Memorandum

Note: Each offeree should be named and numbered so the issuer can keep track of the overall quantity and qualifications of offerees.

Note: The prohibition of reproduction helps limit the number of potential offerees.

Note: Limited Partnership interests are, of course, securities.

Note: This language is similar to what is required in a registration statement.

Note: This language tracks Regulation D requirements.

No._____

Offeree Name _____

PRIVATE PLACEMENT MEMORANDUM

CONFIDENTIAL
Not to be Reproduced

The _____Partnership
Limited Partnership Interests
(Venture Capital Fund)

This memorandum has been submitted confidentially in connection with the private placement of limited partnership interests and does not constitute an offer to sell or the solicitation of an offer to buy such interests in any state or jurisdiction where the offer or sale thereof would be prohibited or to any firm or individual who does not possess the qualifications described within this memorandum.

The date of the Memorandum is _____.

PRIVATE OFFERING TO QUALIFIED INVESTORS

THESE SECURITIES HAVE NOT BEEN REGISTERED WITH THE SECURITIES AND EXCHANGE COMMISSION IN RELIANCE UPON AN EXEMPTION FROM SUCH REGISTRATION SET FORTH IN THE SECURITIES ACT OF 1933. AS AMENDED, PROVIDED BY SECTION 4(2) THEREOF AND REGULATION D OF THE SECURITIES AND EXCHANGE COMMISSION, NOR HAVE THEY BEEN REGISTERED WITH SECURITIES COMMISSIONS OF CERTAIN STATES IN RELIANCE UPON CERTAIN EXEMPTIONS FROM REGISTRATION. NEITHER THE SECURITIES AND EXCHANGE COMMISSION, NOR THE SECURITIES COMMISSION OF ANY STATE HAS APPROVED OR DISAPPROVED THE SECURITIES OFFERED HEREBY OR PASSED UPON OR ENDORSED THE MERITS OF THIS OFFERING OR THE ACCURACY OR ADEQUACY OF THIS MEMORANDUM. ANY REPRESENTATION TO THE CONTRARY IS UNLAWFUL.

These securities are being offered only to investors whom the offerors believe have the qualifications necessary to permit the securities to be offered and sold in reliance upon this exemption.

Qualified offerees must (a) have such knowledge and experience in business and financial matters as will enable them to evaluate the merits and risks of a proposed investment in these securities and (b) be able to bear the economic risk of this investment.

The offerors will be the sole judge as to whether or not an offerree possesses these qualifications. Accordingly, this

Form 20: Private Placement Memorandum (continued)

Memorandum does not constitute an offer to sell or a solicitation of any offer to buy the limited partnership interests to any firm or individual unless and until the offerors have communicated in writing to such investor their belief that that investor possesses these qualifications.

Each investor must confirm and represent that the interest in the partnership is being acquired for long-term investment without any present or foreseeable need to consider disposition of the limited partnership interest.

Each investor will be required to make certain representations to the partnership, including (but not limited to) representations as to investment intent, degree of sophistication, access to information concerning partnership and ability to bear the economic risk of the investment.

Investment advisors and other managers of investment accounts should not consider this investment for any investor that does not possess these qualifications and should not transmit this Memorandum to any such investor without the prior written consent of the offerors.

In no event should this Memorandum be duplicated or transmitted to anyone other than the prospective investor to whom it was directed by written communication of the offerors.

INTRODUCTION

The _____ Partnership (the "Partnership") will be formed by _____ ("General Partners") as a California limited partnership to engage primarily in venture capital investment. The Partnership's objective will be to invest principally in products and companies which offer substantial potention for long-term capital appreciation. (Describe here summary background of the General Partners.)

The Partnership's term will be ____ years, after which it will be liquidated in an orderly and expeditious manner and make distributions to its partners or to a liquidating trust over a term not longer than ____ years, subject to consideration of applicable securities laws.

DESCRIPTION OF OFFERING

The Partnership is offering limited partnership interests privately to selected, highly qualified investors. The following is a summary of certain of its principal assets:

Name	_____
Nature of Investment	Limited partnership interests
Amount of Offering	$_____
Minimum Subscription per Investor	$_____
Term of Partnership	_____ Years
General Partners' Profit Share	_____ %

Annual Management Fee, ____ % up to $10,000,000 of capital plus ____ % above such amount, adjusted for inflation.

Q: Would an investor be able to misrepresent investment intent, destroy the exemption, and then sue the issuer for rescission if the value of the securities declines?

Note: There may be an investment banker acting as the private placement manager and acting like a "best efforts" underwriter in a public offering.

Note: This information would be especially interesting to an investor.

Form 21: Investment Letter

Note: The Investment Letter must be executed by each investor in a private placement.

Q: What is a non-sexist way to address this letter? "Gentlemen" is certainly sexist. "Dear Sir or Madam" is stilted and archaic.

Note: This is all done to help the issuer prove the investment intent of the purchaser.

Note: This chapter contains a sample Rule 144 opinion letter of issuer's counsel. *See* Form 39.

To: Company Issuing Stock

Dear Company Officers:

The Undersigned is acquiring _____ shares of common stock, per value $_____ per share, of the Company.

The Undersigned understands that the aforesaid shares have not been registered under the Securities Act of 1933 (the "Act") on the ground that the transfer of such shares to the Undersigned is exempt under the Act. The Undersigned further understands that reliance on such exemption is predicated in part upon the Undersigned's representation that the Undersigned is acquiring such shares for investment, with no present intention of dividing its interest in said shares (or any part of them) except in accordance with this letter and the Stock Purchase Agreement of even date herewith.

In making the foregoing representation, the Undersigned realizes that in the view of the Securities and Exchange Commission, the statutory basis for exemption would not be present if (notwithstanding such representation) the Undersigned has in mind acquiring the shares for resale upon the occurrence or nonoccurrence of some predetermined event, such as market rise, or at a fixed or determinable time in the future.

In view of the foregoing, the Undersigned agrees that if in the future it decides that a disposition by it of any of the shares appears necessary or advisable in the light of circumstances then existing, it will provide you with either the opinion of counsel satisfactory to you that such disposition does not violate the Act of a letter from the staff of the Securities and Exchange Commission's Division of Corporation Finance to the effect that it will recommend that no action be taken by the Commission with respect to the proposed disposition. Such an opinion or letter shall not be required with respect to any sale or other disposition pursuant to an effective registration statement under the Act.

The Undersigned also acknowledges, with respect to the above-mentioned shares issued to it, that:

(a) Such shares are "restricted securities," as defined in Rule 144 under the Act.

(b) Unless restricted securities are registered under the Act or an exemption from registration is available, restricted securities must be held indefinitely and the holders thereof must therefore bear the economic risk of the investment for an indefinite period of time.

(c) An exemption from the registration requirements of the Act is provided for by Rule 144 thereunder.

Form 21: Investment Letter (continued)

(d) Rule 144 contains limitations on the amount and manner of sales and securities.

(e) Rule 144 may not be available until such time as the Company has been subject to the reporting requirements of Sections 13 or 15(d) of the Securities Exchange Act of 1934 for at least ninety days or has made certain information publicly available.

(f) There is currently no market for shares of common stock or other capital stock and no assurance that such a market will develop.

(g) A notation has been made in the Company's stock transfer ledger indicating that the shares being transferred to the Undersigned are restricted securities and may be transferred only in compliance with this letter, and that similar stop transfer instructions will be given to any person, firm, partnership, or corporation hereafter appointed to act as a transfer agent by the Company.

The Undersigned further acknowledges and agrees that the certificate(s) representing the aforesaid shares being acquired by it shall contain a legend in substantially the following form:

These shares have not been registered under the Securities Act of 1933 (the "Act"). They may not be offered or transferred by sale, assignment, pledge or otherwise, unless

(i) a registration statement for the shares under the Act is in effect, or

(ii) the Company has received an opinion of Counsel satisfactory to the Company that registration is not required under the Act.

For purposes of this letter, where appropriate the singular shall include the plural, and the plural, the singular, and any gender shall include all other genders.

Very truly yours,

s/_____
Name of investor

Note: Each purchaser should sign one of these investment letters.

Q: To what extent does Regulation D involve purchasers rather than mere offerees?

C.   PUBLIC OFFERINGS

When no exemption from registration is available, issuers may choose to make a public offering. In this complex process, the securities to be sold are registered with the SEC. The issuer and its lead underwriter, with their respective counsel, will prepare and file an SEC Registration Statement on one of several forms, the selection of which depends upon the size and history of the issuer. A large part of the Registration Statement is the statutory prospectus, a disclosure document that is distributed in connection with the offer and sale of the securities. Any writing used in connection with the offer to sell securities may be deemed a prospectus and as discussed below in connection with 1933 Act civil liability, the liability for the use of a prospectus that does not satisfy statutory requirements is enormous.

The Closing Memorandum (Form 23) that is prepared at the conclusion of a public offering is presented first here to demonstrate the steps that need to be followed and the documents that need to be prepared for a public offering. The closing memorandum is really a formal version of the checklist that the issuer's lawyer will follow at the beginning of the transaction.

Relevant sections of a sample Registration Statement, Form 25, are included to show the kinds of disclosure that must be made. The SEC letter of comment, and the response from the issuer's counsel, illustrate how the cooperative disclosure process between the SEC and the issuer unfolds. As a result of this process, at least in theory, the public receives disclosure of all material information about the issuer prior to purchasing its securities.

A public offering breaks down into three distinct phases. First is the pre-filing period, before the Registration Statement is filed. Second is the waiting period when a preliminary prospectus is distributed and securities are offered but not sold. Third is the post-effective period, when the securities are actually sold.

During the pre-filing period, the issuer and its lead underwriter cannot make any offer to sell the securities. Offers are broadly defined so that the solicitation of an offer to buy is deemed an offer to sell. Moreover, nothing can even be done to "condition the market" in preparation for the eventual sale of the securities. During this period, if the underwriting is to be on a "firm commitment" basis, in which the underwriters will purchase the securities from the issuers at discount from the offering price and then resell them to the public, the lead underwriter may negotiate with other investment banks to form a syndicate that will purchase and resell the securities once the Registration Statement "becomes effective." The lead underwriter is often called the "representative" of the underwriting syndicate. While it is possible that one underwriter will purchase an entire offering, it is also possible that scores of underwriters will form a syndicate to purchase a large issue. All members of the underwriting syndicate are in privity with the issuer.

The waiting period begins with the filing of the Registration Statement with the SEC. The preliminary prospectus, which comprises much of the Registration Statement, is distributed to the public and the underwriters may offer the securities, accepting indications of interest, but no binding contracts for sale can be made. The SEC's intent is to slow down the sales process so that all material information about the issuer can reach the public market. The Preliminary Prospectus is called a "red herring" prospectus because it contains a legend printed in red on its cover, stating:

"A registration statement relating to these securities has been filed with the Securities and Exchange Commission but has not yet become effective. Information contained herein is subject to completion or amendment. These securities may not be sold nor may offers to buy be accepted prior to the time the registration statement becomes effective. This prospectus shall not consititute an offer to sell or the solicitation of an offer to buy nor shall there be any sale of these securities in any State in which such offer, solicitation or sale would be unlawful prior to registration or qualification under the securities laws of any such State."

The preliminary prospectus will always be incomplete and will have several blank spaces. For example, it will lack the date when it becomes effective ("effective date"), when sales can be made. It will not state the offering price, which is generally subject to market conditions on the date of effectiveness. Also, it will not contain the names of all underwriters in the underwriting syndicate, and the amounts of securities that each will actually agree to purchase.

The effective date, when the securities can be sold, is established by Section 8 of the 1933 Act. Pursuant to that section, a Registration Statement automatically becomes effective 20 days after the last amendment to the Registration Statement is filed unless the SEC approves an earlier date. To avoid waiting the 20 days, the issuer and lead underwriter can request acceleration of the Registration Statement's effective date when they are comfortable with market conditions and when the SEC is satisfied with the disclosure. A practical reason to request acceleration is that once the issuer and lead underwriter have organized the underwriting syndicate and set the price of securities, they cannot afford to wait 20 days during which market conditions are likely to change.

The SEC routinely grants requests for acceleration of effectiveness (see Forms 28 and 29 below) when the final amendment is filed with all blank spaces filled in and when the underwriter states that copies of the preliminary prospectus were furnished to all underwriters and dealers and their salespersons and distributed as required by Rule 460 and SEC 1933 Act Release 4968. The effective date is generally the day that the final amendment is filed.

In the final, post-effective period, after the Registration Statement becomes effective, the securities will actually be sold. Shortly before effectiveness, the issuer and lead underwriter will execute a binding "Underwriting Agreement." Members of the underwriting syndicate execute an "Agreement Among Underwriters" and dealers will sign a "Selling Group Agreement."

The 1933 Act requires that every purchase of securities be accompanied by or preceded with a copy of the final prospectus. The closing for the public offering generally occurs three business days after the Registration Statement becomes effective. The sample closing memorandum in this chapter, Form 23, catalogues the many documents that are prepared, executed, and exchanged at closing. Most importantly, the underwriters receive their stock certificates and the issuer receives the offering price, less the underwriter's discount and expenses.

1. A Cast of Characters for a Sample Transaction

The following is a realistic but fictitious small public offering to show the range of documents that are prepared by the lawyers for the company trying to raise the money, called the Issuer (but generally referred to as the "Company"), and the lawyers for the investment bank that is to act as managing, or lead underwriter.

Issuer	Alison Technologies, Inc. (the "Company") Elvis Thomas, President Bruce Lowe, Secretary
Issuer's Counsel	Peter C. Kostant, Esquire Santoro, Ryan & Kostant
Underwriter	True Aim Securities, Inc. (the "Representative" of the Syndicate of Underwriters) Nick Nieve, President
Underwriter's Counsel	James Froom, Esquire Burton, Froom & Brinsley
Accountants	Charles Parker, CPA Parker & Schwartz, CPAs
Transfer Agent	Confederate Stock Transfer & Trust Co.
SEC	Securities and Exchange Commission
NASD	National Association of Securities Dealers, Inc.
NASDAQ	Automated system of NASD for listing stock price quotes

2. Letter of Intent

Letters of Intent (Form 22) are not legally binding, but are very important in structuring the financial relationship between the lead underwriter and the company that intends to issue securities. Letters of intent are usually drafted by counsel for the lead underwriter. They are seldom mere "boilerplate" forms, but the result of vigorous negotiation between the Issuer and the Underwriter. One important "deal point" is whether the underwriter will agree to a "firm commitment" underwriting in which the lead underwriter, together with the underwriting syndicate that the lead underwriter will put together, will actually purchase the securities from the Issuer, and therefore be at risk if they cannot be resold; or whether the underwriter will just act as selling agent on a "best efforts" basis.

Another "deal point" is the amount and structure of the lead underwriter's compensation. Note that there are limits to the greed or overreaching of the lead underwriter because the National Association of Securities Dealers (NASD) must approve the compensation package, and their approval must be submitted to the SEC.

In the following Alison Technologies deal used as an example, the underwriters will get to purchase the securities for 10 percent below the market offering price (the typical underwriter's "spread" in a small offering), but the lead underwriter will also get the issuer to pay most of the expenses of the public offering plus a three percent non-accountable expense allowance. This three percent allowance may effectively constitute additional compensation to the lead underwriter because it does not have to be accounted for specifically. The lead underwriter is also to get the right to purchase 60,000 Units (equal to 10 percent of the entire offering) for a nominal sum as additional compensation and this will not be shared with the other underwriters in the syndicate. The lead underwriter also gets an exclusive right of first refusal to act as underwriter for the issuer in all financings for five years. Additionally, the issuer must agree to register, at its own considerable expense, securities held by the underwriter, and give it "piggy-back" rights to include the underwriter's securities in any future securities registrations.

The letter of intent allows the underwriter to select the nature and price of the securities to be offered. Note that in the Alison Technologies deal, the letter of intent contemplates the sale of common stock for approximately $5 per share. By the time the Registration Statement was actually filed several months later, the price of the stock had fallen and the lead underwriter innovatively modified the offered securities so that $5 would purchase a Unit consisting of three shares of common stock and one five-year common stock Purchase Warrant that would become valuable and worth exercising if the price of the common stock increased more than 20 percent in the second through fifth year after the public offering. "Warrant" is the term often used in securities practice for options to purchase securities.

The key provisions of the letter of intent are amplified and modified in the subsequent underwriting agreement between the issuer and lead underwriter which only becomes binding months later when it is executed shortly before the registration statement becomes effective, at the close of the waiting period.

One fascinating aspect of the relationship between the issuer and the underwriter is the potential for dynamic shifts in relative power. An initial public offering (IPO) that is not made by a "hot" new company, or a non-IPO made by a weak issuer (like Alison Technologies, Inc.) will put the underwriter in the driver's seat. Once the issuer has taken off, the underwriter, facing competition from other investment banks, is likely to be far more solicitous and "unselfish."

Form 22: Letter of Intent, True Aim Securities, Inc.

Note: Even though the letter is not legally binding, the underwriter leaves itself substantial "outs" It is to be the "sole judge," for example.

Note: Each underwriter in the syndicate will agree to buy only a portion of the total offering. The civil liability of each will thus be severally limited to that amount.

Note: This reflects the current capitalization of the Company.

Note: Seven to ten percent is the typical spread.

True Aim Securities, Inc.
1 Wall Street
New York, NY 10022

November 8, 1993

Elvis Thomas, President
Alison Technologies, Inc.
1 Imperial Avenue
Brooklyn, NY 10102

RE: Letter of Intent
       True Aim Securities, Inc. to Alison Technologies, Inc.

Dear Mr. Thomas:

Reference is made to our recent discussions of a proposed public offering by you of shares of common stock, $.01 par value, (the "Shares") of Alison Technologies, Inc. (the "Company") as herein described (the "Offering"). Based upon our discussions, financial materials which you have and will submit to us, representations which you have made to us, and the favorable operating results of the Company, of which we shall be the sole judge, we hereby confirm in principle our interest in underwriting, on a firm commitment basis, a public offering of the Shares upon the following basic terms and conditions:

1) True Aim Securities, Inc., ("Aim") or the several underwriters for whom Aim may act as representative pursuant to paragraph 6 hereof (the "Underwriters"), will underwrite on a firm commitment basis for the account of the Company and the Company will register and sell approximately 1,000,000 Shares of common stock. The Offering shall be the subject of, and conditioned upon the execution of an Underwriting Agreement between the Company and Aim and the number of the Shares to be publicly offered, the Offering Price and terms are subject to market conditions.

2) You have advised us that immediately prior to the Offering, the Company will have issued and outstanding approximately 4.1 million shares of common stock, $.01 par value and options and warrants outstanding for the purchase of approximately 200,000 shares.

3) The Company will expeditiously take all steps necessary to effectuate this Offering including the preparation and filing of a Registration Statement with the Securities and Exchange Commission (the "Commission") as required by the Securities Act of 1933 (the "Registration Statement").

4) The gross discount to which we shall be entitled shall be a sum equal to ten percent (10%) of the total proceeds resulting from the sale of the Shares.

Form 22: Letter of Intent, True Aim (continued)

5) The Company will grant to Aim individually and not as representative of the Underwriters, upon the closing of the sale of the Shares a five-year warrant (the "Warrant") to purchase up to 15% of the Shares offered for sale. The price of the Warrant shall be one mill per Warrant Share. The Warrant will be exercisable in whole or in part, from time to time, for a period of four years commencing one year after the effective date of the Registration Statement at 120% of the Offering Price. The Warrant shall provide that it cannot be transferred, sold, assigned or hypothecated for one year except that it may be assigned in whole or in part to any officer or employee or affiliate of Aim. The Company agrees to register the Warrant and/or the Warrant Shares at its expense at the request of Aim. This request may be made at any one time during a period of five years beginning one year from the closing of the Offering. In connection with this registration right, Aim will not require the Company to maintain a current registration statement for more than 150 days after any such registration becomes effective. In addition, the Company will grant Aim "piggy back" registration rights for the Warrant and the Warrant Shares. Until such time as the entire Warrant or all of the Warrant Shares shall have been registered, the Company shall give the holder(s) of the Warrant written notice by registered mail not less than thirty (30) days prior to the filing by the Company of any registration statement.

6) Aim shall act as principal in purchasing the securities from the Company under a "firm commitment" (subject to the terms and conditions to be set forth in an Underwriting Agreement). Aim may, at its discretion, negotiate with other underwriters who shall be members in good standing of the National Association of Securities Dealers, Inc. who, acting severally, would contract to purchase as principals portions of the Shares directly from the Company. Pending completion of the Offering, the Company agrees that it will not negotiate with any other underwriter or person relating to a possible private or public offering of securities for a period of one year.

7) Provided that proper corporate action by the Company authorizing the issuance and sale of the Shares shall have been taken and the Registration Statement shall have been filed and declared effective, and subject to the approval of our counsel, we will pay for the Shares no later than ten (10) days after the effective date of the Registration Statement. This tentative commitment is made subject to release of the Underwriter: (1) in the event of war; (2) in the event of any material adverse change in the business, properties or financial condition of the Company, of which event we are to be sole judge; (3) in the event of any action, suit or proceeding at law or in equity against the Company, or by any Federal, State or other commission, board or agency wherein any unfavorable decision would materially adversely affect the business, property, financial condition or income of the

Note: The lead underwriter is getting very valuable warrants for a pittance as part of its compensation. This is because the Company's bargaining position is weak. The registration rights are also very valuable.

Note: This is a typical provision.

Form 22: Letter of Intent, True Aim (continued)

Note: This is called a Green Shoe option. If the offering goes well, the underwriters can increase it by 15 percent to cover overallotments sold. This is completely unrelated to the 15 percent Underwriter's Warrant given as additional compensation in this deal to the lead underwriter.

Note: The Company pays almost all of the expenses of the offering including the underwriter's legal expenses.

Q: What is the cap on the Company's liability if it is at fault?

Note: This protects the underwriter if certain other transactions should occur.

Company; (4) in the event of materially adverse market conditions, of which event we are to be the sole judge.

8) For the purpose of covering overallotments and to be exercisable only for a period of thirty (30) days after the Offering is commenced, Aim shall have the option to purchase a number of Shares equal to up to fifteen percent (15%) of the Shares being offered, at the Offering Price less the underwriting discount.

9) The Company shall be responsible for and shall bear all expenses (including all legal fees) directly and necessarily incurred in connection with the proposed financing, including but not limited to the costs of preparing, printing and filing with the Commission the Registration Statement and amendments, post-effective amendments and supplements thereto; preparing, printing and delivering all underwriting and selling documents, including but not limited to the Underwriting Agreement, the agreement among underwriters, selling agreement, "blue sky" memoranda and stock certificates, "blue sky" fees and disbursements of the transfer agent. You shall pay to us a non-accountable expense allowance of 3% of the gross proceeds resulting from the sale of the Shares (including any Shares sold pursuant to the overallotment option described in Paragraph 8) of which $15,000 will be paid on the execution of this Letter of Intent, to cover the cost of our advertising, mailing, telephone, telegraph, travel, due diligence meetings, and other similar expenses. If the offering is not completed because we prevent its completion (except if such prevention is based upon a breach by the Company of Underwriting Agreement), the Company shall not be liable for our expense allowance set forth in this paragraph except that we may in all events retain our expenses, not in excess of the $15,000 paid to us upon execution of this Letter of Intent. If the Offering is not completed because the Company prevents it or because of a breach by the Company of any such covenant, representation or warranty, the Company's liability for such expense allowance shall be 60% of the 3% non-accountable expense allowance.

10) If the Company prevents the completion of the Offering contemplated herein because the Company is sold, merged or otherwise acquired from the date of this letter prior to effectiveness of the Registration Statement, the Company will pay Aim an investment banking fee equal to 2% of the total consideration received by the Company and/or its shareholders in such sale, merger or acquisition in lieu of the payment set forth in Paragraph 9 hereof, payable in full in cash at the time of consummation of such sale, merger or acquisition.

Form 22: Letter of Intent, True Aim (continued)

11) The Company agrees that if all the Shares are sold in accordance with the terms of the Underwriting Agreement, we shall have a preferential right for a period of five (5) years from the date hereof, to purchase for our account or to sell for the account of the Company or any of its principal shareholders (i.e., shareholders who currently own 5% or more of the currently outstanding common stock of the Company), any securities with respect to which the Company or any of its principal stockholders may seek a private placement or a public offering pursuant to a registration under the Securities Act of 1933. The Company represents and warrants that no other person has any rights to participate in any offer, sale or distribution of its securities with respect to which we shall have the right of first refusal. The Company and its principal stockholders will consult us with regard to any such offering and will offer us the opportunity to purchase or sell any such securities on terms not more favorable to the Company or its principal stockholders than they can secure elsewhere. If we fail to accept in writing such proposal for financing made by the Company or its principal stockholders, within thirty (30) business days after the mailing of a notice containing such proposal by registered mail, addressed to us, then we shall have no further claim or right with respect to the original proposal. Should we not avail ourselves of such opportunity to act as underwriter, this will not affect any preferential rights for future financing.

Note: The underwriter is given a right of first refusal to handle potentially profitable financings for both the Company and its individual principal shareholders.

12) For a period of six (6) months from the closing of the Offering and payment of the proceeds to the Company, the principal shareholders shall agree not to transfer, assign or sell any of their shares without our prior consent.

Note: This is done to stabilize the past offering market price of the securities. The principal shareholders cannot dump their shares. This is often called a "lock-up."

13) The Company will cause at least one million ($1,000,000) dollars of key man life insurance to be written on the life of Elvis Thomas, payable to the Company, which insurance will be kept in force for a minimum period of time equal to the term of the employment contract of Elvis Thomas, but in any case for at least two years from the effective date of the offering.

14) The Company will use Confederate Stock Transfer and Trust Company as its transfer agent. For a period of two (2) years from the effective date of the Registration Statement, the Company at its expense, shall provide us, if so requested, with copies of the Company's daily transfer sheets.

Q: Will the underwriter or the Company select the transfer agent?

15) Aim shall have the right to designate an individual as a director of the Company and, in any event, shall receive from the Company notice of all meetings of the Board of Directors of the Company and the right to attend all such meetings.

Note: In this "deal point," the underwriter is getting the valuable bonus of designating a member of the Company's Board of Directors.

16) Upon the closing of the Offering, Aim will publish, at the expense of the Company, not to exceed $13,000.00, tomb-

Form 22: Letter of Intent, True Aim (continued)

Note: The Underwriting Agreement will be much larger, more detailed and legally binding.

Note: The letter of intent is not legally binding but these provisions as to expenses are binding on the parties.

Q: Since the principal shareholders have agreed to certain conditions, should they also sign?

stone advertisements in financial publications selected by Aim.

17) The foregoing is only a brief outline of the proposed financing and each of the foregoing terms must be interpreted in the form in which it finally appears in the proposed Underwriting Agreement and that a public offering of securities of the Company be made, this letter cannot be construed as a commitment by us to purchase the securities, nor by the Company to sell the securities, and shall be conditioned in its entirety upon the negotiation, execution and delivery of a satisfactory Underwriting Agreement between the Company and us (and this letter is not to be construed as such a contract, nor as an agreement to enter into such a contract) to be entered into immediately prior to the time of the Offering, and shall be conditioned further upon compliance by the Company with the terms contained in this letter and such Underwriting Agreement. The provisions of Paragraphs 9 and 10 hereof shall, however, be effective and binding upon the execution hereof.

If the foregoing conforms to your understanding, please sign, date and return to us the enclosed copy of this letter.

Very truly yours,

TRUE AIM SECURITIES, INC.

By: _____
   Nick Nieve, President

The foregoing is in conformity with our understanding.

ALISON TECHNOLOGIES, INC.

By: _____
   Elvis Thomas, President

Date: _____

Form 23: Memorandum of Closing

MEMORANDUM OF CLOSING

ALISON TECHNOLOGIES, INC.

690,000 Units each consisting of
(a) 3 Shares of Common Stock, par value $.01 per share
and
(b) 1 Common Stock Purchase Warrant

Unit Purchase Option for 60,000 Units

August 3, 1994

I. MATTERS COMPLETED PRIOR TO CLOSING

A. Proceedings Before, and Documents Filed with the
Securities and Exchange Commission

1. On February 10, 1994, a Registration Statement on Form S-1 (File No. X-IIIII)* was filed with the SEC, including the related Preliminary Prospectus bearing such date, covering 600,000 Units, each Unit consisting of three shares of Common Stock, and one Warrant to be sold by the Company. The Registration Statement also covered (a) the Unit Purchase Option to be granted to the Representative, including the underlying securities, for the purchase of 60,000 Units, (b) 90,000 Units which were subject to an option to be granted to the Representative by the Company to purchase such Units to cover over-allotments, if any, and (c) the Common Stock underlying the Warrants.

2. On March 9, 1994, the SEC issued comments on the Registration Statement.*

3. By letters dated March 30, and April 17, 1994, the Company's auditors provided supplemental information and data to the SEC in response to its Letter of Comment dated March 9, 1994.

4. By letter* dated April 23, 1994, transmitted with Amendment No. 1, the Company and counsel for the Company provided supplemental information to the Commission in response to its Letter of Comment dated March 9, 1994.

5. By a letter* dated July 24, 1994, the Company and its counsel requested that the Registration Statement become effective on July 25, 1994, or as soon thereafter as possible.

6. The Registration Statement, as so amended,* became effective at 10:30 a.m. on July 25, 1994, pursuant to order of the SEC.

Note: This includes the 15 percent "Green Shoe" over-allotment that allows the underwriters to sell 15 percent more shares than are formally being offered.

Note: This is part of the lead underwriter's additional compensation.

Note: Documents included in this chapter are marked with an asterisk (*).

Form 23: Memorandum of Closing (continued)

7. On July 26, 1994, ten copies of the final Prospectus were filed with the SEC in compliance with Rule 424(b).

B. Corporate Authorization by the Company

1. By actions taken on October 6, 1993, February 9, 1994, and July 24, 1994, the Company's Board of Directors, among other things, approved all aspects of the public offering of Units (including execution of the Registration Statement, execution of the Underwriting Agreement, and execution of all other documents necessary for such public offering)*, ratified all action taken with respect to the filing of all amendments to the Registration Statement, as well as all action taken to qualify and register the Units for sale in the various states, approved the final form of the Underwriting Agreement, Warrant Agreement and form of Unit Purchase Option and appointed Confederate Stock Transfer & Trust Company as Transfer Agent and Warrant Agent for the Units.

C. Action Taken in Connection with Underwriting and Offering

1. The Company delivered to its Counsel such information and documents as were requested for Blue Sky qualification purposes and the Units were qualified for sale under the Securities or "Blue Sky" laws of certain states, as indicated in the final Blue Sky Memorandum*, dated July 26, 1994, prepared by Counsel for the Company.

2. On July 25, 1994, independent accountants, delivered their "comfort" letter with respect to their independence and the financial statements and certain other information contained in the Registration Statement and Prospectus, as required by Section 4(d) of the Underwriting Agreement.

3. The Underwriting Agreement was executed by the Company and the Representative on July 25, 1994.

4. The Representative commenced the offering on July 25, 1994.

Note: This is generally handled by the underwriter's counsel.

5. Prior to the Closing, Selling Agreements were executed and delivered by various selected dealers and the Underwriters.

6. Prior to the Closing, approval of the underwriting compensation was obtained from the National Association of Securities Dealers, Inc.

D. Other Action Taken Prior to Closing

1. Prior to the Closing, the Company delivered to Counsel for the Underwriter each of the following documents:
    (a) signed copies of the Registration Statement and of the Amendment thereto, including financial statements;

Form 23: Memorandum of Closing (continued)

(b) unsigned conformed copies of the Registration Statement and of the Amendments thereto, including financial statements; and

(c) copies of all exhibits filed with the SEC as part of the Registration Statement.

II. THE CLOSING

A. Persons Present at the Closing

The Closing was held at the offices of True Aim Securities, Inc., 1 Wall Street, New York, New York 10022, at 10:00 a.m. on August 3, 1994. Persons present at the Closing are listed on Schedule A annexed hereto.

B. Action Taken at the Closing

All of the following transactions were considered to have taken place simultaneously, and no delivery or payment was considered to have been made until all steps taken at the Closing had been completed.

Unless otherwise indicated, all documents referred to below are dated August 3, 1994 (the "Closing Date").

1. The Company delivered one original of each of the following documents to the Representative and one copy of the following documents to Counsel for the Representative.

(a) Certificates of the Secretary of State of the State of Delaware, dated July 2, 1994, listing all charter documents on file and certifying that the Company and its Subsidiaries are in good standing with no record of dissolution.

(b) Certificate of the Secretary of State of the State of New York, dated August 1, 1994, as to the qualification of the Company to do business as a foreign corporation in the State of New York.

(c) Copies of the following, certified by the Secretary of the Company:

   (i)   Certificate of Incorporation of the Company and its Subsidiaries, together with all amendments thereto.

   (ii)   By-laws of the Company and its Subsidiaries.

   (iii) Minutes of all meetings of, and all action taken by, the Company's Board of Directors and stockholders with respect to the public offering.

   (iv)   All communications, including enclosures, between the Company, Counsel for the Company or Auditors for the Company and the SEC.

   (v)   Copy of the Warrant Agreement dated as of August 3, 1994, between the Company, the Warrant Agent and the Representative.

   (vi)   Specimens of certificates representing the Common Stock and the Warrants.

(d) Certificate with respect to the incumbency and signatures of certain officers and directors of the Company.

Note: Counsel for the issuer assembles all of these documents.

Form 23: Memorandum of Closing (continued)

(e) Certificates of the Chairman and the principal financial officer of the Company required by Section 4(e) of the Underwriting Agreement.

(f) Original Order of the SEC* declaring the Registration Statement effective under the Securities Act of 1933.

2. Parker & Schwartz, CPAs, independent public accountants, delivered their comfort letter, as required by Section 4(d) of the Underwriting Agreement.

3. The Transfer Agent/Warrant Agent delivered to the Representative its certificate with respect to:

(a) its appointment as Transfer Agent and Warrant Agent; and

(b) the authority of its officers and employees countersigning the certificates for the Common Stock, and the Warrants.

4. The opinion of Santoro, Ryan & Kostant* was delivered to the Representative and Counsel for the Underwriter, as required by Section 4(b) of the Underwriting Agreement.

5. The Warrant Agent completed execution of the Warrant Agreement in counterparts, with the Company and the Representative.

6. The Representative notified the Company that its Unit Purchase Option be issued as 60,000 Units to the Representative.

7. The letters required by Sections 3(k), (1) and (n) of the Underwriting Agreement were delivered by the Principal Stockholder of the Company to the Representative.

8. The Company delivered to the Representative (a) Certificates representing 2,070,000 shares of Common Stock and 690,000 Warrants registered in the names and denominations requested by the Representative; (b) the Unit Purchase Option, duly executed by the Company; and (c) cross receipts which acknowledged receipt of the purchase price for the Units and the Unit Purchase Option.

9. The Representative delivered to the Company (a) a certified or bank cashier's check payable to the order of the Company in New York Clearing House Funds in the amount of $3,381,300.00, representing payment in full for 690,000 Units, net of the $21,000 unpaid balance of the Representative's non-accountable expense allowance; (b) a check in the amount of $60.00 representing a payment in full for the Unit Purchase Option; and (c) a cross receipt which acknowledged receipt of the Units and the Unit Purchase Option.

10. Counsel for the Representative delivered their opinion to the Representative, pursuant to Section 4(c) of the Underwriting Agreement.

Note: These are the "lock-up" letters first referred to in the Letter of Intent.

Note: Notice that the payment for the underwriter's unit purchase option is nominal.

Form 23: Memorandum of Closing (continued)

11. The Company delivered to the Transfer Agent authorization for the delivery of certificates representing the Units.

III. ACTION TO BE TAKEN SUBSEQUENT TO THE CLOSING

1. The twelve months' earnings referred to in Section 3(g) of the Underwriting Agreement will be made available to the Company's security holders and to the Representative as soon as practicable, and in any event, not later than 15 months after the end of the Company's current fiscal quarter.

2. As soon as practicable after the end of each fiscal year and each quarterly fiscal period, respectively, of the Company, for a period of five years after the effective date of the Registration Statement, the Company will mail to the Representative the financial reports set forth in Section 3(d) of the Underwriting Agreement.

3. All documents made available to security holders, filed with the SEC or requested by the Representative pursuant to Section 3(d) of the Underwriting Agreement, will be delivered to the Representative for a period of five years from the effective date of the Registration Statement.

4. Until August 2, 1999, the Company and each holder of 5% or more shares of Common Stock of the Company outstanding prior to the offering ("Principal Stockholders") will consult with True Aim Securities, Inc., in respect of any prospective or actual public or private offering of securities of the Company and will not negotiate the public or private sale of any securities of the Company through any person, firm or corporation other than True Aim Securities, Inc., unless and until they shall have negotiated the sale of such securities with True Aim Securities, Inc., in accordance with Section 3(1) of the Underwriting Agreement.

5. The Principal Stockholders of the Company will not sell any of their shares of the Company's Common Stock until February 3, 1995 without the prior consent of the Representative.

Form 23: Memorandum of Closing (continued)

SCHEDULE A
Present at the Closing

Issuer
    Alison Technologies, Inc.
    Elvis Thomas, President
    Bruce Lowe, Secretary

Counsel for Issuer
    Peter C. Kostant, Esq.
    Santoro, Ryan & Kostant

Representative of Underwriters
    True Aim Securities, Inc.
    Nick Nieve, President

Counsel for Representative
    James Froom, Esq.
    Burton, Froom & Brinsley

Accountants
    Charles Parker, CPA
    Parker & Schwartz, CPAs

Transfer and Warrant Agent
    Confederate Stock Transfer & Trust Company
    Marshall Clapton, Vice President

Form 24: Issuer's Counsel Cover Letter to the SEC

SANTORO, RYAN & KOSTANT
2 Wall Street
New York, NY 10022

February 10, 1994

Securities and Exchange Commission
Judiciary Plaza
450 Fifth Street, N.W.
Washington, DC 20549

Re: Alison Technologies, Inc.

Dear Sir or Madam:

On behalf of our client, Alison Technologies, Inc., a Delaware corporation (the "Company"), we are enclosing in connection with the registration by the Company of 600,000 Units, each Unit consisting of three shares of its Common Stock, par value $.01 per share ("Common Stock"), and one Common Stock Purchase Warrant ("Warrants"), on Form S-1 the following documents:

1. One (1) executed copy of the Registration Statement;
2. Twelve (12) conformed copies of the Registration Statement;
3. Two (2) additional sets of the exhibits filed with the Registration Statement;
4. A certified check in the amount of $1,966.69 made payable to the order of the Commission, in payment of the filing fee.

On behalf of the Company, we advise you as follows:

The Company and the Underwriters desire an effective date in the first half of March 1994.

The Company does not believe any particular disclosure or accounting problems are presented by the Registration Statement.

Please be advised in accordance with Release 5196, that all reports required to be filed by the Company under the Securities and Exchange Act of 1934 have been filed and are complete.

If you have any questions concerning the Registration Statement or information contained in this letter, please do not hesitate to call collect the undersigned at (212) 111-0000.

Please acknowledge receipt of this letter and the enclosures by stamping the duplicate copy of this letter provided

Note: This amount is one twenty-ninth of one percent of the total value of the securities being registered, but this may change in the near future.

Note: The Company is currently a 1934 Act Reporting Company and is current in all of its required reporting.

Form 24: Issuer's Counsel Letter to the SEC (continued)

for such purpose and returning it to our messenger, who has been instructed to wait for such copy.

Thank you very much for your cooperation.

Very truly yours,

Peter C. Kostant
PCK/cm
Enclosures

The next document, Form 25, provides most of a registration statement on SEC Form S-1, including the prospectus. Note that the prospectus is really a disclosure, and not a conventional selling document. The practical impact of all this disclosure has long been disputed. Some argue that the benefits have not been proven.[4] Others believe disclosure has helped make the American securities markets the most transparent and efficient in the world.[5]

Because of the length and complexity of the S-1 form, it varies from other forms presented in this book in that some pages are presented full-page without marginal notes. Also, in some instances notes are superimposed over the document in boxes to focus your attention on certain portions of the text.

Form 25: Excerpts from Registration Statement on Form S-1

As filed with the Securities and Exchange Commission on February 10, 1994.
Registration No. X-V

SECURITIES AND EXCHANGE COMMISSION
Washington, D.C. 20549

Form S-1
Registration Statement
Under
The Securities Act of 1933

Alison Technologies, Inc.
(Exact name of registrant as specified in its charter)

Delaware	3670	XXX
(state or other jurisdiction of incorporation or organization)	(Primary Standard Industrial Classification Code Number)	(I.R.S. employer identification number)

Alison Technologies Inc.
1 Imperial Avenue
Brooklyn, NY 10102
(718) 222-2222

(Address, including zip code, and telephone number, including
area code, or registrant's principal executive offices)

Elvis Thomas, President
Alison Technologies, Inc.
1 Imperial Avenue
Brooklyn, NY 10102
(718) 222-2222

(Name, address, including zip code, and telephone number,
including area code, of agent for service)

Copies to:

Peter C. Kostant, Esq.	James Froom Esq.
Santoro, Ryan & Kostant	Burton, Froom & Brinsley
1 Wall Street	2 Wall Street
New York, NY 10101	New York, NY 10101
(212) 222-2222	(212) 222-3333

Approximate date of commencement of proposed sale to the public: As soon as practicable after the effective date of this Registration Statement.

If any of the securities being registered on the Form are to be offered on a delayed or continuous basis pursuant to Rule 415 under the Securities Act of 1933, check the following box. ☐

Note: Various forms may be available for the issuer. Form S-1 has the broadest application, while Forms S-2 and S-3 are for well-established reporting companies for which public information is already available. Somewhat simpler, Forms SB-1 and SB-2 may be available for small business issuers and would allow for less expensive financial statements.

Note: Many young lawyers are thrilled to see their names on the cover of a registration statement. Lawyers with more experience are less excited, as they recognize that plaintiff's lawyers use these names when listing parties to lawsuits.

Form 25: Registration Statement on Form S-1 (continued)

CALCULATION OF REGISTRATION FEE

Title of Each Class of Securities to Be Registered	Amount to Be Registered	Proposed Maximum Offering Price Per Share (1)	Proposed Maximum Aggregate Offering Price (1)	Amount of Registration Fee
Units (2)	$690,000	$5.00	$3,450,000	$690.00
Common Stock, Par Value $.01 Per Share (2)	2,070,000	—	—	
Common Stock Purchase Warrants (2)	690,000	—	—	
Common Stock, Par Value $.01 Per Share (3)	690,000	$2.00	$1,380,000	$276.00
Underwriter's Unit Purchase Option (4)	60,000	$ .001	$ 60	$ .01
Units (5)	60,000	$6.00	$ 360,000	$ 72.00
Common Stock, Par Value $.01 Per Share (6)	60,000	$2.00	$ 120,000	$ 24.00
Total			$5,310,060	$1,966.69

Note on table, above: It is important to register all the common stock that will underlie the Units to be sold. The registration fee is one twenty-ninth of the maximum public sales price (subject to change soon).

Note to item 7, "Selling Security Holders," on next page: If existing holders of securities are registering them for sale, it is called a "secondary" public offering. Here only the issuer, Alison Technologies, Inc. is registering its own securities for sale.

(1) Estimated solely for the purpose of calculating the registration fee. On February 8, 1994, the closing bid price of the Common Stock quoted on NASDAQ was $1-7/16.

(2) The Units which are being offered hereby consist of an aggregate of 2,070,000 shares of Common Stock and 690,000 Five-Year Common Stock Purchase Warrants (the 1999 Warrants), each Unit to consist of three shares of Common Stock and one 1999 Warrant. The 690,000 Units include 90,000 Units (comprised of 270,000 shares of Common Stock and 90,000 1999 Warrants) which may be issued on exercise of a 30-day option to be granted to the Underwriters or, at the option of True Aim Inc. Securities, Inc., the Representative of the Underwriters, to the Representative in its individual capacity, to cover over-allotments, if any. See "UNDERWRITING."

(3) Issuable upon exercise of the 1999 Warrants included in the Units to be sold to the public. This Registration Statement also covers any additional shares of Common Stock which may become issuable by virtue of the anti-dilution provisions of the 1999 Warrants.

(4) To be issued to True Aim Inc. Securities, Inc. individually and not as the Representative of the Underwriters. Pursuant to Rule 416, there are also being registered such additional securities as may be issued pursuant to the anti-dilution provisions of the Unit Purchase Option.

(5) Issuable upon exercise of the Unit Purchase Option; consists of 180,000 shares of Common Stock and 60,000 1999 Warrants.

Form 25: Registration Statement on Form S-1 (continued)

(6) Issuable upon exercise of the 1999 Warrants to be included in the Units issuable upon exercise of the Unit Purchase Option. This Registration Statement also covers any additional shares of Common Stock which may become issuable by virtue of the anti-dilution provisions of the 1999 Warrants.

The Registrant hereby amends this Registration Statement on such date or dates as may be necessary to delay its effective date until the Registrant shall file a further amendment which specifically states that this Registration Statement shall thereafter become effective in accordance with Section 8(a) of the Securities Act of 1933 or until the Registration Statement shall become effective on such date as the Commission, acting pursuant to said Section 8(a) may determine.

CROSS-REFERENCE SHEET

Item Number and Caption	Heading in Prospectus
1. Forepart of Registration Statement and Outside Front Cover Page of Prospectus	Facing Page of Registration Statement; Outside Front Cover Page of Prospectus
2. Inside Front and Outside Back Cover Pages of Prospectus	Inside Front Cover Page of Prospectus; Outside Back Cover Page of Prospectus
3. Summary Information, Risk Factors and Ratio of Earnings to Fixed Charges	Prospectus Summary; Business; Risk Factors (Not Applicable as to Ratio of Earnings to Fixed Charges)
4. Use of Proceeds	Use of Proceeds
5. Determination of Offering Price	Outside Front Cover Page of Prospectus; Underwriting
6. Dilution	Dilution
7. Selling Security Holders	*
8. Plan of Distribution	Outside Front Cover Page of Prospectus; Underwriting
9. Description of Securities to be Registered	Outside Front Cover Page of Prospectus; Price Range of Common Stock; Description of Securities Item Number and Caption Heading in Prospectus
10. Interests of Named Experts and Counsel	Management; Certain Transactions; Legal Opinions
11. Information with Respect to the Registrant	Prospectus Summary; Price Range of Common Stock; Dividends; Capitalization; Selected Financial Data; Management's Discussion and Analysis of Financial Condition and Results of Operations; Business; Management; Consolidated Financial Statements
12. Disclosure of Commission's Position on Indemnification for Securities Act Liabilities	*

*Item is omitted from the Prospectus because it is not applicable or the answer is in the negative.

Form 25: Registration Statement on Form S-1 (continued)

Note: This section of the registration statement is the preliminary, or "Red Herring," prospectus that will be widely circulated to offerees. In reality it is a disclosure and liability statement rather than a selling document.

Note: The registration statement (including the preliminary prospectus) has cross references to help the reader find all relevant information.

Note: In its comment letter (Form 35, SEC Comment Letter) the SEC deemed this warning insufficient.

Note: Blanks are left for offering price, effectiveness date and underwriters because this information is not available when the registration statement is filed.

A registration statement relating to these securities has been filed with the Securities and Exchange Commission but has not yet become effective. Information contained herein is subject to completion or amendment. These securities may not be sold nor may offers to buy be accepted prior to the time the registration statement becomes effective. This prospectus shall not constitute an offer to sell or the solicitation of an offer to buy nor shall there be any sale of these securities in any State in which such offer, solicitation, or sale would be unlawful prior to registration or qualification under the securities laws of any such State.

PRELIMINARY PROSPECTUS
Dated February 10, 1994

ALISON TECHNOLOGIES, INC.
600,000 Units

Each Unit consists of three shares of Common Stock, par value $.01 per share, and One Five-Year Common Stock Purchase Warrant (the "1999 Warrant") which entitles the holder to purchase one share of Common Stock at a price of $_____. The 1999 Warrants will not be exercisable or separately transferable from the Common Stock included in the Units offered hereby until ninety days after the date of the Prospectus, unless an earlier date is determined by True Aim Securities Inc., the representative of the underwriters (the "Representative").

The Company's Common Stock is traded in the over-the-counter market. The closing bid and asked prices of the Common Stock as quoted by NASDAQ on February 8, 1994 were $1 $7/_{16}$ and $1 $9/_{16}$. There has not been any market for the Units and the 1999 Warrants which are being offered by this Prospectus. See "PRICE RANGE OF COMMON STOCK." The offering price of the Units has been determined by negotiation between the Company and the Representative and is not related to the Company's asset value, net worth or any other established criterion of value. It is expected that the Units will be offered at a price of $5.00 per Unit.

THESE SECURITIES INVOLVE A HIGH DEGREE OF RISK. SEE "RISK FACTORS."

THESE SECURITIES HAVE NOT BEEN APPROVED OR DISAPPROVED BY THE SECURITIES AND EXCHANGE COMMISSION NOR HAS THE COMMISSION PASSED UPON THE ACCURACY OR ADEQUACY OF THIS PROSPECTUS. ANY REPRESENTATION TO THE CONTRARY IS A CRIMINAL OFFENSE.

	Price to Public	Underwriting Discounts and Commissions (1)	Proceeds to Company (2)
Per Unit	_____	_____	_____
Total (3)	_____	_____	_____

TRUE AIM SECURITIES, INC.

The date of this Prospectus is _____, 1994.

Form 25: Registration Statement on Form S-1 (continued)

FOOTNOTES TO COVER PAGE

(1) Excludes additional compensation to be received by the Representative in the form of (i) a non-accountable expense allowance equal to 3% of the public offering price or $_____ ($_____ per Unit) ($_____ if the over-allotment option is exercised in full) and (ii) an option (the "Unit Purchase Option") to purchase up to 60,000 Units exercisable over a period of four years, commencing one year from completion of this offering, at 120% of the public offering price, or $_____ per Unit.

(2) Before deducting expenses of the offering payable by the Company estimated at $_____ (approximately $_____ per Unit), including the Representative's non-accountable expense allowance. See "CERTAIN TRANSACTIONS" and "UNDERWRITING."

(3) The Company has granted the Underwriters or, at the option of the Representative, the Representative in its individual capacity, an option for 30 days to purchase on the same terms up to an additional 90,000 Units solely to cover over-allotments. If such option is exercised in full, the total price to the public will be $_____, the total underwriting discount will be $_____, and the total proceeds to the Company will be $_____. See "UNDERWRITING."

The Units are offered on a "firm commitment" basis, subject to the right of the Underwriters to reject any order in whole or in part and to certain other conditions. It is expected that the delivery of certificates for the Units will take place at the offices of True Aim Securities, Inc., 2 Wall Street, New York, New York 10022, on or about _____,1994.

The Company intends to furnish to its stockholders, after the close of each fiscal year, annual reports containing financial statements certified by its independent accountants. In addition, the Company may furnish to its stockholders quarterly or semiannual reports containing unaudited financial statements.

AVAILABLE INFORMATION

The Company is subject to the informational requirements of the Securities Exchange Act of 1934 and in accordance therewith files reports, proxy statements, and other information with the Securities and Exchange Commission. Such reports, proxy statements and other information may be inspected and copied at the public reference facilities maintained by the Commission at 450 Fifth Street, N.W., Washington, D.C. 20549; and at the Commission's regional offices at 219 South Dearborn Street, Chicago, Illinois 60640; 5757 Wilshire Boulevard, Los Angeles, California 90024; and 26 Federal Plaza, New York, New York 10278. Copies of such material may be obtained from the Public Reference Section of the Commission, 450 Fifth Street, N.W., Washington, D.C. 20549, at prescribed rates. This Prospectus does not contain all the information set forth in the Registration Statement and the exhibits thereto filed by the Company with respect to the offering made hereby. Copies of such Registration Statement are available from the Commission.

Note: The lead underwriter is often called the "Representative." Here it gets the Unit Purchase Option itself, and will not share this compensation with the other underwriters in the underwriting syndicate.

Note: This is a firm commitment underwriting.

Form 25: Registration Statement on Form S-1 (continued)

Note: Sophisticated investors will frequently read the financial statements first and often read no further.

Note: The SEC Comment Letter requested more information.

Note: The SEC Comment Letter requested more emphasis on risk.

PROSPECTUS SUMMARY

The following summary is qualified in its entirety by the more detailed information and consolidated financial statements (and notes thereto) appearing elsewhere in this Prospectus.

The Company

The Company develops, manufactures and markets computer literacy products designed to assist users without specific computer skills in the operation of personal computers, and to enable users to communicate directly with computers by writing on the screen of the computer terminal instead of typing commands on a keyboard. The Company's principal products are a Consumer Light Pen, an Industrial Light Pen, a Big Lite™, complementary software and computer-aided design/drafting systems. The Company also manufactures and sells photo-electronic sensing devices. In addition, the Company provides calibration, servicing and sales of electronic test equipment. The Company is also performing research and development on a 3-D Display, three-dimensional, computer-controlled interactive display system.

The Offering

Units Offered: 600,000 Units, each Unit consisting of three shares of Common Stock and one 1999 Warrant (1).

Securities to be Outstanding After the Offering (1)(2): 5,904,600 shares of Common Stock; 600,000 1999 Warrants.

Use of Proceeds: Advertising and marketing; development of software and hardware for computer literacy products; research and development for 3-D Display; working capital.

NASDAQ Symbol: XXXX

---

(1) Assumes the Underwriters' over-allotment option is not exercised.

(2) Also outstanding are 124,274 Common Stock Purchase Warrants (the "1994 Warrants") issued to the public, and 90,000 warrants issued to Oliver Securities Corp. (the "Oliver Warrants") in connection with the Company's 1991 public offering. See "CERTAIN TRANSACTIONS" AND "DESCRIPTION OF SECURITIES—Outstanding Units and Warrants." The Company's Stock Option Plan (1993) for Incentive Stock Options and Non-Qualified Options provides for the granting of options to purchase no more than 350,000 shares of Common Stock. As of the date hereof, no options have been granted under the Plan. See "MANAGEMENT - Stock Options Plan."

Risk Factors and Dilution

This offering is speculative and involves a high degree of risk. Immediate substantial dilution is net tangible book value

Form 25: Registration Statement on Form S-1 (continued)

per share will be incurred by investors. Persons considering purchasing the Units should review carefully and consider the factors described under "RISK FACTORS" and "DILUTION."

THE COMPANY

The Company develops, manufactures and markets computer literacy products designed to assist users without specific computer skills in the operation of personal computers. The Company's principal products are a Consumer Light Pen, an Industrial Light Pen, a Big Lite, complementary software and computer-aided design/drafting system. The Company also manufactures and sells photo-electronic sensing devices. In addition, the Company provides calibration, servicing and sales of electronic test equipment. The Company is also performing research and development on a 3-D Display, a three-dimensional, computer-controlled interactive display system.

The Company has three wholly-owned subsidiaries, Attractions, Inc. ("Attractions"), LHC ("LHC") and Alison Electronics Instruments Co., Inc. ("Alison Electronics") for which it provides administrative support and is also directly engaged in research and development of the 3-D Display under an exclusive license from its inventor.

Attractions and LHC are actively engaged in the development and sale of computer literacy products and software, including light pens and the Big Lite. A light pen is a hand-held device, shaped like an ordinary pen, which is attached to a personal computer by an electrical cord and enables users to communicate directly with the computer by writing on the screen of the computer terminal instead of typing commands on a keyboard. The Company sells Industrial Light Pens for commercial use, and lower cost Consumer Light Pens designed to be used with many home and personal computers. The Big Lite is a hand-held device which allows the user to organize and process data without using a keyboard of a "mouse." LHC Inc. manufactures all the Company's computer literacy products, including the consumer products which are marketed and sold by Attraction.

Alison Electronics calibrates, services and sells electronic test equipment manufactured by a number of leading makers of such equipment.

The Company, which operated under the name Alison Instrument Co., Inc. prior to January 20, 1994 was incorporated in Delaware in 1988. Its principal office is located at 1 Imperial Avenue, Brooklyn, New York 10102 and its telephone number is (718) 222-2222. The Company's Primary Standard Industrial Clarification Code Number is 3670.

Unless the context otherwise requires, the terms "Alison" and the "Company," as used in this Prospectus, refer to Alison Technologies, Inc. and its subsidiaries.

Form 25: Registration Statement on Form S-1 (continued)

Note: Emphasis on risk and negative information.

Note: The SEC Comment Letter requested more disclosure.

RISK FACTORS

An investment in the securities of the Company is highly speculative in nature and involves a high degree of risk. Anyone considering such purchase should be prepared to suffer loss on his investment and should carefully consider the following risk factors concerning the Company:

1. *Limited Current Operations and Manufacturing Experience.* The Company has recently commenced development, marketing, sales and manufacturing of products in the computer literacy field. The prospective sales of these products are subject to the risks inherent in the establishment of a new business enterprise. An evaluation of the likelihood of the success of the Company must include consideration of the problems, expenses, difficulties, complications and delays frequently encountered in connection with the formation of a new line of business, and the competitive environment in which the Company intends to operate.

While the Company's computer literacy products employ the same technology as certain of the photo-electronic products which the Company has been developing and selling since 1990, many of these computer literacy products are still in the development stage and sales for others have been limited. Of the products sold, the Company has only manufactured and shipped limited quantities, and consequently there is no assurance that the Company will be able to manufacture its products on a cost-effective basis or in a timely manner.

Following the completion of this offering, the Company intends to expand its management and sales teams, but no assurance can be given that the Company will be successful in achieving the many goals which it has set, and the failure to attain one or more of such goals on a timely basis and within the allocated costs could jeopardize the viability of the Company's products. In bringing the computer literacy products to market, the Company will incur substantial costs for the purchase of parts and inventory, advertising and marketing. There is no assurance that the Company will be successful in generating revenues from its computer literacy business activities or that any revenues generated will be sufficient to offset expenses incurred or result in a profit to the Company. See "USE OF PROCEEDS" and "BUSINESS."

2. *Possible Need for Additional Funds.* The proceeds of this offering and funds generated by the Company's existing business are projected to fund the Company's development and working capital requirements for approximately twelve months from the date of this Prospectus. Thereafter, or sooner if costs increase or revenues are not received as anticipated, the Company may require additional financing. There can be no assurance that the Company could successfully obtain such additional funds or, if obtained, that the terms would be attractive to the Company. See "USE OF PROCEEDS."

Form 25: Registration Statement on Form S-1 (continued)

3. *Projected Loss.* The Company lost $195,184 in 1992, and continued to suffer losses of $567,112 through November 3, 1993. It is anticipated that the Company will continue to suffer losses in at least part of 1994.

4. *Dependence on Key Personnel.* Because of the specialized nature of its business, the Company is dependent upon its ability to attract and retain qualified personnel. In particular, the Company is dependent upon the services of its President and Chairman, Elvis Thomas and the Company's business would be adversely affected if it lost his services. Mr. Thomas has no employment contract, but will own in excess of 26.6% of the Company's Common Stock at the conclusion of this offering. Additionally, the Company's success is dependent in large part upon its engineering staff, which must continue to develop new hardware and software for the Company's products. Competition for engineering personnel in the Company's field is intense, and there are many other companies with substantially greater resources. Accordingly, there is no assurance that the Company will be successful in attracting and retaining qualified engineering personnel.

Note: The SEC Comment Letter requested more disclosure.

5. *Potential Obsolescence.* The computer industry, including the development, manufacture and sale of computer literacy products, is characterized by rapid technological change. The Company's ability to compete is dependent, in part, upon its ability to adapt to such change by continuing to enhance and expand its products and services. No assurance can be given that the Company can develop and maintain products and services that are technologically competitive.

6. *Competition.* The Company is a small and insignificant factor in the development and marketing of the products in which it is primarily engaged, and faces competition from many larger companies with vastly greater resources to develop products and to employ more salesmen. Other companies may also be engaged in developing more innovative computer literacy products that could render those of the Company obsolete. The successful development by other companies of competitive products would adversely affect Alison's prospects.

Note: The SEC Comment Letter requested more disclosure.

7. *Limited Patent Protection.* None of the hardware or software for the Company's products, other than the 3-D Display, is protected by patent. Moreover, there is no assurance that the Company's 3-D Display patent would be upheld by the courts if challenged in litigation.

8. *Dilution and Control by Present Owners.* As a result of the sale of the securities offered hereby, there will be an immediate substantial dilution to public investors in that the net tangible book value per share of the Common Stock after the offering will be substantially less than the public

Note: The SEC Comment Letter requested more disclosure.

Form 25: Registration Statement on Form S-1 (continued)

Note: The SEC Comment Letter requested more disclosure.

offering price per share (assuming no part of consideration paid for the Units is attributable to the 1999 Warrants). Further, following completion of this offering, the present officers and directors of the Company, who purchased their shares of Common Stock at prices substantially below the public offering price, will continue to own approximately 27.4% of the outstanding Common Stock.

9. *Effect of Issuance of Warrants and Options.* The Company intends in connection with this offering to grant to the Underwriter, True Aim Securities, Inc., individually and not as Representative, Unit Purchase Options to purchase up to an additional 60,000 Units. Also, pursuant to the Company's Stock Option Plan (1993) for Incentive Stock Options and Non-Qualified Options, the Company may issue options for the purchase of up to an additional 350,000 shares at exercise prices which, in the case of non-qualified stock options, may be at or below the market price for the Company's Common Stock. For the term of the Unit Purchase Options and any incentive of non-qualified stock options, the holders thereof are given an opportunity to profit from a rise in the market price of the Company's Common Stock, with a resulting dilution in the interests of the stockholders. The terms on which the Company may obtain additional financing during that period may be adversely affected. The holders of the Unit Purchase Options and any incentive or non-qualified stock options might be expected to exercise them at a time when the Company would, in all likelihood, be able to obtain needed capital by a new offering of securities on terms more favorable than those provided by the Unit Purchase Options or incentive or non-qualified stock options. In the event that such holders exercise the Unit Purchase Options or incentive or non-qualified stock options at such time, the net tangible book value of the Company's Common Stock might undergo further dilution. See "DESCRIPTION OF SECURITIES" and "UNDERWRITING."

10. *Shares Available for Resale.* Of the 4,104,600 shares of the Company's Common Stock outstanding on the date of this Prospectus, 2,002,800 are "restricted securities" as that term is defined in Rule 144 promulgated under the Securities Act of 1933. In general, under Rule 144 a person (or persons whose shares are aggregated) who has satisfied a two-year holding period may, under certain circumstances, sell within any three-month period a number of shares which does not exceed the greater of 1% of the then outstanding shares of Common Stock or the average weekly trading volume during the four calendar weeks prior to such sale. Rule 144 also permits, under certain circumstances, the sale of shares by a person who is not an affiliate of the Company and who has satisfied a three-year holding period without any quantity limitation. Of the 2,002,800 restricted shares outstanding, approximately 1,729,800 have been held for more than two years and hence are presently available for resale under such Rule. In addition, True Aim, Inc. Securities, Inc., individually, and not in its capacity as Representative, with respect

Form 25: Registration Statement on Form S-1 (continued)

to its Unit Purchase Option, and a former underwriter of the Company with respect to 90,000 shares of Common Stock underlying 90,000 Warrants owned by said former underwriter, have certain demand and "piggy-back" registration rights. For six months after the date of this Prospectus, one major shareholder of the Company has agreed not to sell any of his 1,574,300 shares of Common Stock, under Rule 144 or otherwise, without the prior written consent of the Representative. The Company is unable to predict the effect that sales under Rule 144, pursuant to future registration statements, or otherwise, may have on the then prevailing market price of the Common Stock; it can be expected, however, that such sales of any substantial number of shares of Common Stock would have a depressive effect on the market price of the Common Stock. See "DESCRIPTION OF SECURITIES—Outstanding Units and Warrants" and "UNDER-WRITING."

11. *No Dividends.* There can be no assurance that the proposed operations of the Company will result in sufficient revenues to enable the Company to generate positive cash flow or operate at profitable levels. For the foreseeable future, it is anticipated that any earnings which may be generated from operations of the Company will be used to finance the growth of the Company and that cash dividends will not be paid to stockholders. See "DESCRIPTION OF SECURITIES."

USE OF PROCEEDS

The net proceeds from the sale of the 600,000 Units offered hereby are estimated to be $_____ (after deducting underwriting discounts and commissions of $_____ and expenses payable by the Company estimated at $_____, and without giving effect to the exercise of the Underwriter's over-allotment option or the Unit Purchase Option). The Company intends to use the net proceeds of the offering over approximately the next 12 months, as follows:

Advertising and Marketing (1)	$1,000,000
Development of Computer Literacy and Photo-Electronic Products:	
Software	350,000
Hardware	200,000
Research and Development for 3-D Display System (2)	250,000
Working Capital (3)	$_____
Total	$========

Form 25: Registration Statement on Form S-1 (continued)

(1) Includes approximately $250,000 for the salaries and overhead expenses associated with four additional marketing and two additional support personnel.

(2) Includes $100,000 payable to the inventor of the 3-D Display pursuant to the Company's exclusive licensing agreement. See "BUSINESS-Development of Three-Dimensional, Computer-Controlled Interactive Display."

(3) Includes the salary and associated expenses of a chief financial officer for a period of 12 months.

The foregoing table represents the Company's best estimate of its allocation of the net proceeds of this offering, based upon the current state of its proposed business operations, its current plans and current economic and industry conditions, and is subject to a reapportionment of proceeds realized by the Company among the categories listed above or to new categories.

None of the expenditures described above is a firm commitment by the Company. Projected expenditures are estimates or approximations only. Future events may make shifts in the allocation of funds necessary or desirable. Although the Company has no current plan or intention to reallocate the proceeds of this offering, the management of the Company may reallocate the proceeds of the offering in such manner as it deems appropriate. Any such shifts will be at the discretion of the Company's Board of Directors.

In the opinion of management, the net proceeds of this offering, together with anticipated revenues from operations, will satisfy the Company's projected cash requirements for approximately 12 months following the date of this offering. There can be no assurance that these assumptions will prove to be accurate or that unforeseen events will not occur which might reduce revenues derived over the next 12 months below the assumed level, in which event the proceeds of this offering might satisfy the Company's cash requirements for less than 12 months.

Until used, the Company intends to invest the proceeds of this offering in certificates of deposit and other short-term investments.

DILUTION

At November 30, 1993 the net tangible book value per share of the Company's Common Stock was $.38. Net tangible book value represents total tangible assets less total liabilities, divided by the number of shares of Common Stock outstanding.

The following table illustrates the immediate dilution on a per share basis at November 30, 1993 based upon a public offering price of $_____ per share, less estimated expenses (all of which are being paid by the Company) and less estimated underwritng discounts.

Form 25: Registration Statement on Form S-1 (continued)

Public Offering Price Per Share	$_____ (1)
Net Tangible Book Value at November 30, 1993	$.38
Increase Attributable to Purchase by New Investors	$_____
Net Tangible Book Value Adjusted for the Offering	$_____
Dilution to New Investors	$_____(2)

_____

(1) Attributing no value to the 1999 Warrants.

(2) Assuming non-exercise of the Underwriters' over-allotment option and non-exercise of the 1999 Warrants, and after deducting the underwriting discount and estimated expenses of this offering, and without adjustment for changes in book value attributable to operations after November 30, 1993.

Note: The SEC Comment Letter requested more disclosure. It is important to make clear that the public will likely pay $5.00 for three shares and one warrant, while the existing shareholders only paid $.55 per share. See table on next page.

Note on table below: The SEC Comment Letter requested summary financial information for five rather than three years.

SELECTED FINANCIAL DATA

Operating Results:*	1990	1991	1992	Eleven Months Ended Nov. 30, 1992 (Unaudited)	Eleven Months Ended Nov. 30, 1993 (Unaudited)
Revenues	$1,446,873	$1,562,728	$1,463,863	$1,350,578	$1,299,852
Income (Loss) from Operations	46,779	(39,910)	(185,543)	(152,819)	(556,774)
Other Income (Expenses)	41,412	(47,878)	(4,192)	(5,335)	(10,338)
Net Income	83,562	(86,384)	(195,184)	(158,154)	(567,112)
Weighted Average Shares Outstanding	2,229,330	3,249,333	3,249,333	3,249,333	4,102,818
Earnings (Loss) per Share	.04	(.04)	(.06)	(.05)	(.14)
Balance Sheet Data:					
Working Capital	581,455	1,135,303	938,221	1,019,041	1,141,175
Total Assets	1,159,605	1,676,413	1,655,347	1,685,806	2,439,945
Total Liabilities	782,741	355,998	559,879	553,340	881,899
Stockholders' Equity	376,864	1,320,415	1,095,468	1,132,466	1,558,046

_____

* LHC, Inc., a wholly owned subsidiary of the Company, was acquired on the last business day of August 1990, and the financial results of the Company include the results of LHC, Inc., from the date of its acquisition.

Form 25: Registration Statement on Form S-1 (continued)

MANAGEMENT'S DISCUSSION AND ANALYSIS OF FINANCIAL CONDITION AND RESULTS OF OPERATIONS

The Company's consolidated financial statements reflect significant amounts expended for research and development, licenses and patents, and marketing costs, all in connection with the newly developed product lines in the computer literacy and photo-electronic business segments. All of these costs have been expensed and included as a part of the net loss for the periods presented, although management anticipates future economic benefits as a result of these expenditures. The following table presents by segment the amounts spent and expensed for each of these categories:

Year Ended December 31, 1992 Compared to Year Ended December 31, 1991

	Year Ended Dec. 31, 1991	Year Ended Dec. 31, 1992	Percent Change	Eleven Months Ended Nov. 30, 1992	Eleven Months Ended Nov. 30, 1993	Percent Change
REVENUE:						
Calibration	$831,847	$720,773	(13.4)	$672,550	$443,141	(34.1)
Photo-Electronics and Computer Literacy	730,881	743,090	1.7	678,311	856,711	26.3
SELECTED EXPENSES AND COSTS CHARGED TO EXPENSES:						
Research & Development						
Calibration	—	—	—	—	—	—
Photo-Electronics and Computer Literacy	87,500	95,000	8.6	87,100	180,000	106.7
Marketing						
Calibration	11,365	13,913	22.4	13,544	4,232	(68.8)
Photo-Electronics and Computer Literacy	16,274	25,792	58.5	22,872	179,000	682.6
License and Software Development	—	—	—	—	154,111	—

The following table summarizes the number of Units purchased from the Company, the total consideration paid and the average price per share to be paid by the investors pursuant to this offering (at a public offering price of $_____ per share, attributing no value to the 1999 Warrants) and by the current stockholders:

	Shares Purchased	Percent of Total Shares	Consideration Paid	Percent of Total Consideration Paid	Average Price Per Share
New Investors	1,800,000	30.5	— (1) (2)	—	—
Current Stockholders	4,104,600	69.5	2,261,066 (2)	—	$.55
Total	5,904,600	100.0	— (1) (2)	100.0%	—

(1) These calculations assume that neither the Underwriters' over-allotment option nor the 1999 Warrants are exercised, and that no part of the consideration paid for the Units is attributable to the Warrants. These calculations further assume that none of the Company's currently outstanding 1994 Warrants and none of the Oliver Warrants is exercised. See "DESCRIPTION OF SECURITIES—Outstanding Units and Warrants."

(2) Before deducting underwriting commissions and expense.

Form 25: Registration Statement on Form S-1 (continued)

CAPITALIZATION

The following table sets forth the capitalization of the Company at November 30, 1993 and is adjusted to give effect to the issuance and sale by the Company of 600,000 Units (consisting of 1,800,000 shares of Common Stock and 600,000 1999 Warrants) offered hereby.

	Nov. 30, 1993 Outstanding	As Adjusted
Long-Term Debt and Obligations Under Capital Leases, Less Current Portion	$36,119	$36,119
Stockholders' Equity: Common Stock, Par Value $.01 per Share 10,000,000 Shares Authorized, 4,104,600 Shares Outstanding, 5,904,600 Shares Outstanding as Adjusted	41,120	
Additional Paid-In Capital	2,219,946	
Accumulated Deficit	(703,020)	
Total Stockholders Equity	1,558,046	
Total Capitalization	$1,594,165	

Sales. Sales decreased by $98,865 or 6.3% for fiscal year 1992 over fiscal year 1991. The decrease in sales was due primarily to decreased demand for calibration repair work.

Cost of Sales. Cost of sales increased $57,936 or 5.9% for the fiscal year 1992 over fiscal year 1991 primarily as a result of substantial write-downs or the Company's calibration inventories, consisting chiefly of raw materials and purchased assembly components. These write-downs were in addition to those taken and reflected in the Company's 1991 Consolidated Statement of Operations.

Income. The Company realized a net loss of $195,184 for fiscal year 1992 as compared to $86,384 for fiscal year 1991, a decrease of 226%. The increased losses were due substantially to the write-down of inventories discussed above.

Selling, general administration expenses increased $134,900, which increase is substantially attributable to the marketing costs of the computer literacy products.

For the year ended December 31, 1992, the Company expended $95,000 for the development of technology as opposed to $87,500 in the prior year. As of November 30, 1993, the Company had expanded approximately $180,000 for such development.

Note: The SEC Comment Letter probed Sales, Cost of Sales, Selling, General & Administrative Expenses, Research and Development, and Liquidity & Capital Resources of the Management's Discussion and Analysis for disclosure of more information to clarify possible weaknesses in the issuer.

Form 25: Registration Statement on Form S-1 (continued)

Liquidity and Capital Resources. The Company's short-term borrowings averaged $130,000 at an average interest rate of 15% for the year ended December 31, 1992. For the year ended December 31, 1991, the average short-term borrowings were approximately $82,000 at rates of 9%.

Effects on Inflation. The Company's business is not subject to abnormal inflation or seasonal fluctuation.

BUSINESS

The Company was incorporated in Delaware in 1988 and succeeded to a business which had originally begun in 1981 as the sole proprietorship of Elvis Thomas, the chairman of the board and president of the Company.

Computer Literacy and
Photo-Electronic Products

Existing Computer Literacy Products

Background. The computer literacy field is a developing area of the personal computer market which is geared to the manufacture and sale of products and services designed to make personal computers more "user-friendly." The light pens and Big Lite are designed primarily for users who are not versed in the use of computers.

Industrial and Consumer Light Pens. Alison currently manufactures and markets two light pens, the Industrial Light Pen (LTP105 series), which sells for approximately $100 and is sold in lots of 1,000, and the Consumer Light Pen (LP-10S series), which retails for between $40 and $90 per unit.

The Industrial Light Pen competes with products sold by a number of other manufacturers, including HEI, Inc. and Information Controls Corporation. The company currently believes that the Industrial Light Pen has advantages over its competition because it utilizes photo-optic switching and controlled field of view techniques which result in less distortion or "noise."

Since 1989 the Company has sold approximately 8,000 Industrial Light Pens, and on January 31, 1994 had a backlog of approximately 1,500 units on order. The primary customers are corporations that are competitors of IBM (which manufactures its own light pen but does not sell it to others). Two large companies represent 60% of the Company's Industrial Light Pen orders, and no other individual customer represents 10% of purchases. The Industrial Light Pen is sold primarily to original equipment manufacturers ("OEMs") such as ITT-SEL, Beckman Instruments, Memorex, Hazeltine, and Intermedics. Approximately 20 companies have been purchasers of the Industrial Light Pen.

The Industrial Light Pen is currently sold through seven independent sales representatives who call on manufactur-

Note: The SEC Comment Letter asked for disclosure of the names of the two big customers.

Form 25: Registration Statement on Form S-1 (continued)

ers of terminal, mainframe, mini-sales representatives pursuant to which they receive commissions of approximately 10% of gross sales, which may be terminated by either party upon 60 days' notice.

The Consumer Light Pen is a less expensive version of the Industrial Light Pen. The Company began marketing the Consumer Light Pen in June 1993 and has sold and shipped approximately 6,000 units to date. The market for the low-cost Consumer Light Pen includes users of home and personal computers for educational, office, home and institutional applications. There is currently a backlog of 2,500 units on order. "Toys R Us" and one of the Company's distributors represent 30% of total orders, and units have been sold to hundreds of customers, no one of which represents 10% of purchases.

The Consumer Light Pen and other computer literacy products to be discussed below, including the Big Lite related software and low-cost computer-aided drafting/design systems, are or will be marketed by the Company through a group of six independent sales representatives separate from the group which sells the Industrial Light Pen. The sales representatives, who report to the Company's Eastern and Western Regional Sales Managers, have written contractual agreements with the Company. The independent sales representatives sell to distributors who in turn sell to dealers who sell directly to consumers.

Software. Alison is developing various software programs to allow users of a Consumer Light Pen or Big Lite (as described below) to draw, color, design, move objects, animate and erase directly on a TV screen or computer terminal. Applications include drafting and designing, as well as educational exercises and recreational activities. Materials can either be saved in the computer's memory or printed out.

To date, the Company has developed and sold software packages for two interactive graphics programs, ten computer-aided instruction packages and two entertainment applications. The "Paint 'N Sketch," level 1, interactive graphics program is included with each Consumer Light Pen that is sold. Total sales of these software products to date has been approximately $60,000. The Company has also entered into licensing agreements with two software development companies, Sister Graphics Corporation, of Bethel Island, California, and Luxembourg Graphics Incorporated, of Reston, Virginia, pursuant to which the Company will market two software design packages, the "MICRODRAFTER" and the "ANIMATION DRAFTER."

Developmental Computer Literacy Products
Big Lites. The Big Lite, which the Company plans to market in June 1994, is a hand-held device, which can be quickly mastered and allows the user to organize and process data without having to touch a keyboard. The Big Lite is used like a pen on a desktop to track the cursor, a small white box on

Form 25: Registration Statement on Form S-1 (continued)

the screen of the computer terminal. The Big Lite simplifies the operator's use of the computer by allowing the user to give an instruction to the Central Processing Unit ("CPU") from the "menu" which is displayed on the screen. The command is activated by simply pressing the pen's tip on the desktop, after tracking a function on the "menu." Many functions within the program can be quickly viewed by using the Big Lite.

To the Company's knowledge, there is no other company which currently manufacturers a device similar to the Big Lite. Alison does, however, compete with manufacturers of "mouse" devices such as Mouse House, Mouse Systems Corp., Summagraphics, Logitech and U.S.I. International. The Company believes that the Big Lite while similar in function, may be superior to a "mouse" device because it is designed to fit into the hand of the user like an ordinary pen, thus providing the user with greater dexterity. "Mouse"-type devices are currently used with Apple Computer's Lisa Model, Tele Video's TS 803 personal computer, Visi Corp's Vision software system and Xerox's Star Computer.

Low-Cost Computer Aided Design/Drafting Programs
Alison is developing low-cost computer-aided design/drafting software packages designed to run on the IBM personal computer and on IBM-compatible personal computers. Instead of working at a drafting board, the user sits in front of a CRT and instructs the computer to draw lines and arcs and to store designs by picking coordinates on the face of the CRT with a light pen or Big Lite. This can enable the user to achieve greater accuracy, speed and efficiency than conventional design methods.

Once development is completed, it is anticipated that a program's graphics capability will include storage of the figures and symbols that are needed for a particular type of drawing. The drawings will be user-built from a geometry library in the system and will be stored for recall. Symbols will be assembled or moved on the screen by picking from a "menu" with a light pen or Big Lite. The system will be able to draw various geometric shapes automatically.

The Company currently plans to market a simplified low-cost software package by June 1994. In addition, the Company is developing a sophisticated, professional-level package which will include software, an Industrial Light Pen and a proprietary graphics controller board. The Big Lite and the low-cost, computer-aided design/drafting systems will be marketed through the same independent sales representatives as the Consumer Light Pen.

Photo-Electronic Sensing Devices
The Company's LHC, Inc. subsidiary is involved in the development, manufacture and sale of both traditional and more recently developed photo-electronic equipment, including the Industrial Light Pen, and sensing devices for uses such as the control of elevator doors by the use of a light beam. LHC, Inc. also manufactures the consumer computer literacy products which are marketed and sold by Attractions. The light beam devices produced by LHC are built into convey-

Form 25: Registration Statement on Form S-1 (continued)

ors, burglar alarms, smoke sensors and are utilized in beam breaking, counting, triggering, synchronizing, motion sensing, color sensing, mark sensing, hold sensing, product inspection and other similar uses. The Company also manufactures capacitance proximity sensing devices which measure liquid levels, thickness, moisture and vibration.

The Company stocks a variety of photo-electronic devices, using circuits that are readily adapted to most industrial needs without internal modifications. Modifications to stock items are also produced to adapt them for special control applications, such as web press controllers for printing, and certain industrial smoke detectors.

The company encounters intense competition in the marketing of all its photo-electronic products. There are many competitors who have much greater resources than Alison to develop and market their products, and Alison is only a very small factor in this business.

Calibration, Servicing and Sales of Electronic Test Equipment.

The Company's Alison Electronic subsidiary is engaged in calibration, servicing and sales or electronic equipment, principally low-cost electronic test equipment. Alison's metrology laboratory contains modern equipment and employs technical personnel to perform calibration, certification, conditioning, repair and modification of all types of electrical and electronic test equipment and instrumentation, such as oscilloscopes, digital meters, voltmeters, ohmmeters, signal generators and devices capable of measuring capacitance and inductance.

The calibration and testing methods and procedures employed by the Company meet the requirements of certain military specifications. Alison has reference standards capable of making measurements of AC and DC volts and currents, resistance, capacitance, and inductance which are certified directly by the national Bureau of Standards or indirectly by reference standards in the metrology laboratory traceable to the Bureau or through a third party who has direct traceability to the National Bureau of Standards.

The Company considers its normal marketing area to be the states of New York, New Jersey and Connecticut. Alison believes that there are at least four organizations supplying servicing and recalibration of electronic test equipment in New York, New Jersey and Connecticut, and at least one is larger than Alison. In addition, there are a number of one, or two-man repair shops. As far as sales of test equipment are concerned, Alison encounters competition from many manufacturers, manufacturers' representatives and other sales organizations. Many of these have greater resources than Alison.

Development of Three-Dimensional, Computer-Controlled Interactive Display

On April 2, 1993. The Company acquired an exclusive license under a patent for a three-dimensional, computer-controlled interactive display system capable of producing

Form 25: Registration Statement on Form S-1 (continued)

3-D images and graphics, from J. Robert Teller, Dean of Graduate Studies and Professor of Physics at the Clubland Institute of Technology. Alison has the exclusive right to manufacture and market products derived from the patent or to sublicense the patent to third parties royalty, subject to a minimum of $100,000 per year, on products derived from the patent, and 25% of sublicensing fees paid to Alison.

Since acquiring the license, Alison has expended approximately $150,000 to develop a prototype and intends to use $250,000 of he proceeds of this offering, as well as such additional financing as it may obtain, possibly in the form of joint ventures or sublicenses of the patent, in order to be able to continue development.

The 3-D Display is a light source which originates in a three-dimensional space, can be updated instantly and is not subject to distortion when the viewer changes his position within a 30 range. This system uses an oscilloscope which emits pulses on an axis defined horizontally, vertically and by depth and a computer program which controls the light pulses through a rotating lens so as to transmit updatable spatial shapes within the viewing area of the display.

If the prototype is successfully completed, the system could have many applications. At this time, however, Alison cannot be certain of the commercial applicability of the patent.

Employees

On January 31, 1994, the Company employed 50 persons, of whom 12 were engaged in the development and manufacture of computer literacy products, 3 were engaged in marketing, 13 were engaged in the manufacture and sale of photo-electronic products, 13 were engaged in sales and servicing of electronic test equipment, three were in corporate management and six performed clerical, maintenance, shipping and warehousing functions. None of the employees is represented by a collective bargaining unit, and the Company considers its relations with its employees to be satisfactory.

Patents and Trademarks

In April 1994, the Company acquired the exclusive license to a patent for a three-dimensional, computer-controlled interactive display system. See "BUSINESS Development of Three-Dimensional, Computer-Controlled Interactive Display."

Trademark searches have been completed, and the Company currently is registering the trademarks "Attractions"™ and "Big Lite"™.

Warranty

The Company's computer literacy products carry a 90-day warranty. The photo-electronic sensing products carry a one-year warranty. The electronic test equipment which the Company sells and services carries a 30-day warranty in addition to the manufacturer's warranty. The Company

Form 25: Registration Statement on Form S-1 (continued)

believes that these warranties are consistent with industry standards and, to date, the cost of compliance has not been substantial.

Sources of Supply

The Company purchases the components and supplies necessary for the manufacture and servicing of its products from various domestic sources and has double or triple sources for each item. In the event that a particular supplier became unable to fill orders, the Company would have alternate sources of supply.

Property

The Company leases 15,005 feet of office and plant space in an industrial park at 1 Imperial Avenue, Brooklyn, NY, at an aggregate base rent of $40,162 per annum, plus escalations. The leases expire on August 31, 1998.

CERTAIN TRANSACTIONS

Pursuant to an exclusive licensing agreement, dated April 26, 1993, Dr. J. Robert Teller received $100,000. As part of the same transaction Mr. Teller or his designees were required to purchase 50,000 shares of Restricted Common Stock at a price of $1.00 per share. See "Business-Development of Three Dimensional, Computer-Controlled Interactive Display." As finder for this transaction, on March 2, 1993, Buddy McCartney received 50,000 shares of restricted Common Stock for $.01 per share.

Pursuant to a Prospectus, dated September 22, 1991, the Company made a public offering of 800,000 Units consisting of Common Stock and Warrants. See "DESCRIPTIONS OF SECURITIES - Outstanding Units and Warrants." In connection with such offering, the Company and Oliver Securities Corp. ("Oliver") entered into an Underwriting Agreement, dated September 11, 1991, pursuant to which Oliver received 80,000 Four-Year Warrants exercisable at $1.625 (the "Oliver Warrants"), and which granted certain anti-dilution protection to Oliver. Accordingly, in January 1993, at the time that the Company reduced the exercise price of its outstanding Warrants for a 30-day period, the Company granted to Oliver 10,000 Warrants with the reduced exercise price of $1.275, in addition to the 4-year Warrants exercisable at $1.625 originally granted to Oliver pursuant to the Underwriting Agreement. See "DESCRIPTION OF SECURITIES - Outstanding Units and Warrants."

The law firm of Santoro, Ryan & Kostant has performed legal services to the Company in the past two years for which bills have not been rendered, but said bills will not exceed $100,000.

Note: It is important to disclose the price for which the issuer sold all its currently outstanding securities.

Q: Is it good practice to allow a client to fall so far behind in payments? Could a certified public accountant allow this?

Form 25: Registration Statement on Form S-1 (continued)

DESCRIPTION OF SECURITIES

Common Stock

The Company's Certificate of Incorporation, as amended, authorizes the issuance of 10,000,000 shares of Common Stock, par value $.01 per share. The outstanding shares of Common Stock are, and the shares of Common Stock to be sold by the Company when issued as contemplated by this Prospectus will be fully paid and nonassessable.

Holders of shares of Common Stock are entitled to one vote per share on all matters to be voted on at any meeting of shareholders. The shares of Common Stock do not have cumulative voting rights, which means that the holders of more than 50% of the shares of Common Stock voting for the election of directors can elect all the directors, in which event the holders of the remaining shares of Common Stock will not be able to elect any director.

Holders of shares of Common Stock are entitled to receive such dividends when, as and if declared by the Board of Directors out of funds of the Company legally available for the payment of dividends. The company has not paid any cash dividends on its Common Stock and intends to retain earnings, if any, to finance the development and expansion of its business.

Upon any liquidation, dissolution or winding up of the Company, holders of shares of Common Stock are entitled to receive pro rata all of the assets of the Company available for distribution to shareholders. Shareholders of the Company do not have preemptive rights to subscribe for or purchase any stock, obligations, warrants or other securities of the Company.

Outstanding Units and Warrants

Pursuant to a Prospectus dated September 22, 1991, the Company sold 800,000 Units consisting of one share of Common Stock, $.01 par value and one immediately severable Three-Year Redeemable Warrant (the "1994 Warrants") to purchase one share of Common Stock at $1.50 per share. The Warrant price was protected against dilution and would be adjusted upon the happening of certain events, including stock splits, stock dividends, mergers, consolidations or other recapitalizations. The 1994 Warrants are traded separately from the Units and the Common Stock, and 124,274 1994 Warrants are currently outstanding. In connection with the 1991 public offering, the Company and Oliver Securities Corp. ("Oliver") entered into an Underwriting Agreement dated September 11, 1991, pursuant to which Oliver received 80,000 Four-Year Warrants exercisable at $1.625 (the "Oliver Warrants"), and which granted certain anti-dilution protection, and certain demand and "piggyback" registration rights, to Oliver. Accordingly, in January 1993, at the time that the Company reduced the exercise price of its outstanding 1994 Warrants for a 30-day period, the Company granted to Oliver 10,000 Warrants with the reduced exercise price of $1.275, in addition to the 80,000

Form 25: Registration Statement on Form S-1 (continued)

Oliver Warrants exercisable at $1.625 originally granted to Oliver to the Underwriting Agreement.

On or after one year from the date of issuance of the Warrants, the Company could, at its election, call the Warrants in whole or in part at a price of $.75 per Warrant at any time upon 30 days' notice. Any Warrants called for redemption may be exercised in accordance with the terms on or before the redemption date.

In January 1993, for a 30-day period ending February 21, 1993, the Company reduced the exercise price of its Three-Year Redeemable Warrants from $1.50 to $1.125. During that period, 675,726 Warrants were exercised. The Company paid a management fee to Senior Service & Co., Inc. of $35,272 in connection with the transaction.

New Units

Each Unit consists of three shares of Common Stock and one 1999 Common Stock Purchase Warrant. The Common Stock and 1999 Warrants will be separately transferable after _____, 1994, or such earlier date as may be designated by the Representative.

1999 Warrants

The 1999 Warrants will be issued in registered form under a Warrant Agreement (the "Warrant Agreement"), to be dated as of the date of this Prospectus, among the Company, the Representative and Confederate Stock Transfer & Trust Company (the "Warrant Agent"). Each 1999 Warrant entitles the registered holder to purchase one share of Common Stock at any time commencing on the date it is separately transferable (or such earlier date as may be designated by the Representative) until the close of business on _____ 1999, at a price of $_____ per share.

The Company has the right to redeem the 1999 Warrants at a price of $.10 per Warrant at any time after the first anniversary of the closing date of this offering if the average of the mean of the closing bid and asked prices for the Company's Common Stock as reported by NASDAQ for any 20 consecutive trading days after the first anniversary of the closing date of this offering exceeds $_____ per share. The Company is required to give Warrantholders 30 days' written notice of its intention to redeem the 1999 Warrants, and prior to expiration of this 30-day period the Warrantholders may exercise the 1999 Warrants. All 1999 Warrants must be redeemed if any are redeemed. The Company has authorized and reserved for issuance the shares of Common Stock purchasable upon exercise of the 1999 Warrants. Such shares of Common Stock, when issued, shall be fully paid and nonassessable.

The exercise price and the number and kind of shares of Common Stock to be obtained upon exercise of the 1999 Warrants are subject to adjustment in the event of a stock dividend or on a split of the Common Stock, or in the event of a reorganization of recapitalization of the Company or of the merger or consolidation of the Company in accor-

Form 25: Registration Statement on Form S-1 (continued)

dance with the Warrant Agreement Certificates for the 1999 Warrants are interchangeable without service charge for certificates of different denominations at the office of the Warrant Agent, Confederate Stock Transfer & Trust Company, 3 Wall Street, New York, NY 10022.

Fractional shares will not be issued upon exercise of 1999 Warrants and, in lieu thereof, a cash adjustment based on the market price of the Common Stock on the date of exercise will be made. The 1999 Warrants do not confer upon the holder any voting or preemptive rights, or any other rights of a shareholder of the Company.

A 1999 Warrant may be exercised upon the surrender of a duly completed certificate on or prior to its expiration at the office of the Warrant Agent, accompanied by cash or a certified or official bank check payable to the order of the Warrant Agent for the exercise price.

The above summary does not purport to be complete. The Warrant Agreement containing all of the terms and conditions applicable to the 1999 Warrants, has been filed as an exhibit to the Registration Statement of which this Prospectus is a part.

Tax Considerations Regarding Units

The cost of each Unit will be allocable between each of its two elements (three shares of Common Stock and one 1999 Warrant) in accordance with their relative fair market values to determine the adjusted basis of each element for federal income tax purposes. The sale or redemption of a 1999 Warrant will result in the recognition of gain or loss to the holder in an amount equal to the difference between the amount realized and its adjusted basis. Provided the holder is not a dealer in the 1999 Warrants and the Common Stock is a capital asset to the holder or would be a capital asset to the holder if acquired by him, such gain or loss will be a capital gain or loss (long-term if the 1999 Warrant has been held for more than one year). While uncertainty exists under present law, redemption of a 1999 Warrant by the Company should yield the same tax treatment a sale; there may, however, be a risk that gain or loss upon the redemption would be ordinary, rather than capital, in character.

Effects of Exercise of 1999 Warrant on Holders. No gain or loss will be recognized to a holder of a 1999 Warrant on his purchase of Common Stock for cash pursuant to the exercise of the Warrant. The adjusted basis of a share plus the exercise price; the holding period of the share for long-term capital gain purposes will begin on the date after the Warrant is exercised.

Expiration of 1999 Warrants. Loss on the expiration of a 1999 Warrant which, if sold by the holder would have resulted in capital gain or loss, would be a long-term or short-term capital loss to the holder, depending on whether the 1999 Warrant was held for more than one year. Under published rulings of the Internal Revenue Service, the Company would

Form 25: Registration Statement on Form S-1 (continued)

be required to recognize gain on the expiration of an unexercised 1999 Warrant equal to the consideration which it received therefor.

Other Tax Considerations. There may, in addition, be federal tax considerations, or state, local or foreign tax considerations, applicable to the circumstances of a particular prospective investor, and prospective investors are urged to consult their own tax advisers before determining whether to purchase the Units.

Transfer Agent, Registrar and Warrant Agents

The Transfer Agent, Registrar and Warrant Agent of the shares of Common Stock and the 1999 Warrants of the Company is Confederate Stock Transfer & Trust Company, 3 Wall Street, New York, NY 10012.

UNDERWRITING

The underwriters named below have severally agreed to purchase from the Company the following respective numbers of Units:

Underwriter	*Number of Units*
True Aim Inc. Securities	
Total:	600,000

Note This space is blank because the lead underwriter does not yet know what underwriters will be in the underwriting syndicate.

Through the Representative, the Underwriters have advised the Company that they propose to offer the Units to the public at the public offering price set forth on the cover page of this Prospectus and that they may allow to certain dealers, who are members of the National Association of Securities Dealers, Inc., concessions of not in excess of $_____ per Unit, of which not in excess of $_____ may be reallowed to other dealers who are members of the National Association of Securities Dealers, Inc. After the commencement of this offering, the public offering price, the concessions and the reallowances may be changed.

The Underwriters are committed to purchase all the Units offered hereby on a "firm commitment" basis, if any are purchased.

The Underwriting Agreement provides for reciprocal indemnification between the Company and its controlling persons on the one hand and the Underwriters and their respective controlling persons on the other hand against certain liabilities in connection with this offering, including liabilities under the Securities Act of 1933.

The Company has granted an option to the Underwriters or, at the Representative's option, to the Representative in its individual capacity, exercisable during the 30-day period after the date of this offering, to purchase up to a maximum of 90,000 additional Units at the public offering price, less the

Note: Each underwriter that joins the underwriting syndicate will purchase only a portion of the securities to be offered because Section 11 of the 1933 Act places a cap on liability of each underwriter at the aggregate offering price of the securities purchased by each underwriter.

Note: The SEC Comment Letter requested additional information about indemnification which the SEC opposes as a matter of public policy.

Note: This is the Green Shoe over-allotment option.

Form 25: Registration Statement on Form S-1 (continued)

Q: What are "piggyback" registration rights?

underwriting discount, to satisfy over-allotments in the sale of the Units.

The Company has agreed to pay to the Representative a non-accountable expense allowance of three percent of the aggregate offering price of the Units offered hereby (including any shares purchased pursuant to the over-allotment option), of which $15,000 has been paid to date.

In connection with this offering, the Company has agreed to sell to True Aim Inc. Securities ("Aim") individually and not as Representative of the Underwriters, upon the closing of the sale of the Units for $60, a five-year Unit Purchase Option (the "Unit Purchase Option") to purchase up to 10% of the number of Units offered for sale. The Unit Purchase Option will be exercisable in whole or in part, from time to time, for a period of four years commencing one year after the effective date of the Registration Statement at 120% of the Offering Price. The Unit Purchase Option provides that it cannot be transferred, sold, assigned or hypothecated for one year except that it may be assigned in whole or in part to any officer, employee or affiliate of Aim. The Company has agreed to register the Unit Purchase Option and/or the securities underlying such option at its expense at the request of Aim. This request may be made any one time during the period of four years beginning one year from the closing of this offering. In connection with this registration right, Aim will not require the Company to maintain a current registration statement for more than 150 days after any such registration becomes effective. In addition, the Company will grant Aim "piggyback" registration rights for the Unit Purchase Option and the underlying securities. Until such time as the entire Unit Purchase Option or all of the underlying securities shall have been registered, the Company shall give the holder or holders of the Unit Purchase Option written notice by registered mail not less than 30 days prior to the filing by the Company of any registration statement.

For the life of the Unit Purchase Option and the Warrants contained therein, the holder will be given the opportunity to profit from a rise in the market value of the Common Stock with a resulting dilution in the interest of the other holders of Common Stock. The holder of the Unit Purchase Option and the Warrants contained therein can be expected to exercise them at a time when the Company would, in all likelihood, be able to obtain any needed capital from an offering of its unissued Common Stock on terms more favorable to the Company than those provided by the Unit Purchase Option. Such facts may adversely affect the terms on which the Company can obtain additional financing. To the extent that the Underwriters realize any gain from the resale of the Unit Purchase Option or the securities underlying the Unit Purchase Option, the gain may be deemed additional underwriting compensation.

The Company also agreed that if, at the time of exercise of any of the Warrants more than one year after the closing

Form 25: Registration Statement on Form S-1 (continued)

of this offering, (i) the market price of the Company's Common Stock is more than the exercise price, (ii) the holder of the Warrants indicates in writing that his exercise was solicited by a member of the National Association of Securities Dealers, Inc., and (iii) the Warrant was not held in a discretionary account, then the Company will pay a fee of 4% of the exercise price to Aim, a portion of which may be reallowed by Aim, to the dealer involved (which may also be Aim). As a condition of payment of this fee, Aim or the soliciting dealer will be required to represent that the solicitation of the Warrant exercise was not in violation of Rule 10b-6 promulgated under the Securities Exchange Act of 1934.

The Company and each of its principal stockholders have granted to Aim a right of first refusal for five years to act as underwriter for subsequent public or private offerings of the Company's securities regardless of whether such securities are offered by the Company or by such stockholders.

The Underwriting Agreement provides that the Company obtain a key-man life insurance policy on the life of Elvis Thomas, president and chairman of the board, in the amount of $1 million, and that it keep this policy in effect for at least two years from the effective date of this Prospectus. The beneficiary of this policy is the Company.

The foregoing does not purport to be a complete statement of the terms and conditions of the Underwriting Agreement, copies of which are on file at the offices of the Representative, the Company, and the Securities and Exchange Commission.

The public offering price of the Units has been determined by negotiation between the Company and the Representative and is not related to the Company's asset value, net worth or any other established criterion of value. Factors considered in determining the offering price of the Units included the amount of dilution per share of Common Stock to the public investors and the estimated amount of proceeds believed by management of the Company to be necessary to accomplish its proposed goals. See "DILUTION" and "USE OF PROCEEDS."

EXPERTS

The consolidated financial statements and schedules of Alison Technologies, Inc. and subsidiaries included in this Prospectus and the Registration Statement, for the periods indicated in their reports, have been examined by Parker & Schwartz, CPAs, independent accountants, whose reports thereon appear elsewhere herein and in the Registration Statement. Such financial statements and schedules have been included in reliance upon the reports of Parker & Schwartz, CPAs, given upon their authority as experts in accounting and auditing.

Form 25: Registration Statement on Form S-1 (continued)

Note: Part II is not part of the preliminary prospectus that gets widely distributed to the public.

Note: The NASD one-time company listing fee for NAS-DAQ Small Cap Market is $5,000 and a minimum variable fee of $1,000.

LEGAL OPINIONS

The legality of the shares of Common Stock offered hereby will be passed upon for the Company by Messrs. Santoro, Ryan & Kostant, 1 Wall Street, New York, New York, 10101, counsel for the Company. The firm of Burton, Froom & Brinsley, 2 Wall Street, New York, New York 10101, counsel for the Underwriters, will pass upon the legality of the shares of Common Stock for the Underwriters.

PART II
INFORMATION NOT REQUIRED IN PROSPECTUS

Item 13. Other Expenses of Issuance and Distribution

Registration Fee — Securities and Exchange Commission	$1,966.69
Filing Fee — N.A.S.D.	$6,000.00
Blue Sky Fees and Expenses (including Legal Fees)	_____
Cost of Printing and Engraving	_____
Legal Fees and Expenses	_____
Accounting Fees and Expenses	_____
Transfer Agent's and Registrar's Fees and Expenses	_____
Miscellaneous Expenses	_____
Total	========

Item 14. Indemnification of Directors and Officers

The Registrant's Certificate of Incorporation, as amended, provides that the Registrant shall indemnify, to the full extent permitted by Section 145 of the Delaware General Corporation Law, as amended from time to time, all persons whom it may indemnify pursuant to such Section. The provisions of Section 145 of the Delaware General Corporation Law are set forth in Exhibit 28 hereto.

The Underwriting Agreement, filed as Exhibit 1.1 to this Registration Statement, provides for indemnification and contribution by the Underwriters with respect to certain liabilities of directors and officers of the Registrant.

Insofar as indemnification for liabilities arising under the Securities Act of 1933 may be permitted to directors, officers and controlling persons of the Registrant pursuant to the foregoing provisions or arrangements, such provisions or arrangements may be limited by the Registrant's undertaking Statement.

Item 15. Recent Sales of Unregistered Securities

Pursuant to an exclusive licensing agreement, dated April 26, 1993, Dr. J. Robert Teller and his designees received 50,000 shares of restricted Common Stock at the price of $1.00 per share. As finder for this transaction, Buddy McCartney, on March 2, 1993, received 50,000 shares of restricted Common

Form 25: Registration Statement on Form S-1 (continued)

Stock at $.01 per share. Pursuant to the anti-dilution provisions of the Underwriting Agreement, dated September 21, 1991, in January 1993 the Company granted to Oliver Securities Corp. 10,000 additional Common Stock Purchase Warrants with the reduced exercise price of $1.275.

Item 17. Undertakings.

The undersigned Registrant hereby undertakes:

(1) to file, during any period in which offers or sales are being made, a post-effective amendment to this Registration Statement:

   (i) to include any prospectus required by Section 10(a)(3) of the Securities Act of 1933;

   (ii) to reflect in the Prospectus any facts or events arising after the effective date of the Registration Statement (or the most recent post-effective amendment thereof) which, individually or in the aggregate, represent a fundamental change in the information set forth in the Registration Statement;

   (iii) to include any material information with respect to the plan of distribution not previously disclosed in the Registration Statement or any material change to such information in the Registration Statement, including (but not limited to) any addition or deletion of the managing underwriter.

Insofar as indemnification for liabilities arising under the Securities Act of 1933 may be permitted to directors, officers and controlling persons of the Registrant pursuant to the foregoing provisions, or otherwise, the Registrant has been advised that in the opinion of the Securities and Exchange Commission such indemnification is against public policy as expressed in the Act and is, therefore, unenforceable. In the event that a claim for indemnification against such liabilities (other than the payment by the Registrant of expenses incurred or paid by a director, officer or controlling person of the Registrant in the successful defense of any action, suit or proceeding) is asserted by such director, officer or controlling person in connection with the securities being registered, the Registrant will, unless in the opinion of its counsel the matter has been settled by controlling precedent, submit to a court of appropriate jurisdiction the question whether such indemnification by it is against public policy as expressed in the Act and will be governed by the final adjudication of such issue.

SIGNATURES

Pursuant to the requirements of the Securities Act of 1933, the Registrant certifies that it has reasonable grounds to believe that it meets all of the requirements for filing on Form S-1 and has duly caused this Registration Statement to be signed on its behalf by the undersigned, thereunto duly

Note: The SEC will not grant acceleration unless the issuer makes the representation about indemnification.

Form 25: Registration Statement on Form S-1 (continued)

Note: The registration statement must be signed by the Principal Executive Officer, the Chief Financial Officer, the Chief Accounting Officer and a majority of the directors.

Q: Is a director who does not sign the registration statement liable under Section 11 of the 1933 Act?

authorized, in the City of New York, State of New York, on February 10, 1994

Alison Technologies,
By /s/ Elvis Thomas
Chairman of the Board, President
and Principal Executive Officer

The undersigned officers and directors hereby make, constitute and appoint Elvis Thomas and Bruce Lowe, and each of them, as their agents, proxies and attorneys-in-fact to sign and cause to be filed with the Securities and Exchange Commission any and all amendments (including post-effective amendments) to the Registration Statement to which this signature page relates in all capacities which the undersigned have signed said Registration Statement.

Pursuant to the requirements of the Securities Act of 1933, this Registration Statement has been signed by the following persons in the capacities and on the dates indicated.

Signature	Title	Date
/s/ Elvis Thomas	Chairman of the Board, President, Principal Executive Officer, Chief Financial Officer and Director	Feb. 10, 1994
/s/ Bruce Lowe	Secretary, Treasurer, Chief Accounting Officer and Director	Feb. 10, 1994
/s/ Napoleon Dynamite	Director	Feb.10, 1994

CONSENTS OF INDEPENDENT
CERTIFIED PUBLIC ACCOUNTS

We consent to the inclusion of our report dated March 1, 1992 relating to the financial statements of Alison Technologies, Inc. as at December 31, 1992, 1991, and 1990, to Registration Statement being filed under the Securities Act of 1933 on Form S-1 by Alison Technologies, Inc.

We also consent to the reference to our firm under the caption "Experts" in the Prospectus.

Parker & Schwartz
Certified Public Accountant

New York, New York
4/10/94

Form 26: SEC Comments on Registration Statement

Securities and Exchange Commission
Judiciary Plaza
450 Fifth Street, N.W.
Washington, DC 20549

March 9, 1994

Peter C. Kostant
Santoro, Ryan & Kostant
2 Wall Street
New York, NY 10022

Re: Alison Technologies, Inc. (the "Company")
        File No. X-11111
        Registration Statement on Form S-1

Dear Mr. Kostant:

The staff has the following comments concerning the above referenced registration statement filed with the Company.

Cover Page of Prospectus
(1) Please indicate that an investor should be able to afford a substantial loss on his investment due to the highly speculative nature of the offering.

The Company - Page 4
(2) Indicate the Company's date of inception, its place of business, and briefly discuss any significant events in chronological order since inception.

Prospectus summary - Pages 4-5
(3) Under the risk factors section on page 5, please indicate that any person investing in these securities should be able to afford a loss on their entire investment.

Risk Factors - Pages 8-10
(4) Limited Current Operations & Manufacturing Experience, Page 8
Please add to the discussion of the Company's computer literacy products the quantities of these products manufactured, sold and/or shipped to date.

Dependence on Key Personnel - Page 9
(5) Please indicate that no key man insurance policy is currently in effect, but that one is required under the agreement with the underwriters. Please note by what point in time the Company plans to have one in place, the identity of the person(s) involved, and the dollar amount of such insurance.

Competition - Page 9
(6) Please identify those firms that the Company considers to be its major competitors.

Note: In an offering of this type the staff of the SEC will comment in writing to the Issuer's counsel. These comments are quite representative.

Note: The SEC wants the risky nature of the investment to be stressed even more.

Note: Again, the emphasis on risk.

Note: This would clarify the current status of the business.

Form 26: SEC Comments (continued)

Note: Further stress on risks.

Note: This makes it easier for the reader to find out about dilution of the value of the reader's investment.

Note: The SEC wants more disclosure about a prior transaction by the Company.

Note: Again, this further clarifies dilution.

Limited Patent Protection
(7) Please discuss if any competitor currently holds a patent for a product similar to those of the Company, and whether there may exist any grounds for an infringement action.

Dilution and Control by Present Owners
(8) Please provide appropriate cross references to Dilution and Description of Securities.

Shares Available for Resale - Page 10
(9) Please indicate, if true, that the 1,729,800 shares which may be sold are held by management.

(10) Please identify the former underwriter who has the demand and/or piggy-back registration rights, and briefly outline those rights.

(11) Please identify the major shareholder who agreed not to sell any stock for 6 months after the prospectus date.

Use of Proceeds - Page 11
(12) Identify the Chief Financial Officer in Footnote No. 3 and specify the dollar amount or percentage of proceeds from the offering attributable to his salary.

Dilution - Page 12-13
(13) Please indicate in the table on page 13 the consideration and average price paid by the current stockholders after deducting the underwriter's commissions and all expenses.

(14) Please provide in the narrative a discussion of the results of dilution, including figures, to illustrate the contrast between the price paid by new shareholders versus the book value of their shares.

Selected Financial Data - Page 16
(15) Please include selected financial data for a 5 year period if available.

The Business - Pages 18-23
(16) Please identify the two (2) large companies who comprise 60% of the Company's industrial light pen orders, as discussed on page 19.

(17) Please indicate the extent to which development of the low-cost computer-aided design/drafting software packages has progressed, and whether the June 1994 market introduction date of the product is still attainable.

Management's Discussion and Analysis - Pages 17-18
Sales - Page 18
(18) Please discuss more fully in the narrative the increase in both volume and/or price, if applicable, in the photo-electronic and computer literacy segment.

Form 26: SEC Comments (continued)

(19) A discussion of the decrease in calibration revenues should also indicate the Company's plans, if any, to phase out or increase its revenues from this segment.

Cost of Sales
(20) Please explain why the inventory write-downs occurred and what action has been taken to prevent future write-downs. In addition, please include a discussion under this caption for the photo-electronic and computer literacy segments.

Note: This would further clarify a business weakness of the Company.

Selling, General & Administrative Expenses
(21) Please discuss how long the Company anticipates the increased spending levels for the computer literacy products to continue and the specific reasons for the decrease in the calibration costs.

Research and Development
(22) Please discuss the Company's timetable for the continuation of significant expenditures for product development, and explain the impact of the computer-aided design/drafting software package product development.

Liquidity & Capital Resources
(23) Please discuss the Company's liquidity position on a short and long-term basis.

Underwriting - Pages 32-34
(24) Please expand the explanation and discussion of any indemnification provisions.

Note: The SEC opposes indemnification as against public policy.

(25) The staff is currently considering certain aspects of the plan of distribution and may have further comments at a later time.

(26) Please indicate on page 34 if the Company will have the key man life insurance in place by the date of the prospectus.

General
(27) It appears that the provisions of Rule 415 are applicable and therefore the box on the outside cover page should be checked and the Undertakings required by Item 512(a) of Regulation S-K should be provided.

Financial Statements
(Four pages of comments, requiring a response from Charles Parker, CPA of Parker & Schwartz, CPAs, the Company's auditors, followed.)

Please key the Registrant's letter of response to the staff's letter of comment. Furnish NASD letter indicating approval of the underwriter arrangements.

Any request for acceleration should be filed in accordance with Rule 461 of Regulation C. Any such request should be accompanied or immediately preceded by a

Note: The SEC requires that the National Association of Securities Dealers, Inc., has approved the Underwriter's compensation.

Form 26: SEC Comments (continued)

Note: The SEC will make acceleration a quid pro quo for distributing the "red herring" prospectus.

Note: The SEC has designated specific attorneys with whom the Company's counsel can work.

description of the steps taken to comply with Rule 15c2-8 under the 1934 Act and Release 33-4968 concerning distribution and redistribution of prospectuses.

Requests for acceleration should also be accompanied or immediately preceded by a letter from the Registrant's chief financial officer stating whether there has been any material change in the Registrant's operating or financial condition since the date of the latest financial data in the prospectus. Of course, any such material change should be fully disclosed in the prospectus.

If you have any questions regarding the above comments, please contact Roy Dylan, Esq. at (202) 111-1111; questions concerning the accounting comments may be directed to Elmore Richards at (202) 111-1112.

Sincerely,

Terry E. Jagger
Branch Chief

Form 27: Issuer's Counsel Response to SEC Comments

SANTORO, RYAN & KOSTANT
2 Wall Street
New York, NY 10022

April 23, 1994

Securities and Exchange Commission
Judiciary Plaza
450 Fifth Street, N.W.
Washington, DC 20549
Attention: Messrs. Roy Dylan and Elmore Richards

Re: Alison Technologies, Inc.
        Registration Statement on
        Form S-1 File, No. X-11111

Dear Sirs:

Enclosed herewith are the following documents in connection with the above-described Registration Statement:

(1) One signed and two conformed copies of Amendment No. 1, with exhibits; and

(2) Ten extra copies of the Registration Statement, of which three have been marked to show changes from the prior filing.

We believe that we have responded to all of the Commission's comments in its letter, dated March 9, 1994. A copy of this letter is annexed hereto, with paragraph numbers inserted on the Commission's letter for easy reference.

Letter, dated March 9, 1994
Cover Page of Prospectus
1. We have complied with these comments.

The Company
2. The text has been expanded to include the date of the Company's inception and its principal place of business. The principal activities of the Company are outlined in the summary, and there is a discussion of the significant events of the Company since inception under the "COMPANY."

Prospectus Summary
3. We have complied with these comments.

Risk Factors — Limited Current Operations and
Manufacturing Experience
4. We have complied with these comments. We have inserted a cross-reference to "BUSINESS" — Computer Literacy and Photo-Electronics Products" which contains a discussion of the quantities of computer literacy products manufactured, sold and shipped to date.

Note: Issuer's counsel respond to the SEC comments in this format.

Note: Amendment No. 1 includes all the changes that the SEC requested. This letter shows how, paragraph by paragraph, every SEC comment was addressed.

All these changes will be in the final prospectus that purchasers of the securities will receive.

Form 27: Response to SEC Comments (continued)

Dependence on Key Personnel

5. This section now states that there will be a $1,000,000 key-man life insurance policy on the life of Elvis Thomas, with the Company as beneficiary, in effect prior to the completion of the Offering.

Competition

6. We have inserted a cross-reference to "BUSINESS — Computer Literacy and Photo-Electronics Products" where we describe the competing companies in the computer literacy field.

Limited Patent Protection

7. We have complied with these comments. The Company is aware of only one competitor, Information Controls Corporation, which holds a patent on a photodiode light pen which is approximately 20 years old. The management of the Company does not believe that it is infringing this patent.

Dilution and Control by Present Owners

8. We have complied with these comments.

Shares Available for Resale

9. We have indicated that of the 1,729,800 shares which are available for resale, 1,616,800 are currently held by the management of the Company.

10. We have complied with these comments. Oliver Securities Corp., the underwriter in connection with the Company's 1991 public offering, holds 90,000 warrants to purchase 90,000 shares of Common Stock, which expire on November 24, 1996, 80,000 of which are exercisable at $1.625 and 10,000 of which are exercisable at $1.275.

Oliver also has the right to request one registration of these warrants and the underlying shares by the Company until November 24, 1996, and also has "piggyback" registration rights until that time.

11. We have complied with these comments.

Use of Proceeds

12. The Company no longer intends to hire a Chief Financial Officer.

Dilution

13. We have complied with these comments.

14. We have complied with these comments.

Selected Financial Data

15. We have complied with these comments.

Form 27: Response to SEC Comments (continued)

The Business

16. We have complied with these comments.

17. We have complied with these comments, and have stated that the Company currently intends to introduce the low-cost computer-aided design/drafting software package by August 1994.

Management's Discussion and Analysis — Sales

18. We have complied with these comments.

19. We have complied with these comments.

Cost of Sales

20. We have complied with these comments.

Selling, General and Administrative Expenses

21. We have complied with these comments.

Research and Development

22. We have complied with these comments. The Company will be able to complete the development of the low-cost computer-aided design/drafting software package by August 1994, and the Company has postponed for an indefinite period the development of the professional-level computer-aided design/drafting package referred to in the initial filing.

Liquidity

23. We have complied with these comments.

Underwriting

24. We believe that we have complied with this comment by supplying the information contained in the Underwriting section, and in Part II, Item 17.

25. We believe that we have complied with the additional comments concerning the plan of distribution which we received during telephone conferences with Mr. Roy Dylan, of the Commission.

26. The key-man life insurance policy will be in place prior to the completion of this Offering.

General

27. Pursuant to the provisions of Rule 415, we have checked the box on the outside cover page, and have provided the undertakings required by Item 512(a) of Regulation S-K.

Financial Statements

28. Parker & Schwartz, the Certified Public Accountant for the Company, has responded to the accounting questions of the Commission by its letters to Elmore Richards, dated March 30, 1994, and April 17, 1994.

Form 27: Response to SEC Comments (continued)

We will furnish to the Commission a letter from the NASD indicating the approval of the Underwriting arrangements prior to the time that the Registration Statement becomes effective.

If you have any questions, please do not hesitate to telephone the undersigned.

Very truly yours,

Peter C. Kostant

PCK/cm

Form 28: Issuer's Counsel Request for Acceleration

SANTORO, RYAN & KOSTANT
2 Wall Street
New York, NY 10022

July 24, 1994

VIA FEDERAL EXPRESS
Securities and Exchange Commission
Judiciary Plaza
450 Fifth Street, N.W.
Washington, D.C. 20549
Attention: Messrs. Dylan and Richards

Re: Alison Technologies, Inc.
        Registration Statement on Form S-1
        (File No. X-11111)

Dear Sirs:

Enclosed please find the request from our client, Alison Technologies, Inc., to accelerate the effective date of 10:00 a.m. on July 25, 1994 or as soon thereafter as is practicable. Please acknowledge receipt of the enclosure on the enclosed copy of this letter and return the same to the undersigned in the stamped, addressed envelope provided.

If you have any questions, please do not hesitate to contact the undersigned.

With best personal regards.

Sincerely,

Peter C. Kostant

PCK/cam
Enclosures

Note: Acceleration requests must come from the issuer and its counsel.

Form 29: Issuer's Request for Acceleration

Alison Technologies, Inc.
1 Imperial Avenue
Brooklyn, NY 01050

July 24, 1994

Securities & Exchange Commission
Judiciary Plaza
450 5th Street N.W.
Washington, D.C. 20549
Attn: Mssrs. Dylan & Richards

Ref.:   Alison Technologies, Inc.
          Registration Statement on Form S-1
          File No. X-11111

Gentlemen:

In my capacity as President, Chief Executive Officer and Chief Financial Officer of Alison Technologies, Inc. (the "Company"), I hereby confirm that there has been no material adverse change in the financial condition of the Company since March 31, 1994, except as set forth in the prospectus. In addition, I am not aware of any material information concerning the Company which is not included in the most recent amendment to the Company's above referenced Registration Statement.

The Company hereby requests acceleration of the effective date of Registration Statement to 10:00 A.M. on July 25, 1994 or as soon thereafter as is practicable.

Very truly yours,

ALISON TECHNOLOGIES, INC.

by: _____
Elvis Thomas
Chief Executive Officer and Chief Financial Officer

ET/sm
via: Federal Express

Form 30: SEC Order Declaring Registration Statement
         Effective

PETER KOSTANT, Esq.

July 31, 1994

SANTORO, RYAN & KOSTANT
2 WALL STREET
NEW YORK, NY

ISSUER: ALISON TECHNOLOGIES, INC.

1933 ACT REGISTRATION STATEMENT FILE NO.: X-11111

1939 ACT TRUST INDENTURE
QUALIFIED FOR DEBT OFFERING: N/A

EAST COAST EFFECTIVE TIME AND DATE: 10:30 A.M. ON
    JULY 25, 1994

BONNIE RONSTADT, DEPUTY DIRECTOR
SECURITIES AND EXCHANGE COMMISSION

VIA GRAPHIC SCANNING COLLECT

Note: This is a written certification from the SEC that the Registration Statement became effective.

3.   *Opinion Letters of Counsel*

In addition to providing informal advice and generally coordinating all of the steps necessary for a complex public offering, the Issuer's counsel must provide a formal opinion letter to the Issuer which is executed by the law firm and is an exhibit to the filing with the SEC. (Form 31.) In addition, the underwriting agreement will generally require that the issuer's counsel provide a detailed opinion letter to the underwriters, and that underwriter's counsel provide an opinion letter to the issuer. (See Forms 32 and 33.) The language in opinion letters is carefully crafted and lawyers must satisfy themselves as to the factual and legal validity of all assertions.

The opinion does not constitute a guarantee of accuracy or legality by the lawyers to the company, but counsel will be liable if the opinion was prepared negligently, and professional standards can be very exacting. Thus, while one senior Wall Street lawyer joked in a $500 million transaction, "I don't know why they are getting so excited, we told them it was only an opinion," the law firm or its insurance carrier will be liable for negligence.

The following opinion letter was filed with the SEC as an exhibit to the Registration Statement on Form S-1, in connection with the Alison Technologies Public Offering.

Form 31: Issuer's Counsel Opinion Letter for the SEC

SANTORO, RYAN & KOSTANT
2 Wall Street
New York, NY 10022

July 25, 1994

Alison Technologies, Inc.
1 Imperial Avenue
Brooklyn, New York   01051

Re: Registration on Form S-1 Relating to the Issuance of up to 690,000 Units, Consisting of Common Stock and Common Stock Purchase Warrants

Dear Sir or Madam:

We have acted as counsel to Alison Technologies, Inc., a Delaware corporation (the "Company"), in connection with the preparation of a registration statement (the "Registration Statement") on Form S-1 (File No. X-11111) filed by the Company on February 10, 1994 under the Securities Act of 1933, as amended (the "Securities Act") to register the public offering of up to 690,000 units (the "Units"), each Unit consisting of three shares of common stock of the Company, par value $.01 per share (the "Common Stock"), and one warrant to purchase an additional share of Common Stock. Also being registered is a Unit Purchase Option to be sold to the Underwriter to purchase up to 180,000 shares of Common Stock, and 60,000 warrants to purchase 60,000 shares of Common Stock, hereinafter referred to the "Unit Purchase Option." The shares of Common Stock and warrants comprising the Units are hereinafter referred to as the "Shares" and the "Warrants," respectively, and the shares issuable upon the exercise of the Warrants are hereinafter referred to as the "Underlying Shares."

In such capacity, we have examined the form of certificate for the Units, the Shares and the Warrants and the form of warrant agreement (the "Warrant Agreement") between the Company and Confederate Stock Transfer & Trust Company, 3 Wall Street, New York, New York as warrant agent (the "Warrant Agent"), pursuant to which the Warrants are to be issued. We have also examined such records, documents, statutes and decisions as we have deemed relevant.

In our opinion

(i) the Shares, when issued in accordance with the terms of the Registration Statement against payment of the purchase price therefor, will be validly issued, fully paid and non-assessable shares of the Company's Common Stock,

(ii) the Warrants, when duly executed and delivered by the Company and countersigned by the Warrant Agent, will be the legal, valid and binding obligations of the Company, except as may be limited by bankruptcy, insolvency, moratorium or other laws now or hereafter in effect affecting the

Note: Many law firms have committees of partners that review all opinion letters before they are executed by the firm.

Note: Terms are carefully defined.

Q: What due diligence should the lawyers perform? *See* Due Diligence Memorandum, Form 49.

Form 31: Issuer's Counsel Opinion Letter (continued)

rights of creditors generally and subject to equitable principles,

(iii) the Underlying Shares, when issued upon the exercise of the Warrants in accordance with their terms and upon full payment of the exercise price, will be validly issued, fully paid and non-assessable shares of the Company's Common Stock, and

(iv) the 180,000 shares of Common Stock underlying the Unit Purchase Option when issued pursuant to the terms of the Registration Statement will be validly issued, fully paid and non-assessable shares of the Company's Common Stock, and the 60 Warrants contained in the Unit Purchase Option upon their exercise in accordance with their terms and upon full payment of the exercise price will be 60,000 validly issued, fully paid and non-assessable shares of the Company's Common Stock.

We hereby consent to the use of this opinion and to all references to our firm in the Registration Statement.

In giving such opinion, we do not thereby admit that we are acting within the category of persons whose consent is required under §7 of the Securities Act or the rules and regulations of the Securities and Exchange Commission thereunder.

Very truly yours,

SANTORO, RYAN & KOSTANT

Note: Counsel expressly allows its client to file the letter with the SEC as part of the offering.

Q: Why are they not admitting this?

Form 32:   Issuer's Counsel Opinion Letter for Underwriter at Closing

SANTORO, RYAN & KOSTANT
2 Wall Street
New York, NY 10022

August 3, 1994

True Aim Securities, Inc.
As Representative of the Underwriters
2 Wall Street
New York, NY 10022

Dear Sir or Madam:

This opinion is rendered to you pursuant to Section 4(b) of the Underwriting Agreement dated July 25, 1994 (the "Underwriting Agreement") between True Aim Securities Inc., the Representative of the Underwriters (the "Representative" as buyer and Alison Technologies, Inc. (the "Company"), a Delaware Corporation, as seller, which Underwriting Agreement relates, among other things, to the sale by the Company to the Underwriters of 600,000 Units (the "Units"), each Unit consisting of three shares of its authorized but unissued Common Stock, $.01 per value, and one Warrant, each entitling the holder to purchase one share of Common Stock for $1.00, and the Unit Purchase Option to purchase an aggregate of 60,000 Units (the "Unit Purchase Option"). The shares of Common Stock and Warrant included in the Units are referred to in the aggregate as the Shares and Warrant, respectively. The Shares issuable upon exercise of the Warrant are, respectively, included in the Shares and referred to as the Warrant Shares.

In this matter we have been and are acting as counsel for the Company and as such we have participated in the preparation of the registration statement (File No. X-1111) filed by the Company with the Securities and Exchange Commission under the Securities Act of 1933, as amended (the "Act"), covering the Units and the amendments thereto, including the prospectus dated July 25, 1994, filed as a part thereof pursuant to Rule 424 under the Act (said registration statement and prospectus, as so amended, being hereinafter for convenience referred to as the "Registration Statement" and "Prospectus," respectively).

In so acting, we have made inquiry of officers and directors of the Company with respect to various matters described in the Registration Statement and Prospectus and have examined the originals or copies, certified to our satisfaction, of all such corporate instruments and certificates of public officials and of officers and representatives of the Company, as we have deemed relevant and necessary as a basis for the opinion hereinafter set forth. In such examination, we have assumed the genuineness of all signatures and authenticity of all documents submitted to us as originals

Note: This much more extensive opinion letter of issuer's counsel is required in the Underwriting Agreement between the issuer and the underwriter. Receipt of this letter is a condition of closing.

Note: The Company's counsel gives this opinion to the underwriter, not to their client.

Note the caveats.

Form 32: Opinion Letter for Underwriter (continued)

and the conformity to original documents of documents submitted to us as certified or photostatic copies.

In rendering this opinion, we have relied as to factual matters which have not been independently established on certificates from public officials and certificates and written statements of officers and representatives of the Company and other responsible persons, in each case to the extent deemed appropriate.

Note the caveats.

On the basis of the foregoing inquiry and examination and in reliance thereon and on all such other matters as we deem relevant in the circumstances, we are of the opinion that:

Note: A substantial due diligence investigation must be made before such an opinion can be given.

(i) the Company has been duly incorporated and is validly existing and in good standing under the laws of the State of Delaware, and the Company's subsidiary, Alison Electronic Instrument Co., Inc. have been duly incorporated, are validly existing and in good standing under the laws of the State of New York, and the Company and its subsidiaries have full corporate power and authority to own their properties and conduct their business as described in the Registration Statement and Prospectus and are qualified as a foreign corporation in each jurisdiction in which the ownership or leasing of properties or conduct of their business requires such qualification;

(ii) All of the issued and outstanding shares of capital stock of each of the subsidiaries named above are owned by the Company free and clear of any mortgage. pledge, lien, charge or encumbrance and all such shares are duly authorized, validly issued, fully paid and non-assessable;

(iii) to our best knowledge (a) the Company and its subsidiaries have obtained or are in the process of obtaining, all licenses, permits and other government authorizations necessary to the conduct of their business as described in the Prospectus, (b) such licenses, permits and other government authorizations obtained are in full force and effect, and (c) the Company and its subsidiaries are in all material respects complying therewith;

Note the caveat.

(iv) the authorized capitalization of the Company as of March 31, 1994 is as set forth under "Capitalization" in the Prospectus; all shares of the Company's outstanding stock requiring authorization for issuance by the Company's board of directors have been duly authorized, validly issued, are fully paid and non-assessable and conform to the description thereof contained in the Prospectus; the outstanding shares of Common Stock of the Company have not been issued in violation of the preemptive rights of any shareholder and the shareholders of the Company do not have any preemptive rights or other rights to subscribe for or to purchase, nor are there any restrictions upon the voting

Form 32: Opinion Letter for Underwriter (continued)

or transfer of any of the Shares; the Common Stock, the Warrant, the Unit Purchase Option and the Warrant Agreement conform to the shares of Common Stock to be issued upon exercise of the Warrant and the Unit Purchase Option, upon issuance in accordance with the terms of such Warrant, the Warrant Agreement and Unit Purchase Option have been duly authorized and, when issued and delivered, will be duly and validly issued, fully paid, non-assessable, free of preemptive rights and no personal liability will attach to the ownership thereof; a sufficient number of shares of Common Stock has been reserved for issuance upon exercise of the Warrant and Unit Purchase Option and to the best of our knowledge, neither the filing of the Registration Statement not the offering or sale of the Units as contemplated by the Underwriting Agreement gives rise to any registration rights or other rights, other than those which have been waived or satisfied for or relating to the registration of any shares of Common Stock.

(v) this Agreement, the Unit Purchase Option and the Warrant Agreement have been duly and validly authorized, executed and delivered by the Company and, assuming due execution and delivery of the Underwriting Agreement by the Representative, are the valid and legally binding obligations of the Company, except no opinion is expressed as to the enforceability of the indemnity provisions contained in Section 6 or the contribution provisions contained in Section 7 of the underwriting Agreement;

(vi) the certificates evidencing the shares of Common Stock are in valid and proper legal form; the Warrant will be exercisable for shares of Common Stock of the Company in accordance with the terms of the Warrant and at the prices therein provided for; at all times during the term of the Warrant the shares of Common Stock of the Company issuable upon exercise of the Warrant have been duly authorized and reserved for issuance upon such exercise and such shares, when issued upon such exercise in accordance with the terms of the Warrant and at the price provided for, will be duly and validly issued, fully paid and non-assessable;

(vii) we know of no pending or threatened legal or governmental proceedings to which the Company is a party which could materially adversely affect the business, property, financial condition or operation of the Company; or which question the validity of the securities of the Company, the Underwriting Agreement, the Warrant Agreement or the Unit Purchase Option, or of any action taken or to be taken by the Company pursuant to the Underwriting Agreement, the Warrant Agreement of the Unit Purchase Option; and no such proceedings are known to us to be contemplated against the Company; there are no governmental proceedings or regulations required to be described or referred

Form 32: Opinion Letter for Underwriter (continued)

to in the registration Statement which are not so described or referred to;

(viii) the Company is not in violation of or default under, nor will the execution and delivery of the Underwriting Agreement, the Unit Purchase Option or the Warrant Agreement, and the incurrence of the obligations therein set forth and the consummation of the transactions therein contemplated, result in a violation of, or constitute a default under the certificate or articles of incorporation or by-laws, in the performance or observance or any material obligations, agreement, covenant or condition contained in any bond, debenture, mortgage, loan agreement, lease, joint venture or other agreement or instrument to which the Company is a party or by which it or any of its properties may be bound or in violation of any material order, rule, regulation, writ, injunction, or decree of any government, governmental instrumentality or court, domestic or foreign;

(ix) the Registration Statement has become effective under the Act and to the best of our knowledge, no stop order suspending the effectiveness of the Registration Statement is in effect, and no proceedings for that purpose have been instituted or are pending before or threatened by, the Commission; the Registration Statement and the Prospectus (except for the financial statements and other financial data contained therein, or omitted therefrom, as to which we need express no opinion) comply as to form in all material respects with the applicable requirements of the Act and the Rules and Regulations;

(x) we have participated in the preparation of the registration statement and the prospectus and nothing has come to our attention to cause us to have reason to believe that the Registration Statement or any amendment thereto at the time it became effective contained any untrue statement of a material fact required to be stated therein or omitted to state any material fact required to be stated therein or necessary to make the statements therein not misleading or that the Prospectus or any supplement thereto contains any untrue statement of a material fact or omits to state a material fact necessary in order to make statements therein, in light of the circumstances under which they were made, not misleading (except, in the case of both the Registration Statement and any amendment thereto and the Prospectus and any supplement thereto, for the financial statements, notes thereto and other financial information and statistical data contained therein, as to which we need express no opinion);

(xi) all descriptions in the Registration Statement and the Prospectus, and any amendment or supplement thereto, of contracts and other documents are accurate and fairly represent the information required to be shown, and we are

Form 32: Opinion Letter for Underwriter (continued)

familiar with all contracts and other documents referred to in the Registration Statement and the Prospectus and any such amendment or supplement or filed as exhibits to the Registration Statement, and we do not know of any contracts or documents of a character required to be summarized or described therein or to be filed as exhibits thereto which are not so summarized, described or filed;

(xii) no authorization, approval, consent, or license of any governmental or regulatory authority or agency is necessary in connection with the authorization, issuance, transfer, sale or delivery of the Units by the Company, in connection with the execution, delivery and performance of the Underwriting Agreement by the Company or in connection with the taking of any action contemplated therein, or the issuance of the Unit Purchase Option or the Securities underlying the Unit Purchase Option other than registrations or qualifications of the Units under applicable state of foreign securities or Blue Sky laws and registration under the Act; and

(xiii) the statements in the Registration Statement under the captions "Business," "Use of Proceeds," "Management," and "Description of Securities" have been reviewed by us and insofar as they refer to descriptions of agreements, statements of law, descriptions of statutes, licenses, rules or regulations or legal conclusions, are correct in all material respects.

Very truly yours

Santoro, Ryan & Kostant

Form 33: Underwriter's Counsel Opinion Letter Requirement

Note: The Underwriting Agreement required the underwriter's counsel to provide this opinion.

All corporate proceedings and other legal matters relating to this Underwriting Agreement, the Registration Statement, the Prospectus and other related matters shall be satisfactory to or approved by counsel to the several Underwriters, and you shall have received from such counsel a signed opinion, dated as of the Closing Date, together with copies thereof of each of the Underwriters, with respect to the validity of the issuance of the Units, the form of the Registration Statement and Prospectus (other than the financial statements and other financial data contained therein), the execution of this Agreement and other related matters as you may reasonably require. The Company shall have furnished to counsel for the several Underwriters such documents as they may reasonably request for the purpose of enabling them to render such opinion.

To review briefly, Alison Technologies, the Issuer, and its lead underwriter, True Aim Securities, executed an Underwriting Agreement that required opinion letters to be prepared by counsel for each of the parties to the transaction.

In addition to the opinion letter above from the Issuer's counsel, Burton, Froom & Brinsley, the Underwriting Agreement also required the Underwriter's counsel to write a letter as a condition of closing. The opinion letter from the Underwriter's counsel was required to contain the preceding specific provision, found in Form 33.

The Company's auditors are also required to provide what are called "comfort letters." These generally provide support for all numerical assertions in the Registration Statement and affirm that the financials comply with SEC requirements. The auditors must also update the audited financial statements and state that as to unaudited financial statements, and for the period subsequent to the last unaudited statement, that after a specified limited examination, nothing has come to the auditor's attention that would render the financial information in the Registration Statement as amended, materially misleading. Because these negative assurances may be of somewhat limited value, until recently the auditor's comfort letter was often referred to as a "cold" comfort letter. For whatever reason, this term has largely been dropped from securities law parlance.

4.   Corporate Housekeeping in Connection with Public Offerings

Counsel for the issuer will need to prepare for various corporate actions in connection with various steps of a public offering. It may be necessary to amend the issuer's Articles of Incorporation to authorize a sufficient number of shares of stock for the public offering. This generally requires shareholder approval. The Board of Directors should also formally approve the filing of the Registration Statement with the SEC and the final price for the securities and underwriting arrangements. All these actions by the issuer, and an opinion letter from issuer's counsel that they were validly taken will be a condition to final closing required by the lead underwriter in the underwriting agreement that is executed when the Registration Statement becomes effective.

Form 34: Amendment of Corporate Charter

**CERTIFICATE OF AMENDMENT
OF INCORPORATION OF
ALISON TECHNOLOGIES, INC.**

The undersigned, ELVIS THOMAS, President, and BRUCE LOWE, Secretary, of ALISON TECHNOLOGIES, INC., a corporation organized and existing under and by virtue of the General Corporation Law of the State of Delaware,

DO HEREBY CERTIFY as follows:

FIRST: At a meeting of the Board of Directors of said Corporation, the directors adopted the following resolution:

RESOLVED, that it is advisable and best in the interest of the Corporation to amend Article FOURTH of the Certificate of Incorporation to read as follows:

"FOURTH: The total number of shares of capital stock which the Corporation shall have authority to issue is 10,000,000 all of which shall be Common Stock, $.01 par value per share."

SECOND: That the proposed amendment was adopted by the shareholders of the Corporation and this Certificate is being filed in accordance with Section 242 of the General Corporation Law.

IN WITNESS WHEREOF, ALISON TECHNOLOGIES, INC. has caused its corporate seal to be hereunto affixed and this Certificate to be signed by Elvis Thomas, its President, and Bruce Lowe, its Secretary, this 6th day of October, 1993.

ALISON TECHNOLOGIES, INC.

By: _____
    Elvis Thomas, President

Attest: _____
    Bruce Lowe, Secretary

Note: Shareholder approval was required and received.

Note: Signed by the president, attested to by the secretary.

Form 35:   Board of Directors' Resolutions in Preparation
            for SEC Filing

ALISON TECHNOLOGIES, INC.

Resolutions of the Board of Directors
Adopted February 9, 1994

RESOLVED, that the officers of ALISON TECHNOLOGIES, INC. (the "Company") be, and they hereby are, authorized and empowered to take any and all action which may be necessary or advisable to prepare and file a registration statement, and any required amendments, under the Securities Act of 1993 covering not more than 2,760,000 shares of Common Stock consisting of: 690,000 Units (the "Units") each Unit consisting of three shares of Common Stock and one Five-Year Common Stock Purchase Warrant.

RESOLVED, that the proper officers of the Company be, and they hereby are, authorized in the name and on behalf of this Company, to take any and all action which they may deem necessary or advisable in order to effect the registration of qualification (or exemption therefrom) of the Company's Units for issue, offer, sale or trade under the Blue Sky or securities laws of any of the States of the United States of America and in connection therewith to execute, acknowledge, verify, deliver, file or cause to be published any applications, reports, consents to service of process, appointments of attorneys to receive service of process and other papers and instruments which may be required under such laws, and to take any and all further action which they may deem necessary or advisable in order to maintain any such registration or qualification for as long as they deem necessary or as required by law or by the Underwriters of such securities.

RESOLVED, that the officers of the Company be, and they hereby are, authorized to negotiate an underwriting agreement with True Aim Securities, Inc. as Representative of several underwriters relating to the sale and exchange of the Company's Common Stock, but said Agreement shall not be executed and delivered until pricing arrangements have been approved by the Board of Directors of the Company.

RESOLVED, that subject to the sale of not more than 690,000 Units pursuant to said Underwriting Agreement, the Board authorizes the original issuance of not more than 240,000 shares of authorized and unissued Common Stock of the Company as a reserve to cover the Unit Purchase Option granted to True Aim Securities, Inc. pursuant to said agreement, which Unit Purchase Option shall consist of 60,000 Units, each Unit consisting of three shares of Common Stock and one Five-Year Common Stock Purchase Warrant and which shall be delivered to True Aim Securities, Inc.

Note: The Board of Directors met and adopted these resolutions just prior to filing the Registration Statement with the SEC.

Q: Should the Minutes recite that all three directors were present, name them, and state that the vote was unanimous (or describe what the vote actually was)?

Note: The exact price of the securities to be offered has not yet been established.

Form 35:   Board of Directors' Resolutions in Preparation
           for SEC Filing (continued)

RESOLVED, that the Chairman of the Board and the Secretary of the Company are authorized to instruct Confederate Stock Transfer & Trust Company, as transfer agent, to issue and deliver to True Aim Securities, Inc. certificates for said securities in such names and denominations as True Aim Securities, Inc. may designate, and said officers are hereby authorized to adopt the forms of the aforementioned securities of the Company.

RESOLVED, that the Board of Directors does hereby ratify any and all actions which have been taken to date by the officers of the Company in furtherance of the resolutions.

There being no further business to come before the meeting, upon motion made and seconded, the meeting was adjourned.

By: _____
    Bruce Lowe, Secretary

Form 36:   Minutes of Board of Directors' Special Meeting
           in Preparation for Closing

**MINUTES OF THE SPECIAL MEETING OF THE BOARD OF
DIRECTORS OF ALISON TECHNOLOGIES, INC.**

Held via Telephone Conference
Tuesday, July 24, 1994, at 11:00 a.m.

The following members of the Board were legally present:

Elvis Thomas
Bruce Lowe
Napoleon Dynamite

constituting the entire Board and quorum. All persons participating in the meeting could hear each other at the
same time, and the special meeting thus met the requirements for a meeting via telephone pursuant to the
Delaware General Corporation Law. Peter C. Kostant, Esq., of
counsel, was also on the telephone line.

Mr. Thomas, President of the Board of the Company,
presided; Mr. Lowe, Secretary of the Company, kept the minutes of the meeting.

Mr. Thomas stated that one of the purposes of the meeting
was to ratify and to approve the filing, pursuant to the
Securities Act of 1933, of the Registration Statement on Form
S-1 (File No. X-11111) and all amendments thereto (and the
related Prospectus) covering the issuance and sale of up to
690,000 Units of the Company's securities.

Mr. Kostant then presented to the meeting the following
documents, copies of which had been previously forward-
ed to all directors:

(1) Proof of Amendment No. 1 to the Registration State-
     ment on Form S-1;
(2) Form of Underwriting Agreement between the Com-
     pany and True Aim Securities, Inc., as Representative of
     the Underwriters;
(3) Form of Certificate for the Units being offered;
(4) Form of Warrant Agreement for the 1999 Warrants
     being issued (the "1999 Warrants").

Thereupon, on motion duly made and seconded, it was

RESOLVED, that the Board hereby approves the proposed
public offering of up to 690,000 Units, each Unit consisting of
three shares of Common Stock and one 1999 Warrants enti-
tling the holders to purchase additional shares of Common
Stock, all as described in the Amendment No. 1 to
Registration Statement (No. X-11111) on Form S-1 of the
Securities and Exchange Commission.

Note: This meeting was held
to approve everything necessary for the closing of the
public offering, including the
price of the units. It was held
by telephone, as permitted
under Delaware law.

Form 36: Minutes of Special Meeting (continued)

RESOLVED, that the Board hereby authorizes the officers to file said Amendment to the Registration Statement (and additional amendments, if necessary) and cause said Registration Statement to become effective as soon as practicable.

RESOLVED, that the Board hereby approves the issuance and sale of up to 690,000 of its Units on the terms set forth in the form of Underwriting Agreement with True Aim Securities, Inc., as Representative, the form of which had earlier been submitted to the Board of Directors. The Board hereby also approves the issuance and sale of a Unit Purchase Option for an aggregate of 60,000 Units to be substantially in the form as submitted to the Board.

RESOLVED, that the form of Underwriting Agreement for the sale of up to 690,000 Units submitted to the Board of Directors is approved and the President, Vice President and the Secretary, and each of them, are authorized to execute and deliver said Underwriting Agreement to True Aim Securities, Inc. on behalf of the Company.

RESOLVED, that the Warrant Agreement between the Company, the Representative of the Underwriters and Confederate Stock Transfer and Trust Company, pursuant to which the Units will be issued is hereby approved, and the President, and the Secretary, and each of them, are authorized to execute and deliver the Warrant Agreement on behalf of the corporation to Confederate Stock Transfer and Trust Company.

RESOLVED, that the form of certificates for the Units being offered submitted to the meeting be and it hereby is approved as the form of certificates to represent the Units being issued.

RESOLVED, that the officers of the Company be, and they hereby are, authorized to execute and deliver any and all documents on behalf of the Company and to take all steps as in their judgment, acting with the advice of counsel, may be necessary or advisable to obtain an effective Registration Statement covering the Units, concluding an Underwriting Agreement with True Aim Securities, Inc., selling the Units pursuant to said Underwriting Agreement, issue the Units, including the shares of Common Stock and 1999 Warrants, and consummating the public financing.

RESOLVED, that the Board hereby approves, ratifies and confirms all actions taken by the officers of the Company in furtherance of said public offering.

There being no further business to come before the meeting, it was, on motion duly made, seconded and carried, adjourned.

_____

Bruce Lowe, Secretary

5. *Blue Sky Matters*

Many states have state securities laws which require that public offerings of securities be registered. These are often called Blue Sky laws because prior to their enactment, the only limit on what promoters could promise an investor was the blue sky above.

While the federal securities laws are based upon the requirement that there be adequate disclosure for an investor to evaluate the merit of an investment, many states have a judgment and valuation system in which state securities commissioners have wide discretion to determine whether an offering is "fair, just and equitable." Federal and state jurisdiction overlap, and there is no federal preemption.

A Blue Sky Memorandum is usually prepared by the issuer's counsel, stating what must be done to qualify the public offering for sale in various states. Some states will largely rely upon the SEC requirements as sufficient. Securities will often not be offered in states with difficult requirements.

Form 37: Blue Sky Memorandum

600,000 Units
ALISON TECHNOLOGIES, INC.

BLUE SKY MEMORANDUM

True Aim Securities, Inc.
As Representative of the Several Underwriters
1 Wall Street
New York, NY 10022

May 24, 1994

In connection with the proposed distribution to the public of the above Units (each Unit consisting of three shares of Common Stock, $.01 par value, and one five year Common Stock Purchase Warrant), and up to an additional 90,000 Units as to which Underwriters have been granted an over-allotment option, we, as counsel for Alison Technologies, Inc., have prepared this Memorandum. It supplies information concerning the extent to which and the conditions upon which (i) before the Regisration Statement is effective, offers to sell and solicitations of offers to buy the Units (herein collectively called "offers"), made orally or through written

Note: This memorandum was prepared as a guide for due diligence by the underwriter.

Form 37: Blue Sky Memorandum (continued)

material complying with the Securities Act of 1933 and the rules and regulations thereunder ("offering material"), will be permissible under the Blue Sky or securities laws of certain States, and (ii) after the Registration Statement is effective, sales or contracts of sale ("sales") of the Units will be permissible under such Blue Sky or securities laws.

STATES WHERE FILINGS NOT REQUIRED

It is believed that offers of the Units to the public may be made before the Registration Statement is effective except as otherwise indicated, and sales to the public may be made after it is effective, in the following States without registration of the Units or any filings being made, but only by dealers or brokers registered or licensed in the respective States except as otherwise indicated:

District of Columbia
Nevada (registration or licensing as a dealer or broker is not required)
New Jersey (offers may not be made before the Registration Statement is effective)
Utah

STATES WHERE FILINGS ARE REQUIRED

It is believed that sales of the Units to the public after the Registration Statement is effective may be made in the following States only after certain requirements as to filings or registrations have been met with respect to the Units to be sold therein, only if made by dealers or brokers registered or licensed in the respective States, and only if limited to the number of Units indicated. Pending the completion of such filings or registrations and before the Registration Statement is effective, offers by dealers or brokers registered or licensed in the respective States will be permissible except as otherwise indicated. Before any of the Units are sold to the public in these States, inquiry should be made of True Aim Securities, Inc. as to whether such action has been completed.

State	No. of Units
California	100,000
Connecticut	100,000
Delaware	entire issue
Florida	18,000
Maryland	30,000
Massachusetts	entire issue
New York	entire issue

(Offers may be made following the filing of a Further State Notice with the New York Department of State by the underwriting syndicate manager on behalf of the syndicate.)

State	No. of Units
Ohio	60,000
Oregon	20,000
Pennsylvania	entire issue
Texas	80,000
Vermont	20,000

Form 37: Blue Sky Memorandum (continued)

Arrangements are being made to qualify the Units for sale in the above States, to file where required the Preliminary Prospectus, such Prospectus as amended and the Final Prospectus and to file a Further State Notice on behalf of the syndicate with the New York Department of State. No dealer should proceed as if such action has been completed until information has been obtained from the administrative authorities in the respective States or from True Aim Securities, Inc. to that effect.

Other offering material must be filed where required by each dealer desiring to use such material.

STATES NOT COVERED BY THIS MEMORANDUM

This Memorandum does not cover the requirements with respect to offers or sales to the public under the Blue Sky or securities laws of the following States. Therefore, offers or sales of the Units should not be made to the public therein:

Alabama	Kentucky	North Dakota
Alaska	Louisiana	Oklahoma
Arizona	Maine	Puerto Rico
Arkansas	Michigan	Rhode Island
Colorado	Minnesota	South Carolina
Georgia	Mississippi	South Dakota
Hawaii	Missouri	Tennessee
Idaho	Montana	Virginia
Illinois	Nebraska	Washington
Indiana	New Hampshire	West Virginia
Iowa	New Mexico	Wisconsin
Kansas	North Carolina	Wyoming

This Memorandum is furnished only for the general information of the several Underwriting. It has been prepared on the basis of an examination of the Blue Sky or securities laws of certain States and of the published rules and regulations (if any) of the authorities administering such laws, as reported in standard compilations, communications with such authorities in certain instances and information set forth in the Registration Statement relating to the Units as initially filed under the Securities Act of 1933. This Memorandum is subject to the existence of broad discretionary powers of the authorities administering such laws, authorizing them, among other things, to withdraw exemptions accorded by statute, to impose additional requirements, to refuse registration and to issue stop orders.

This Memorandum does not cover the requirements under any such laws with respect to advertising matter other than offering material or with respect to the form or contents of any Offering material.

SANTORO, RYAN & KOSTANT

Note: The lead underwriter put together an underwriting syndicate that purchased the securities, at a discount, from the Company. The syndicate also used a Selling Group of broker/dealers to help sell the securities. Everyone was careful not to offer the securities for sale in these states.

D.   CIVIL LIABILITY UNDER THE 1933 ACT AND DUE DILIGENCE

There is a great deal of difference between liability under the 1933 Act and the 1934 Act. For example, liability under Section 10(b) and Rule 10b-5 of the 1934 Act applies to all purchases and sales of securities using instrumentalities of interstate commerce. Even if securities or transactions are exempt from the registration requirements of Section 5 of the 1933 Act, purchases and sales will still be covered by Rule 10b-5 of the 1934 Act.

In addition to the criminal liability contained in Section 17 of the 1933 Act, three major sections provide for civil liability. Section 11 of the 1933 Act provides liability for an untrue statement of material fact or the omission of a material fact required to be stated in a registration statement. The liability, which is joint and several, extends to the issuer, its chief executive, financial and accounting officers, each director, each underwriter (in an amount not to exceed the aggregate offering price of the securities it underwrites), and each accountant or other expert who has taken responsibility for preparing some portion of the registration statement.

While this language from the 1933 Act would seem to open a floodgate of litigation, the section was not really tested judicially until *Escott v. Bar Chris Constr. Corp.*, 283 F. Supp. 643 (S.D.N.Y. 1968). There is little actual case law about Section 11 liability, perhaps because issuers, their underwriters, and legal counsel have been so careful to provide full and accurate disclosure.

The defenses to Section 11 liability are especially important. While the issuer itself has no defense for material misstatements or omissions, each other party has what is called a "due diligence" defense if it exercised "due diligence" in making a reasonable investigation of the accuracy of the registration statement. The level of what constitutes due diligence varies as to whether the party is an expert (for example, an accountant) and whether the misstatement or omission is contained in an expertized or non-expertized portion of the registration statement. The highest standard of investigation is reserved for experts in the expertized portions. Inside directors are also likely to be held to a higher standard than outside directors, but some investigation is required by all parties.

Section 12(1) provides for civil liability when a person offers or sells a security in violation of Section 5, the registration requirement of the 1933 Act. Accordingly, if a security is sold without registration when an exemption did not apply, the buyer is entitled to rescission and a return of the full purchase price from the seller. The buyer will certainly exercise this option if the price of the security declines. If the buyer has already sold the security at a loss, she is entitled to recover the difference between the offering price and the price at which she sold the security.

Section 12(2) provides for civil liability, rescission, or damages for material misstatements or omissions in any prospectus or oral communication. It would seem to be broader than Section 11, which only applies to registration statements, but its scope may recently have been narrowed by the Supreme Court in *Gustafson v. Alloyed Co.*, 115 S. Ct. 1061 (1995).

Careful due diligence can reduce the possibility of making mistakes that can lead to liability. Form 37 provides good due diligence procedures for underwriter's counsel.

Form 38: Due Diligence Investigation Guidelines

SANTORO, RYAN & KOSTANT

GUIDELINES FOR CONDUCTING
DUE DILIGENCE INVESTIGATIONS

A. GENERAL

1. This memorandum sets forth a comprehensive list of items that could be reviewed in connection with an underwriter's due diligence investigation. The list is neither exhaustive nor indicative of all of those items that must, at a minimum, be reviewed in connection with each due diligence investigation.

2. Whether a due diligence investigation is sufficient will depend upon what constitutes a "reasonable investigation" under the circumstances. The scope (including the items reviewed and the period of time covered) of each due diligence investigation will vary, depending upon such factors as the type of issuer, the type of security being issued (whether debt or equity and, if debt, its maturity), and when (if ever) the issuer did its last public offering of securities. In addition, the scope of the investigation by underwriter's counsel will vary, depending on the nature of the legal opinion it is being asked to render in connection with the offering.

3. If possible, the due diligence investigation should be completed before the Registration Statement is filed with the Securities and Exchange Commission. If there is a substantial period of time between the initial filing of the Registration Statement and the date on which the securities are issued, the managing underwriter and its counsel should discuss with the issuer's officers and accountants the need to update the disclosure in the Registration Statement.

B. PRELIMINARY PROCEDURES

Early in the process (perhaps before the managing underwriter, the issuer, and counsel for the issuer begin drafting the Registration Statement) the managing underwriter or its counsel could:

1. Check the issuer's credit rating (including a review of all submissions to rating agencies) and its general reputation with its creditors, customers, and suppliers.

2. Interview the issuer's accountants regarding the issuer's accounting system and practices.

3. Review research reports on the issuer.

Note: This memorandum was prepared as a guide for due diligence by the underwriter and its counsel.

Q: What level of due diligence would be required for executive officers of the issuer? Inside directors? Outside directors? Accountants?

Form 38: Due Diligence Guidelines (continued)

4. If stock is to be sold, obtain historical quotations for the issuer's securities.

5. Review the issuer's annual reports on Form 10-K, quarterly reports on Form 10-Q, and reports to shareholders. Determine whether these filings were made in a timely manner.

6. Review the issuer's reports on Form 8-K filed since the issuer's most recent annual report.

7. Review other filings by the issuer under the Securities Act or the Securities Exchange Act.

C. CHARTER DOCUMENTS

1. Counsel could review a long-form good standing certificate of the issuer (and of each material subsidiary) and certified copies of each document mentioned to determine:

   a. Whether the issuer and such subsidiary are duly incorporated (this will also require review of the relevant state statute for the state of incorporation).

   b. Whether the issuer and such subsidiary are in good standing.

   c. Whether the name of the issuer (and, where applicable, of each such subsidiary) and the place and date of incorporation referred to in the Registration Statement are correct.

   d. Whether any shareholder has preemptive rights, and, if so, whether such rights have been properly waived or preserved.

   e. Whether the capitalization disclosed in the Registration Statement is correct.

   f. Whether the documents were properly adopted and amended.

   g. Whether the charter restricts stock issuance or transfer.

   h. Whether the charter contains any provisions (such as cumulative voting provisions, preemptive rights provisions, or anti-acquisition provisions) that should be complied with or disclosed in the Registration Statement.

2. Counsel could review certified copies of the current by-laws of the issuer and of each material subsidiary. The by-laws could be checked against the charter and state law to

Form 38: Due Diligence Guidelines (continued)

determine that they are not defective. In addition, the by-laws could be reviewed to determine whether:

a. They contain any provisions limiting the powers of the issuer's officers and directors.

b. They contain any provisions that should be disclosed in the Registration Statement.

D. MINUTES

1. The official minutes of all meetings of shareholders, board of directors, and committees of the issuer and of the issuer's material subsidiaries could be read to determine whether:

a. Charter, by-law, and statutory proceedings were followed (i.e., quorum, notice of meetings, percentage of votes).

b. Events were discussed that should be disclosed in the Registration Statement (such as long-term obligations, material litigation, or other material transactions).

2. If stock is being issued, all minutes of the issuer since the date of its incorporation could be reviewed to determine whether each share of the issuer's stock has been duly authorized, validly issued, and fully paid for. In this connection, certificates of the transfer agent or registrant could be reviewed regarding the number of shares issued, and certificates of the issuer's accountants could be reviewed concerning full payment for each share.

3. Counsel could attempt to establish that the facts and figures in the issuer's minutes match those in the Registration Statement concerning:

a. Pension plans;

b. Officers' remuneration;

c. Options to purchase securities;

d. Stock option plans; and

e. Transactions between the issuer and its officers and directors.

E. VARIOUS DOCUMENTS

The following types of documents concerning the issuer and material subsidiaries could be reviewed:

Form 38: Due Diligence Guidelines (continued)

1. Proposed exhibits to the Registration Statement.

2. Exhibits to Exchange Act documents (See B-5 and B-6 above).

3. Material contracts.

4. Pension and employee benefit plans' stock option, profit sharing, and other employee or management compensation plans.

5. Management employment contracts and agreements not to compete.

6. Material labor contracts.

7. Material lease agreements, licensing and franchise agreements, joint venture agreements, and distributor agreements.

8. Recent title and appraisal reports with respect to material properties and assets (including Uniform Commercial Code searches on major assets).

9. Debt instruments, including loan agreements, revolving credit agreements, and indentures (the covenants could be reviewed to determine if (i) the proposed offering would violate any covenant, and (ii) the issuer or subsidiary is in violation of any financial covenant).

10. Material insurance policies.

11. Letters of counsel to the issuer's accountants delivered in connection with recent audits.

12. Documentation concerning recent private placements of securities.

13. Files concerning pending litigation and administrative proceedings involving the issuer or subsidiary.

14. Recent news releases relating to the issuer or subsidiary.

15. Other documents that will verify the information in the Registration Statement (such as reports showing projected construction costs, occupancy rates, backlog orders).

F. MISCELLANEOUS OTHER MATTERS

1. Counsel could determine that the Registration Statement conforms with the requirements of the Securities Act form being used and that the issuer is qualified to use the form.

Form 38: Due Diligence Guidelines (continued)

2. If there are material patents or trademarks, an opinion from patent and trademark counsel could be considered.

3. Counsel could consider the effect of pending legislation or litigation on the issuer and its material subsidiaries.

4. Counsel could review prospectuses and Exchange Act reports of competitors to determine if issues discussed in such documents were not covered by the issuer's draft Registration Statement.

5. Counsel could determine whether the issuer has complied with environmental, health, safety, and civil rights laws.

G. DUE DILIGENCE MEETINGS

1. The managing underwriter and counsel should meet with the issuer's operating officers to discuss issues related to the issuer's investigations and management's projection of the issuer's future business results, what effects the economy and competition may have on operations and results in the future, and plans the issuer may have concerning its present business or new areas of business.

2. The managing underwriter and counsel should meet with the issuer's accountants and financial officers to discuss the issuer's financial condition and prospects and its accounting practices, standards, and controls.

3. After counsel has completed its investigation of the issuer's and material subsidiaries' contracts and minutes, the managing underwriter and counsel could discuss any issues or questions raised in the course of such review.

1.   Sale of Restricted Securities

As discussed above in connection with private placements, securities that were purchased from an issuer in a non-public transaction are restricted, and must be purchased for investment purposes. One who purchases from an issuer with a view to a distribution of the security is an "underwriter" under the relevant definition in the 1933 Act, and underwriters are required, under Section 5, to register securities before they can be offered or sold. The important factual question is how long must a purchaser hold securities before they will not be deemed an underwriter for whom the sale of the securities will not be with a view to a distribution. SEC Rule 144 clarifies this problem and provides a safe harbor.

One who is not an affiliate of the issuer (i.e., not an officer, director or shareholder in a control position) may sell the "restricted" securities after holding them two years, providing that four conditions are met: (1) the issuer must be current in its 1934 Act reporting requirements; (2) the sale must be made in a broker's transaction or to a market maker; (3) no more than the greater of one percent of the outstanding issue or the average weekly trading volume for the preceding four weeks may be sold in any three month period; and (4) a form must be filed with the SEC if more than 500 shares are sold or the total sales price exceeds $10,000.

These conditions do not apply, and a non-affiliate can freely sell, restricted securities after holding them for three years.

As discussed in connection with private placements, since the restricted securities will have a legend on them, and there will be a Stop Transfer Order with the transfer agent, an opinion of issuer's counsel will be needed before the transfer agent will remove the legend and transfer the securities.

Form 39:   Issuer's Counsel's Opinion Letter Regarding
            Compliance with Rule 144 for Sale of Stock

SANTORO, RYAN & KOSTANT

December 10, 1990

To: Stock Transfer Agent

Attention:

In connection with the proposed sale by _____ of an aggregate of 10,000 shares of the 20,000 shares of Class A common stock of _____ Company registered in the name of _____ and represented by Certificate No. _____ we have been provided with the following, and provide you with copies of the same herewith:

   1. Letter representations of _____ dated December 7, 1995.
   2. Seller's representation letter dated December 6, 1995.
   3. Forms 144 filed with the Securities and Exchange Commission on behalf of _____.

According to our records, the 10,000 shares being sold by _____ were acquired by him on October 6, 1993 in connection with his exercise of a non-qualified stock option theretofore granted to him by _____, and that the consideration for such shares was paid in full on the date of exercise.

To the best of our knowledge, after due inquiry, (i) _____ is not an affiliate of _____ and (ii) _____ Company has been subject to the reporting requirements of Section 13 of the Securities Exchange Act of 1934 for a period of at least 90 days prior to December 6, 1990, and has filed all the reports required to be filed thereunder during the twelve months preceding December 6, 1995.

Assuming that, according to your records, one percent of the outstanding shares of Class A common stock of _____ is more than 10,000 shares, we are of the opinion that all of the relevant requirements of Rule 144 as adopted by the Securities and Exchange Commission under the Securities Act of 1933 have been satisfied with respect to the proposed sale by _____ and that upon the surrender of the certificate referred to above in connection with such sale, you may properly issue a new certificate to the purchaser of the 10,000 shares referred to above without further restrictions on their transfer. However, the certificate which will be issued to _____ to reflect the balance of 10,000 shares to be held by him following the subject sale should be marked with the usual and customary legend indicating the continuation of the restrictions on their transfer without compliance with the registration provisions of the

Note: The transfer agent will not transfer securities that have a restrictive legend prohibiting transfer without receipt of this letter from issuer's

Form 39:   Issuer's Counsel's Opinion Letter (continued)

Securities Act of 1933 or the availability of an exemption therefrom.

If you need any additional information with respect to the foregoing, please advise.

Very truly yours,

Peter Kostant

2.   *No Action Letters*

The commissioners of the SEC vote on formal action to be taken by the Commission but they are advised by the SEC staff. The SEC staff will often provide an interpretation of a provision of law for an interested party. Counsel for the interested party will write to the SEC describing the relevant facts in detail. Based upon these facts, the SEC staff may respond that it would not recommend an enforcement action to the Commission. Thus, "No Action" letters are a kind of private law. They may not be legally binding, but the SEC has always honored them. By reading existing No Action letters, which are public documents, lawyers can learn how the SEC would be likely to interpret statutes, rules, and regulations.

In the following illustrative transaction, a company called Gensia, Inc. was about to settle two class action lawsuits. Part of the settlement to plaintiffs consisted of their receipt of Gensia stock.

As part of the settlement, the attorneys for Gensia agreed to request a No Action letter from the SEC Division of Corporation Finance that the shares would not be restricted securities because of the Section 3a(10) exemption from regulation. The issuer's counsel wrote, in relevant part:

[W]e respectfully request the written advice of the Staff of the Division of Corporation Finance (the "Division") that it will not recommend enforcement action to the Securities and Exchange Commission (the "Commission") based upon the following facts and that the Division concurs with our opinion that (i) the Company may issue shares (the "Settlement Stock") to members of the plaintiff class ("Settlement Class") and to their counsel ("Class Counsel") in exchange for the settlement of claims of the Settlement Class without registration under the Securities Act of 1933, as amended (the "Act"), in reliance upon the exemption under Section 3(a)(10) thereof; (ii) the Settlement Stock as so issued will not be deemed to be "restricted securities" within the meaning of Rule 144(a)(3) under the Act; and (iii) the Settlement Stock as so issued will be freely transferable except that, if any transferee of the Settlement Stock is deemed to be an "affiliate" of the Company within the meaning of Rule 144(a)(1) under the Act, then any public sale of Settlement Stock by such transferee without registration under the Act will be required to comply with the provisions of Rule 144 except for the holding period requirements under Rule 144(d). . . .

The Division has articulated the following four requirements that must be met in order for the Section 3(a)(10) exemption to be available to an issuer that issues securities in settlement of pending class action litigation: (i) the Court must hold a hearing on the fairness of the terms and conditions of the issuance of all such securities; (ii) the persons to whom such securities are to be issued must receive notice of the hearing and of the right to be heard; (iii) the Court must be advised prior to the hearing that if the terms and conditions of the settlement are approved, registration of the securities will not be required under the Act by virtue of the Court's approval; and (iv) the Court must approve the fairness of the terms and conditions of the settlement.

Accordingly, issuer's counsel requested a No Action letter based upon approximately ten pages of factual representations.

The SEC Division of Corporation Finance provided the following No Action letter (Form 40).

Form 40: SEC No Action Letter

June 23, 1995

Publicly Available June 23, 1995

Re: Gensia Inc. (the "Company")
        Incoming letter dated June 22, 1995

Based on the facts presented in your letter, and contingent upon the approval of the Settlement Agreement, the Plan of Allocation and the individual allocations of cash and the Company's common stock ("Settlement Stock") by the Court following hearings on each of the foregoing, as described in your letter, the Division will not recommend any enforcement action to the Commission if the Company, in reliance upon your opinion as counsel that registration is not required, issues Settlement Stock in connection with the settlement of the class action suit pending against the Company, as described in your letter, without registration under the Securities Act of 1933.

Recipients of Settlement Stock who are not deemed to be affiliates of the Company may resell such stock for their own accounts without regard to Rule 144. Recipients of Settlement Stock who are deemed to be affiliates may resell such stock pursuant to Rule 144. However, because the Settlement Stock will not be restricted securities, the holding period requirement of Rule 144(d) is inapplicable.

Note: The SEC staff expressly limits its opinion to the facts as represented, and purports not to reach a legal conclusion.

Because these positions are based on the representations made to the Division in your letter, it should be noted that any different facts or conditions might require different conclusions. Further, our response regarding registration of the Settlement Stock only expresses the Division's position on enforcement action and does not purport to express any legal conclusion on the question presented.

Sincerely,

Cecilia D. Blye
Special Counsel
Securities and Exchange Commission (SEC)

E. COMPLIANCE WITH THE SECURITIES EXCHANGE ACT OF 1934

Unlike the Securities Exchange Act of 1933, which governs proposed sales of securities to the public, the 1934 Act generally regulates the flow of information concerning securities that are already owned by the public. One purpose served by the 1934 Act is that the initial information provided by the 1933 Act's disclosure requirements would become outdated but for the 1934 Act's continuous reporting requirements. Many provisions of the 1934 Act apply to companies which have securities that are traded on a national securities exchange (Section 12(b)) and companies which have assets exceeding $5 million and a class of equity security held of record by 500 persons.

The SEC requires these public companies, called "reporting companies," to file an annual report on Form 10-K. Reporting companies must also file quarterly reports on Form 10-Q, mostly of financial information prepared by their accountants. Another non-periodic but very important report is the 8-K, which must be filed in the event of any material change in the company. A material change might be a change in control; acquisition or disposition of significant assets; the event of bankruptcy or receivership; a change of certifying accountant; resignation by a director due to disagreements over operations, policy or practices; or any other important event. The company has either five or fifteen days to file a report for most of these events.

Because SEC Regulation S-K disclosure provisions apply to both the 1933 and 1934 Act filings, as part of integrated disclosure, these periodic reporting requirements essentially keep all registration statements current.

Form 41: Management's Discussion and Analysis of Operations from Form 10-K (excerpt of sample)

Note: This is the Management's Discussion and Analysis (MD&A) portion of a 10-K for a reporting company. The requirements for the MD&A are set forth in Part II, item 7 of Form 10-K, which cross-references to the disclosure required i item 303 of Regulation S-K.

Note: Are the new hardwood distribution centers the equivalent of "new units"? Why not be clearer? This is confusing.

Q: Overproduction and price-wars would drive the market price down. Why would this reduce inventory? Wouldn't it be a good time to buy more inventory?

Note: Increased costs volume should not affect "new units" profits. The statement says "new units" increased their contribution to profits.

Note: Adding the accounts of "Mystery Properties" to what? This sentence makes it sound like the accounting rules forced a merger.

Note: This is repetitive.

Note: Where supply conditions are strengthened, can we infer that prices will go back up?

DISCUSSION AND ANALYSIS OF OPERATIONS

UNUSUAL, INFREQUENT OR SIGNIFICANT CHANGES

Continued improvements in results of new hardwood lumber distribution centers added since 1983 plus a 6% increase in sales of the School Shop Equipment segment caused revenues to increase 5% to $109 million. While new units increased their contribution to profits, overall company earnings were affected by:

1) over-production of certain domestic hardwoods plus a price war in Genuine Mahogany, both of which necessitated sizable downward adjustments in inventories,

2) increased costs associated with higher volume of new units,

3) increased insurance, interest and bad debt expenses, and

4) start-up costs of Mystery-Mill, the new hardwood dimension cut-up plant in Louisville, Kentucky.

Adoption of new accounting requirements for consolidation of subsidiaries resulted in adding the accounts of Mystery Properties, Inc. Since this low-leverage real estate operation also produces profits and exceptional cash flow, consolidated ratios and comparisons were not significantly changed.

TRENDS OR UNCERTAINTIES

Mild winters over the past two years coupled with the drought allowed logging of domestic hardwoods to reach an all-time high. Over-production and a decrease in selling prices of certain domestic hardwoods coupled with a price war in Genuine Mahogany necessitated sizeable downward adjustments in inventories. Supply conditions strengthened in late months of Fiscal 1989, eliminating the need for additional inventory adjustments.

Seriously depressed economies of Texas, Oklahoma, and Louisiana are improving slowly while the economy in Colorado continues to weaken.

Form 41: Discussion of Operations (continued)

LIQUIDITY FACTORS AND PROBABILITIES

Net working capital exceeds $21 million, up slightly over last year. Record-setting cash flow (net earnings plus depreciation) of $6.9 million paid for: 1) capital expenditures of $2.4 million, 2) cash dividends of $1.7 million and retirement of long-term debt of $447,000. Note also that short term bank borrowing was reduced $2.4 million with little change in combined inventory and accounts receivable totals. Unused bank lines are adequate to finance seasonal working capital needs.

CAPITAL EXPENDITURES, IMPROVEMENTS AND EXPANSIONS

Internally generated funds (cash flow) paid for capital expenditures of $2.4 million including
1) $392,000 for expansion of mill capabilities at the Louisville Processing Center for production of Mystery-Mill hardwood lumber dimension products and,
2) amounts to purchase additional mill and transportation equipment and warehouse storage/handling equipment at other distribution center.

IMPACT OF INFLATION ON OPERATIONS

Supply and demand conditions continue to be the primary factors in determining the prices and costs of Company products. Inflation did not have a significant effect on the Company's operations during Fiscal 1988/89.

Note: Pure padding.

FORWARD-LOOKING DATA

The Company intends to aggressively market Mystery-Mill hardwood dimension products through existing distribution networks to better serve existing customers and identify potential new opportunities for sales and earnings growth.

Expansion opportunities for the School Shop Equipment segment will be pursued as identified for potential to broaden product offerings and increase gross margin dollars.

Note: Apparently this means, "In the future, we're going to try to sell more stuff."

Note: This Management's Discussion and Analysis of Operations is adapted from a profitable and highly ethical company's submission, but note how sketchy and confusing the disclosure is.

Form 42: Form 8-K Disclosing Adverse Court Rulings

SECURITIES AND EXCHANGE COMMISSION
WASHINGTON, D.C. 20549

_____

FORM 8-K

CURRENT REPORT

Pursuant to Section 13 or 15(d) of the
Securities Exchange Act of 1934

Date of Report (Date of earliest event reported)   January 4, 1993

Eagle Hardware & Garden, Inc.
(Exact name of registrant as specified in its charter)

Washington
(State of other jurisdiction of incorporation)

0-00000   00-0000000
(Commission File Number)   (IRS Employer Identification No.)

101 Andover Park East, Suite 200
Tukwila, Washington   98188
(Address of principal executive offices)   (Zip Code)

Registrant's telephone number, including area code
(206) 431-0000

Item 5. Other Events

On January 4, 1993, King County Superior Court Judge Michael C. Hayden granted summary judgment for a Bellevue citizens' group opposed to the construction of the proposed Eagle hardware & Garden, Inc. ("Eagle" or the "Company") store in Bellevue, Washington. In a memorandum opinion, Judge Hayden ruled as a matter of law that Eagle's proposed store is a permitted use in Bellevue's light industrial zone and that Bellevue's Design and Development Department followed the proper due process procedures in determining this issue. Judge Hayden also ruled, however, that the City of Bellevue did not comply with the State Environmental Policy Act when it adopted an Environmental Impact Statement from a previous proposal, instead of completing a new EIS.

If Judge Hayden's decision is upheld, the City of Bellevue would be required to prepare a supplemental Environmental Impact Statement, and further appeals with respect to the store are possible. As a result of Judge Hayden's decision, the Company believes that the opening of its proposed Bellevue store, previously scheduled for the first quarter of fiscal 1993, may be delayed by as much as six months.

Q: How would you determine whether the adverse judgment was a material event?

Form 42: Form 8-K Disclosing Adverse Court Rulings
          (continued)

```
SIGNATURES:

Pursuant to the requirements of the Securities Exchange Act
of 1934, the registrant has duly caused this report to be
signed on its behalf by the undersigned hereunto duly
authorized.

EAGLE HARDWARE & GARDEN, INC.




January 7, 1993  By_____
Date                     Richard T. Takata
                         President and Chief Operating Officer
```

Drafting Exercise 16

Your firm is general counsel to the Possession National Bank. One of your partners has lunch with the senior partner of the bank's auditors, Waters, Price & House, and is told that the auditors have serious questions about the bank's financial viability because of risks inherent in their business strategy. The audit firm resigns but declines to give anything but an innocuous explanation, simply stating that it cannot continue to audit the bank profitably.

Prepare the 8-K to file with the SEC.

F.   SECTION 16(B) LIABILITY FOR SHORT-SWING PROFITS

Often, one responsibility of corporate counsel for a reporting company is to make certain that the company's officers, directors, and beneficial owners of more than ten percent of any class of equity securities, file Form 3 with the SEC to disclose their initial ownership interests, Form 4 to disclose any changes in ownership, and Form 5 to disclose ownership on an annual basis. Section 16(b) prohibits these persons from profiting from any purchase and sale made within less than a six-month period.

In an action brought under Section 16(b) by the company or on its behalf, the company will recover all profits derived from the transactions. This is an absolute liability provision, and proof of the absence of inside information is not a defense. Section 16(a) requires that officers, directors, and ten-percent beneficial shareholders must report when they buy or sell securities.

Notes

1. An excellent short treatise that students will find helpful is Larry D. Soderquist, Understanding the Securities Laws (3d ed. Practicing Law Institute).

2. Section 5 of the 1933 Act reads as follows:

(a) Unless a registration statement is in effect as to a security, it shall be unlawful for any person, directly or indirectly—

(1) to make use of any means or instruments of transportation or communication in interstate commerce or of the mails to sell such security through the use or medium of any prospectus or otherwise; or

(2) to carry or cause to be carried through the mails or in interstate commerce, by any means or instruments of transportation, any such security for the purpose of sale or for delivery after sale.

(b) It shall be unlawful for any person, directly or indirectly—

(1) to make use of any means or instruments of transportation or communication in interstate commerce or of the mails to carry or transmit any prospectus relating to any security with respect to which a registration statement has been filed under this title, unless such prospectus meets the requirements of section 10; or

(2) to carry or cause to be carried through the mails or in interstate commerce any such security for the purpose of sale or for delivery after sale, unless accompanied or preceded by a prospectus that meets the requirements of subsection (a) of section 10.

(c) It shall be unlawful for any person, directly or indirectly, to make use of any means or instruments of transportation or communication in interstate commerce or of the mails to offer to sell or offer to buy through the use or medium of any prospectus or otherwise any security, unless a registration statement has been filed as to such security, or while the registration statement is the subject of a refusal order or stop order or (prior to the effective date of the registration statement) any public proceeding or examination under Section 8.

3. For an example of such restrictive language, see the Notes to Form 11 below.

4. *See, e.g.,* George J. Benston, Required Disclosure and the Stock Market: An Evaluation of the Securities Exchange Act of 1934, 63 Am. Econ. Rev. 132 (1973); Homer Kripke, Fifty Years of Security Regulation in Search of a Purpose, 21 San Diego L. Rev. 257 (1984); Homer Kripke, The Myth of the Informed Layman, 28 Bus. Law. 631 (1973); Frank H. Easterbrook & Daniel R. Fischel, Mandatory Disclosure and the Protection of Investors, 70 Va.L. Rev. 669 (1984). The last two are excerpted in Larry D. Soderquist, Securities Regulation (3d ed. 1993) at 115-117 and 124-127.

5. *See, e.g.,* John C. Coffee Jr., Market Failure and the Economic Case for a Mandatory Disclosure System, 70 Va. L. Rev. 717 (1984), excerpted in Larry D. Soderquist, Securities Regulation (3d ed. 1993) at 128-129.

Chapter 9

Acquisitions

A. MERGERS AND ACQUISITIONS

In a merger, the board of directors of each corporation agrees on a plan of merger that complies with the relevant corporation statute. One corporation will survive the merger and the shareholders of the non-surviving corporation(s) will receive cash or securities.

Shareholder approval is often necessary, but in a statutory "short form" merger in which the acquiring corporation owns a large portion of the acquired corporation, as specified in the relevant statute, shareholder approval is not required. Dissenting shareholders have statutory appraisal rights under which they will receive a court-approved value for their shares.

In many acquisitions, the acquiring corporation is at risk in one way or another for the contingent (and all other) liabilities of the acquired corporation. This will certainly occur in a merger or, as a possible diminution of value, when one corporation purchases the stock of another. To avoid this, the acquiring corporation may hold part of the purchase price in escrow or may accept a guarantee from a third party. Certain liabilities may also be specifically excluded from the transaction. The acquiring corporation may protect itself from liability to some extent by merging the acquired corporation into a new wholly-owned subsidiary formed for that purpose.

Acquisitions are sometimes accomplished by purchase of the acquired corporation's assets in order to avoid liability for unknown or contingent liabilities of the acquired corporation. However, this technique may be unsuccessful because of the doctrine of "de facto merger" pursuant to which the acquiring corporation may be liable to the creditors of the acquired corporation. The acquiring corporation must also comply with the "bulk sales" provisions of Article 6 of the Uniform Commercial Code if it is to escape the liabilities provided in the UCC.

Form 43: Letter of Intent for Purchase of a Corporation

Q: How does this letter of intent compare with the underwriter's letter, Form 33? To what extent, if any, is this letter intended to be legally binding?

ABC Industries
Number, Street
City, State, Zip

Date

Ms. Johnette A. Smith, President
XYZ Corporation
Number, Street
City, State, Zip

Re: Proposed Purchase of Stock of XYZ Corporation and Subsidiaries by ABC Industries, Inc.

Dear Ms. Smith:

This letter will confirm the various discussions that we have had with you relative to the proposed purchase by ABC Industries, Inc. ("ABC") of all of the issued and outstanding shares of stock of XYZ Corporation ("XYZ"). The objective of our discussions has been the execution and consummation, as soon as feasible, of a formal Purchase Agreement between ABC and all of the shareholders of XYZ (the "Purchase Agreement") which, among other things, would provide for the various matters set forth below:

(1) In the proposed transaction, the Buyer will be ABC, or a new wholly-owned subsidiary of ABC to be organized and properly financed for the purpose of such acquisition, and the Sellers will be yourself and all of the other shareholders of XYZ. If the Buyer should be a wholly-owned subsidiary of ABC, the obligations of the Buyer to make the payments descried in Paragraph 3 below will be guaranteed by ABC.

Q: Should each side be obligated to pay its own expenses?

(2) By its purchase of the XYZ stock, the Buyer will also be acquiring all of the outstanding shares of XYZ's subsidiaries (i.e., Subco Corporation, ZYX, Inc., and XYZ International, Inc.). XYZ and said subsidiaries are hereinafter collectively referred to as "XYZ." It is, of course, understood that the Sellers' legal and accounting fees, and their other expenses incurred in connection with the proposed transaction, shall be paid by the Sellers.

(3) For the shares of XYZ stock to be purchased by the Buyer, the Buyer shall pay the total sum of $5,500,000. Such total purchase price shall be payable as follows:

(a) On the date of the consummation of the Purchase Agreement (the "Closing Date"), the Buyer shall pay an amount equivalent to the "Total stockholders' equity" set forth in the audited balance sheet of XYZ referred to below in Paragraph 5(b).

(b) The balance of such total purchase price shall be paid in such installments, at such times and pursuant to

Form 43: Letter of Intent for Purchase of a Corporation
(continued)

such other terms and conditions as shall be set forth in the Purchase Agreement.

(4) Upon the execution by you and return to us of this Letter of Intent, counsel for the Sellers and ABC's counsel shall prepare, and the parties shall execute, a formal Purchase Agreement containing provisions in accord with the foregoing, together with such further appropriate terms and conditions as such counsel may mutually determine. The Purchase Agreement shall be subject, in all respects, to the approval of all parties thereto. The Purchase Agreement shall specify the Closing Date (which shall not be later than October 1, 1995), and shall contain the normal and usual warranties as to the absence of undisclosed liabilities; merchantability of inventory; usability and good operating condition of all land, buildings, and leasehold improvements; etc. The Purchase Agreement shall also provide that, pending the Closing Date, ABC and its representatives shall have, at all times, access to XYZ's premises and to the books and records of XYZ, and that XYZ and the Sellers shall furnish to ABC and its representatives such financial and operating data, and such other information with respect to the business and properties of XYZ, as ABC shall, from time to time, reasonably request. In connection therewith, ABC and its representatives shall be privileged to contact and communicate with XYZ's vendors, its customers, manufacturers of its machinery and equipment, and other persons having business dealings with XYZ. It is, of course, understood that all such access, investigations, contacts, etc., to be conducted by ABC and its representatives shall be conducted in such manner as not to interfere unduly with the normal conduct of XYZ's business; and further, that, if the Purchase Agreement shall not be consummated for any reason whatsoever, ABC shall keep confidential any information (unless ascertainable from public or published information or trade sources) obtained from XYZ (or such vendors, customers, manufacturers, and other persons) concerning XYZ's operations and business.

(5) The Purchase Agreement shall also provide that the obligations of the Buyer thereunder are expressly subject to the following:

(a) A favorable review by ABC's counsel of the corporate status and proceedings of XYZ and the good and marketable title of XYZ to its real property and other assets;

(b) The receipt by ABC of the joint certification of XYZ auditors (Stone & Company) and ABC's auditors (Able Baker & Co.) as to the amount of the "Total Stockholders' Equity" of XYZ as at the most recent practicable date prior to the Closing Date. Such certification (i) shall be based upon an audit of XYZ utilizing generally

Q: Should there be cross-indemnification for breach?

Q: Does one usually include "etc." in an agreement?

Note: The Agreement should be drafted so that confidentiality provisions survive even if the deal is not completed.

Form 43: Letter of Intent for Purchase of a Corporation
(continued)

accepted accounting principles applied on a consistent basis and (ii) shall reflect a continuation to the date thereof of the favorable trend of operations shown in the XYZ Condensed and Consolidated Income Statement for the period of three (3) months ending March 31, 1995, heretofore delivered to ABC;

(c) The approval of the transaction by the board of directors of ABC; and

Note: A more detailed job description might be necessary.

(d) The execution of a mutually satisfactory Employment Agreement between XYZ or the Buyer and you, such Employment Agreement to be effective as of the Closing Date.

(6) As stated above, the Closing Date of the Purchase Agreement is expected to be October 1, 1995, or sooner if possible. In consideration for the substantial expenditures of time, effort, and expense to be undertaken by ABC in connection with the preparation and execution of the Purchase Agreement, and the various investigations and reviews referred to above in paragraphs 4 and 5, the Sellers undertake and agree

(a) that neither they nor XYZ shall, between the date of the execution by you of this Letter of Intent and the Closing Date, enter into or conduct any discussions with any other prospective purchaser of the stock or assets of XYZ (except for the Dorset, Maryland, property of Subco Corporation), and

(b) that they shall cause XYZ to use its best efforts to preserve intact its business organization and the good will of its customers, suppliers, and others having business with it.

(7) ABC considers that time is of the essence in consummating the proposed transaction. Accordingly, we have instructed our counsel to work with the Sellers' counsel promptly after your execution of this Letter of Intent, to prepare the Purchase Agreement, which shall contain provisions in accord with the foregoing. It is, of course, understood

(a) that this letter is intended to be, and shall be construed only as, a Letter of Intent summarizing and evidencing the discussions between XYZ and ABC to the date hereof and not as an offer to purchase the stock or assets of XYZ or an agreement with respect hereto, and

Q: Should there be a clear time limit on this?

(b) that the respective rights and obligations of the Sellers, XYZ, the Buyer, and ABC remain to be defined in the Purchase Agreement, into which this Letter of Intent and all prior discussions shall merge, provided,

Form 43: Letter of Intent for Purchase of a Corporation
(continued)

however, that the respective obligations of the Sellers and XYZ under Paragraph 6 shall be binding upon them, respectively, when this Letter of Intent shall be executed and delivered to ABC.

Q: Should this be binding on both sides?

If the foregoing meets with the approval of yourself and the other shareholders of XYZ, kindly so signify by signing and returning the enclosed duplicate copy of this letter, where-upon this letter shall constitute a Letter of Intent between the parties in accordance with the terms and provisions set forth above.

Note: There should probably be a clause stating that there are no brokers or finders.

We shall look forward to receiving your prompt advices.

Very truly yours,

By _____
     James B. Jones
     Vice-President

CONFIRMED: July _____, 1995

_____
Johnette A. Smith, individually and on behalf of the share-holders of XYZ Corporation

Q: Why isn't it necessary to bind XYZ Corporation?

Form 44: Due Diligence Request Form

Note: The documents requested for review are very similar to those described in the underwriter's due diligence memorandum, Form 38.

AMERICAN BUSINESS ASSISTANCE, INC.
(THE "COMPANY")

PRELIMINARY LIST OF DOCUMENTS
TO BE REVIEWED IN CONNECTION
WITH DUE DILIGENCE INVESTIGATION

1. The Company's charter, as amended to date.

2. The Company's by-laws, as amended to date.

3. Minutes of meetings of the Company's board of directors for the last five years.

4. Minutes of meetings of all committees of the Company's board of directors for the last five years.

5. Minutes of meetings of the Company's shareholders for the last five years.

6. The Company's stock ledger.

7. All budgets prepared by the Company during the last five years.

8. All cash flow projections prepared by the Company during the last five years.

9. All materials (including proxy statements) sent by the Company to the Company's shareholders during the last five years.

10. The Company's annual reports, reports in connection with the Company's interim financial reports, and all letters from the Company's outside auditors to the Company, together with the Company's responses (if any) to such letters, for the last five years.

11. All documents (including exhibits thereto) filed by the Company with the Securities and Exchange Commission (the "Commission") during the last five years, and all correspondence between the Company and the Commission during the last five years.

12. All documents filed by the Company with the National Association of Securities Dealers, Inc. (the "NASD") or with any exchange on which the Company's securities have been listed during the last five years, and all correspondence between the Company and the NASD or any such exchange during the last five years.

13. All press releases issued by the Company during the last five years.

Form 44: Due Diligence Request Form (continued)

14. Files concerning all pending litigation and administrative proceedings involving the Company or its properties. Be sure to include all letters covering the last two years concerning pending claims, litigations, and judgments involving the Company (together with related complaints and answers), from law firms retained by the Company.

15. Current questionnaires of the Company's officers, directors, and significant shareholders.

16. All corrupt practices studies and memoranda prepared by or on behalf of the Company during the last five years.

17. All available reports (e.g., marketing reports, engineering reports, analysts' reports, and title and appraisal reports) on the Company or its properties prepared by the Company or by third parties (including trade publications) during the last five years.

18. All available industry studies of the Company's business segments.

19. All contracts and agreements (including title insurance policies) pertaining to any material purchase or lease of property by the Company.

20. All agreements and instruments to be referred to in the Registration Statement on Form S-1 (including the exhibits and schedules to the Registration Statement on Form S-1).

21. All significant contracts and agreements (not otherwise provided pursuant to Items 18 or 19 hereof) to which the Company is a party, including but not limited to:

(a) acquisition and disposition agreements;

(b) other agreements relating to issuance of additional shares of the Company's securities;

(c) debt instruments (including loan agreements, revolving credit agreements, and indentures);

(d) union contracts;

(e) purchase and supply contracts;

(f) pension and employee benefit plans; stock option, profit sharing, and other employee or management compensation plans;

(g) employment contracts and agreements not to compete;

(h) agreements between the Company and its management or controlling shareholders;

Form 44: Due Diligence Request Form (continued)

Q: What does this definition say?

(i) government contracts;

(j) licensing and franchise agreements;

(k) joint venture agreements;

(l) distributorship agreements; and

(m) insurance policies.

22. Documents comparable to the documents described in Items 1 through 20 hereof, but with respect to:

(a) each "significant subsidiary (as such term is defined in Rule 405 promulgated under the Securities Act of 1933) of the Company, and

(b) each other subsidiary of the Company which has accrued any liability (contingent or otherwise) which could have a material effect on the Company's business or prospects.

Form 45: Agreement and Plan of Merger

AGREEMENT AND PLAN OF MERGER

THIS AGREEMENT AND PLAN OF MERGER, dated the _____ day of _____, 199____, is entered into and adopted by and between ABC, Inc., a Missouri corporation, ("ABC") and XYZ, Inc., a Missouri corporation, ("XYZ").

WHEREAS, ABC is a corporation duly organized and existing under the laws of the State of Missouri, and has on the date hereof an authorized capital consisting of 300,000 shares of common stock of the par value of $1.00 per share, of which on the date hereof 75,000 shares are issued and outstanding and ABC has no right or options for the issuance of any additional shares; and

WHEREAS, XYZ is a corporation duly organized and existing under the laws of the state of Missouri and has on the date hereof an authorized capital consisting of 30,000 shares of common stock of the par value of $1.00 per share, of which on the date hereof 22,772 shares are issued and outstanding and XYZ has not rights or options for the issuance of any additional shares; and

WHEREAS, ABC and XYZ desire to merge ABC into XYZ in order to combine the financial strength of the two companies, consolidate the management and other functions, expand the operations of the surviving company, and provide greater opportunity for future growth.

NOW, THEREFORE, in consideration of the mutual representations, covenants, and conditions contained herein, the parties agree as follows:

I. MERGER

Subject to the terms and conditions in this Agreement and Plan of Merger on the effective date as provided below, and pursuant to the General and Business Corporation Law of Missouri, ABC shall be merged with and into XYZ and XYZ shall be the Surviving Corporation. The corporate existence, franchises and rights of XYZ, as the Surviving Corporation, with its purposes, privileges, powers and objects, shall continue unimpaired by the Merger, and XYZ, as the Surviving Corporation shall succeed to and be fully vested with the corporate existence, identity and all rights, privileges, powers, franchises, assets, liabilities and obligations of ABC. The separate existence and corporate organization of ABC shall cease upon the effective date (as defined herein), and thereupon ABC and XYZ shall become a single corporation.

Note: This is a merger in which XYZ will be the surviving corporation.

Note: This should be included as a representation and warranty.

Note: This should be included as a representation and warranty.

Note: This is a more typical recital.

Form 45: Agreement and Plan of Merger (continued)

Note: The Articles should be attached as an exhibit.

II. TERMS AND CONDITIONS OF MERGER

The terms and conditions of the merger, the mode of carrying the merger into effect, and the manner and basis of converting the shares of stock of ABC into shares of stock of XYZ are as follows:

(a) *Shareholder Votes.* After the Agreement and Plan of Merger has been approved by the holders of at least two-thirds of the outstanding shares of common stock of XYZ and by at least two-thirds of the outstanding shares of ABC, Articles of Merger shall be certified, executed and acknowledged by ABC and XYZ and filed in accordance with the laws of Missouri in the office of the Secretary of State of Missouri.

(b) *Effective Date.* The merger shall become effective on the later of the 1st day of December, 199____, or the date the Articles of Merger are filed with the Secretary of State of Missouri (the "effective date").

(c) *Manner of Conversion.* The 75,000 issued shares of ABC common stock shall be converted into a total of 5,000 shares of XYZ common stock on the basis of fifteen (15) shares of ABC common stock for each one (1) share of XYZ common stock.

(d) *Issued Shares of XYZ.* The shares of XYZ common stock issued and outstanding shall remain issued and outstanding.

(e) *Surrender and Exchange of Share Certificates.* Following the effective date of the merger, certificates representing 75,000 issued shares of ABC common stock of $1.00 par value, may be exchanged for certificates representing (5,000) issued shares of XYZ common stock of $1.00 par value. After the effective date, each holder of an outstanding certificate or certificates of ABC (the "Old Certificates"), upon surrender thereof to XYZ or its designated agent, shall be entitled to receive, as soon as practicable, in exchange a certificate or certificates representing the number of shares of XYZ common stock (the "New Certificates") into which the shares of ABC common stock previously represented by such surrendered Old Certificates have been converted and exchanged. Until surrendered and exchanged, each outstanding Old Certificate shall be deemed for all corporate purposes, other than the payment of dividends or other distributions, if any, to holders of record of XYZ common stock of XYZ to represent the number of shares of XYZ common stock into which the shares of ABC common stock previously represented by such Old Certificates shall have been converted and exchanged. No dividend or other distribution, if any, payable on or after the effective date to holders of record of shares of XYZ common stock shall be paid to the holders of outstanding Old Certificates; provided, however, that after the surrender and exchange of such outstanding

Form 45: Agreement and Plan of Merger (continued)

Old Certificates there shall be paid to the record holders of the new Certificates issued in exchange therefor the amount, without interest thereon, of dividends and other distributions, if any, which previously have become payable to holders of record on or after the effective date with respect to the number of shares of XYZ common stock represented by such New Certificates. If outstanding Old Certificates are not surrendered and exchanged for New Certificates by the close of business on the day immediately prior to the date, if any, on which the dividends and distributions would otherwise escheat or become the property of any governmental unit or any agency, the amount of the dividends and other distributions which (i) previously have become payable with respect to the shares of XYZ common stock into which the shares of ABC common stock previously represented by such Old Certificates shall have been converted, and/or (ii) subsequently become payable with respect to such shares of XYZ common stock, shall become the property of XYZ, and, to the extent not in the possession of XYZ, shall be paid over to XYZ, free and clear of all claims or interest of any person previously entitled thereto. If any holder of an outstanding certificate or certificates representing ABC common stock shall deliver to XYZ such affidavits, indemnity agreements or surety bonds as XYZ shall reasonably require in conformity with its customary procedure with respect to lost stock certificates of XYZ, XYZ shall treat such delivery as surrender of any lost or misplaced or destroyed certificate or certificates representing ABC common stock.

(f) *Fractional Shares.* No fractional shares of common stock and no scrip certificates therefor shall be issued to represent any fractional interests in common stock of XYZ, and such fractional interests shall not entitle the owners to vote, receive dividends, or exercise any other right of shareholders. Each person entitled to a fractional share interest in the common stock of XYZ shall receive from XYZ a cash payment for such fractional interest equal to the respective fractional share interest times $13.72 per share.

(g) *ABC's Operations.* Upon Merger, the assets, properties, rights, privileges, immunities, debts, liabilities, obligations and all other interests of ABC shall be deemed to be transferred to and vested in XYZ in accordance with the law of the State of Missouri.

III. DIRECTORS AND OFFICERS

The directors and principal officers of XYZ shall from and after the effective date of the merger be as follows:

Albert Able, President and Director
Bob Baker, Vice President, Secretary and Director
Carol Charley, Vice President, Treasurer and Director

Q: What does "escheat" mean?

Q: Is it necessary to cover stock splits, dividends and recapitalizations?

Form 45: Agreement and Plan of Merger (continued)

and they shall serve in office until their successors are duly qualified and elected at the next annual meeting of shareholders and directors of XYZ.

If, on the effective date of the merger, any of the above listed persons is unable to serve in the capacity designated, the vacancy shall be filled in the manner provided by the Bylaws of XYZ.

IV. ARTICLES OF INCORPORATION AND BYLAWS

The Articles of Incorporation of XYZ shall be amended as follows:

"Article IV

The total number of shares of stock which the corporation shall have authority to issue is Fifty Thousand (50,000) shares and the par value of each share is One Dollar ($1.00)."

No change in the Bylaws of XYZ shall be effected by the merger, and the Bylaws in effect on the effective date of the merger shall remain in full force and effect until repealed, amended, or modified.

V. CORPORATE ACTION PRIOR TO MERGER

Neither party shall prior to the effective date of the merger, without the written consent of the other party:

(a) make any change in its authorized capital stock; issue or sell, or agree to issue or sell any shares of any class of stock; grant any option, warrant, or any other right to purchase or to covert any obligation into any of its capital stock; issue or sell, or agree to issue or sell any evidence of indebtedness or other security;

(b) declare or pay any dividend, or authorize or make any other distribution or distributions of assets to its shareholders;

(c) liquidate or dissolve the corporation;

(d) encumber or mortgage any of its property, or enter into any transaction that is out of the ordinary course of business;

(e) repeal, amend, and/or modify the Articles of Incorporation and/or Bylaws of the corporation;

(f) approve, adopt, or otherwise participate in another merger, consolidation or reorganization of the corporation;

(g) sell all or substantially all of the assets of the corporation; or

(h) pay or promise to pay any bonuses or special compensation to any officer, employee or agent.

Form 45: Agreement and Plan of Merger (continued)

VI. REPRESENTATION AND WARRANTIES OF ABC

ABC represents and warrants to XYZ the following:

(a) *Existence.* As of the date of this Agreement and Plan of Merger, ABC is a corporation validly organized in Missouri and duly qualified to conduct business in the jurisdictions in which its business operations require qualification under applicable law, with capital stock authorized, issued, and outstanding as stated in the preamble.

(b) *Operation.* ABC possesses all of the appropriate right, title and interest in its properties now being used in the regular conduct of its business operations necessary to permit the continuance of such operations.

(c) *Financial Statement.* ABC has heretofore delivered to XYZ its balance sheets as of October 1, 199_____, and the related statement of income and surplus for the fiscal year ended 19_____, all certified to by MNO&P, certified public accountants, and all prepared without audit. The foregoing financial statements have been prepared in accordance with generally accepted accounting principles consistently applied and fairly represent the financial position and results of operations of ABC and XYZ as of the dates and for the periods indicated.

(d) *Property.* ABC has title to all of its property, including all property reflected in its balance sheets as of October 1, 199_____, and not sold in the ordinary course of business after that date free and clear of any mortgage, lien, pledge, charge, claims, or encumbrance, except as shown on the balance sheets and minor liens, encumbrances, and adverse claims which do not materially impair the value of the property.

(e) *No Material Litigation.* There are no actions, suits, or proceedings pending, or to the knowledge of ABC, threatened against or affecting ABC, at law or in equity, or before or by any federal, state, municipal, or other governmental department, commission, board, bureau, agency, or instrumentality, that can reasonably be expected to result in any materially adverse change in the business, properties, operations, prospects, or assets or in the condition, financial or otherwise, of ABC.

(f) *Taxes.* ABC has filed all tax returns and reports required to be filed, including, without limitation, returns of federal and state income, employment, sales and use taxes; and all taxes, interest, penalties, assessments, or deficiencies that have become due will have been paid in full, or adequate provision(s) for the payment have been made.

(g) *No Material Change. Since October 1, 199_____,* ABC has continued actively the conduct of its business, meeting and

Q: Should this be broadened to include all assets?

Q: Should this be broadened to include any violation of law?

Form 45: Agreement and Plan of Merger (continued)

performing all its obligations in the regular course of business, and (1) there will have been no material decrease in net assets, (2) there has been no material adverse change in the financial condition, business, properties, or assets of ABC, (3) ABC has not entered into any transaction or incurred any indebtedness or obligation that is out of the ordinary course of business, (4) ABC has not declared or paid any dividend or authorized or made any other distribution of any kind to its shareholders.

(h) *No Default.* The merger of ABC with XYZ shall not result in default under any condition, covenant, obligation, or agreement relating to ABC's stock, securities, indebtedness, or any material contract, lease, or license. ABC has delivered to XYZ true and accurate copies of all material contracts, leases, and licenses.

(i) *Assignment.* All of the rights and interest of ABC under all material contracts, leases, licenses, and choses in action are assignable to XYZ (to the extent assignment is necessary) or, appropriate consents to such assignment have been obtained; and no default in any indenture, loan agreement, or any other obligation will result from consummation of the merger.

VII. REPRESENTATIONS AND WARRANTIES OF XYZ

XYZ represents and warrants to ABC the following:

(a) *Existence.* As of the date of this Agreement and Plan of Merger, XYZ is a corporation validly organized in Missouri and duly qualified to conduct business in the jurisdictions in which its business operations require qualification under applicable law, with capital stock authorized, issued and outstanding as stated in the preamble.

(b) *Operations.* XYZ possess all of the appropriate right, title and interest in its properties now being used in the regular conduct of its business operations necessary to permit the continuance of such operations.

(c) *Financial Statement.* XYZ has heretofore delivered to ABC its balance sheets as of October 1, 19____, and the related statements of income and surplus for the fiscal years ended December 31, 19____, all certified to by MNO&P, certified public accountants, and all prepared without audit. The foregoing financial statements have been prepared in accordance with generally accepted accounting principles consistently applied and fairly represent the financial position and results of operations of XYZ and ABC as of the dates and for the periods indicated.

(d) *Property.* XYZ has title to all of its property, including all property reflected in its balance sheets as of October 1,

Form 45: Agreement and Plan of Merger (continued)

199_____ and not sold in the ordinary course of business after that date free and clear of any mortgage, lien, pledge, charge, claim, or encumbrance, except as shown on the balance sheets and minor liens, encumbrances, and adverse claims which do not materially impair the value of the property.

(e) *No Material Litigation.* There are no actions, suits, or proceedings pending, or to the knowledge of XYZ, threatened against or affecting XYZ, at law or in equity, or before or by any federal, state, municipal, or other governmental department, commission, board, bureau, agency, or instrumentality, that can reasonably be expected to result in any materially adverse change in the business, properties, operations, prospects, or assets, or in the condition, financial or otherwise, of XYZ.

(f) *Taxes.* XYZ has filed all tax returns and reports required to be filed, including, without limitation, returns of federal and state income, employment, sales and use taxes; and all taxes, interest, penalties, assessments, or deficiencies that have become due have been paid in full, or adequate provision(s) for the payment have been made.

(g) *No Material Change. Since October 1, 199_____,* XYZ has continued actively the conduct of its business, meeting and performing all its obligations in the regular course of business, and (1) there has been no material decrease in net assets, (2) there has been no material adverse change in the financial condition, business, properties, or assets of XYZ, (3) XYZ has not entered into any transaction or incurred any indebtedness or obligation that is out of the ordinary course of business, (4) XYZ has not declared or paid any dividend or authorized or made any other distribution of any kind to its shareholders.

Note: This should be in a representation and warranty.

(h) *No Default.* The merger of XYZ with ABC shall not result in default under any condition, covenant, obligation, or agreement relating to XYZ's stock, securities, indebtedness, or any material contract, lease, or license. XYZ has delivered to ABC true and accurate copies of all material contracts, leases, and licenses.

(i) *Assignment.* All of the rights and interest of XYZ under all material contracts, leases, licenses, and choses in action are assignable to ABC (to the extent assignment is necessary) or, appropriate consents to such assignment have been obtained; and no default in any indenture, loan agreement, or any other obligation will result from consummation of the merger.

Form 45: Agreement and Plan of Merger (continued)

VIII. CONDITIONS PRECEDENT TO ABC'S OBLIGATIONS

ABC's obligation to merge with XYZ is subject to the fulfillment prior to or on the effective date of each of the following conditions:

(a) *Representations and Warranties.* The representation and warranties of XYZ shall be true at and as of the effective date as though such representations and warranties were made at and as of such time.

(b) *Compliance.* XYZ has performed all obligations and agreements and complied with all covenants contained in this Agreement to be performed or complied with prior to the effective date. The President of XYZ shall have delivered to ABC a certificate, certifying to the best of such person's knowledge that, as of the effective date, the representation and warranties with respect to XYZ are true in all material respects and that the conditions set forth in this Agreement and Plan of Merger have been fulfilled and accomplished.

(c) *Opinion of Counsel.* XYZ shall have delivered to ABC an opinion of its legal counsel stating that as of the effective date:

> (i) XYZ is duly organized, validly existing, and in good standing under the laws of the State of Missouri;

> (ii) The capital stock of XYZ is authorized, issued and outstanding as stated in the preamble; and

> (iii) This Agreement has been duly and validly authorized by, and will be effective and binding upon XYZ, in accordance with its terms and the provisions of the laws of the State of Missouri upon due filing and recording in the office of the Secretary of State.

(d) *No Emergency.* There shall not have been subsequent to the date of this Agreement and Plan of Merger, any state of war declared or the commencement of any hostilities or any other national or international calamity directly or indirectly involving the United States, any declaration of a national emergency, general banking moratorium or suspension of trade on the New York Stock Exchange, or general limitation on the extension of credit by lending institutions in the United States that would materially affect the conduct of business or the properties, operations or assets of either party.

(e) *Approvals.* ABC shall be satisfied that all agreements, clearances or approvals by governmental authorities or other persons, and all corporate proceedings of the Boards of Directors and shareholders of XYZ, which ABC deems necessary or advisable, have been duly and validly taken or obtained upon such conditions or terms, if any, as are acceptable to ABC.

Form 45: Agreement and Plan of Merger (continued)

(f) *No Injunction.* At the effective date there shall be no effective injunction, writ, or preliminary restraining order or any order of any nature issued by a court or governmental agency of competent jurisdiction directing that the transactions contemplated herein, or any of them, not be consummated; and there shall not be pending or threatened before any court or governmental agency, any action or proceeding directly or indirectly challenging the proposed acquisition or otherwise directly or indirectly relating to it or any other action or proceeding which could in the judgment of ABC's management materially and adversely affect ABC or XYZ or impair the merger contemplated by this agreement and Plan of Merger.

(g) *No Adverse Action.* There shall not have been any action taken, or any statute, rule, regulation or order proposed, or enacted or entered into by any state, federal or foreign government, agent or instrumentality which would render the parties unable to effectuate the merger or, in the judgment of ABC's management, prohibit, restrict or delay consummation of the merger and other transactions contemplated hereby or make such consummation unduly burdensome to ABC.

IX. CONDITIONS PRECEDENT TO XYZ'S OBLIGATIONS

XYZ's obligation to merge with ABC is subject to the fulfillment prior to or on the effective date of each of the following conditions:

(a) *Representations and Warranties.* The representation and warranties of ABC shall be true at and as of the effective date as though such representations and warranties were made at and as of such time.

(b) *Compliance.* ABC has performed all obligations and agreements and complied with all covenants contained in this Agreement to be performed or complied with prior to the effective date. The President of ABC shall have delivered to XYZ a certificate, certifying to the best of such person's knowledge that, as of the effective date, the representation and warranties with respect to ABC are true in all material respects and that the conditions set forth in this Agreement and Plan of Merger have been fulfilled and accomplished.

(c) *Opinion of Counsel.* ABC shall have delivered to XYZ an opinion of its legal counsel stating that as of the effective date:

    (i) ABC is duly organized, validly existing, and in good standing under the laws of the State of Missouri;

    (ii) The capital stock of ABC is authorized, issued and outstanding as stated in the preamble; and

Form 45: Agreement and Plan of Merger (continued)

(iii) This Agreement has been duly and validly authorized by, and will be effective and binding upon ABC, in accordance with its terms and the provisions of the laws of the State of Missouri upon due filing and recording in the office of the Secretary of State.

(d) *No Emergency.* There shall not have been subsequent to the date of this Agreement and Plan of Merger, any state of war declared or the commencement of any hostilities or any other national or international calamity directly or indirectly involving the United States, any declaration of a national emergency, general banking moratorium or suspension of trade on the New York Stock Exchange, or general limitation on the extension of credit by lending institutions in the United Stats that would materially affect the conduct of business or the properties, operations or assets of either party.

(e) *Approvals.* XYZ shall be satisfied that all agreements, clearances or approvals by governmental authorities or other persons, and all corporate proceedings of the Boards of Directors and shareholders of ABC, which XYZ deems necessary or advisable, have been duly and validly taken or obtained upon such conditions or terms, if any, as are acceptable to XYZ.

(f) *No Injunction.* At the effective date there shall be no effective injunction, writ, or preliminary restraining order or any order of any nature issued by a court or governmental agency of competent jurisdiction directing that the transactions contemplated herein, or any of them, not be consummated; and there shall not be pending or threatened before any court or governmental agency, any action or proceeding directly or indirectly challenging the proposed acquisition or otherwise directly or indirectly relating to it or any other action or proceeding which could in the judgment of XYZ's management materially and adversely affect XYZ or ABC or impair the merger contemplated by this agreement and Plan of Merger.

(g) *No Adverse Action.* There shall not have been any action taken, or any statute, rule, regulation or order proposed, or enacted or entered into by any state, federal or foreign government, agent or instrumentality which would render the parties unable to effectuate the merger or, in the judgment of XYZ's management, prohibit, restrict or delay consummation of the merger and other transactions contemplated hereby or make such consummation unduly burdensome to XYZ.

X. ABANDONMENT OF MERGER

Anything herein to the contrary notwithstanding, this Agreement may be terminated and the merger abandoned at any time prior to the effective date of the merger (either before or after submission to or approval by the shareholders of ABC and XYZ):

Form 45: Agreement and Plan of Merger (continued)

(a) By mutual agreement of the Boards of Directors of ABC and XYZ.

(b) At the election of Board of Directors of either ABC or XYZ if:

(i) the merger shall not have been consummated before December 1, 199____, or such later date as shall be mutually agreed upon from time to time by the Board of Directors of XYZ and ABC; or

(ii) any of the representation and warranties contained in this Agreement and Plan of Merger made by one corporation shall as of the effective date of the merger be untrue in any respect that would adversely and materially affect the corporation abandoning the merger or any of its shareholders; or

(iii) any condition or covenant set forth in this Agreement and Plan of Merger to be complied with, performed or met by the other corporation or any other person (not a party hereto) or governmental body or agency shall not have been complied with, performed or met; or

(iv) the holders of more than ten percent (10%) of the outstanding common stock of XYZ shall, prior to the vote for approval of the merger file appropriate written notice of their objections to the merger, including a statement of their intention to demand payment for their shares.

XI. SUBMISSION TO SHAREHOLDERS

This Agreement shall be submitted as promptly as practicable to the shareholders of ABC and to the shareholders of XYZ as prescribed in section 351.420 of the General and Business Corporation Law of Missouri.

XII. GENERAL

(a) *No Fees.* Each of the corporations represents to the other that it has not incurred, and will not incur, any liability for brokerage fees or agents; commissions in connection with this Agreement and the transaction contemplated herein.

(b) *Counterparts.* For the convenience of the parties and to facilitate the filing and recording of this Agreement of Merger, any number of counterparts hereof may be executed, and each such counterpart shall be deemed an original instrument.

(c) *Notices.* All notices, requests, consents, and other communications hereunder shall be in writing, and shall be

Form 45: Agreement and Plan of Merger (continued)

mailed postage prepaid, addressed (i) if to XYZ, at (Number Street, City, State, Zip Code), attention: Albert Able, President; or (ii) if to ABC, at (Number Street, City, State, Zip Code), attention: Bob Baker, President.

(d) *Further Action.* From time to time prior to the effective date, each corporation shall permit the other to make and will cooperate and assist such other corporation in making, such investigations as may be appropriate to enable such corporation to determine compliance with the terms of this Agreement.

(e) *Waiver.* Any failure of either of the corporations to comply with any of its obligations, agreements, or conditions as set forth herein may be waived only by a writing signed by the other corporation.

(f) *Governing Law.* This Agreement shall in all respects be governed by and construed in accordance with the laws of the State of Missouri.

(g) *Amendment.* The corporations, by mutual consent of their respective Board of Directors, may amend, modify and supplement this Plan of Merger in such manner as may be agreed upon by them in writing at any time before approval or adoption thereof by the stockholder of any of the corporations or all of them.

IN WITNESS WHEREOF, each of the corporations, pursuant to a resolution passed by its Board of Directors at a meeting thereof duly called and held, has caused this instrument to be executed as of the day and year first above written.

ABC, Inc.

By: _____

Name: _____

Title: _____

(SEAL)

ATTEST: _____

Name: _____

Title: _____

XYZ, Inc.

By: _____

Name: _____

Title: _____

(SEAL)

ATTEST: _____

Name: _____

Title: _____

Note: Unlike the transaction in Form 44, here both corporations are to be parties.

Form 46: Articles of Merger

ARTICLES OF MERGER

Secretary of State
State of Missouri
Jefferson City, Missouri 65101

Pursuant to Sections 351.410 through 351.458, Revised Statutes of Missouri, 1986, as amended, of the General and Business Corporation Law of Missouri, the undersigned corporations certify the following:

1. That THE XYZ CORPORATION, a Missouri corporation and WIDGETS, INC., a Missouri corporation are hereby merged and that the above-named THE XYZ CORPORATION is the Surviving Corporation.

2. The Board of Directors of THE XYZ CORPORATION met on _____ and by resolution adopted by majority vote of the members of such Board approved the plan of Merger set forth in these Articles.

3. That the Board of Directors of WIDGETS, INC., met on _____ and by resolution adopted by majority vote of the members of such Board approved the Plan of Merger set foth in these Articles.

4. The Plan of Merger thereafter was submitted to a vote at a special meeting of the shareholders of THE XYZ CORPORATION held on _____ at 1371 Main Street, Kansas City, Missouri, and at such meeting there were two thousand (2,000) shares entitled to vote and two thousand (2,000) shares voted in favor and no shares voted against the Plan.

5. The Plan of Merger thereafter was submitted to a vote at a special meeting of the Shareholders of WIDGETS, INC. held on _____ at 1200 Main Street, Kansas City, Missouri, and at such meeting there were one thousand (1,000) shares entitled to vote and one thousand (1,000) shares voted in favor and no shares voted against such Plan.

6. Plan of Merger.

a. THE XYZ CORPORATION, a Missouri corporation, is the survivor.

b. All the property, rights, privileges, leases and patents of WIDGETS, INC., are to be transferred to and become the property of THE XYZ CORPORATION, the survivor. The officers and Board of Directors of the above-named corporation are authorized to execute all deeds to effectuate a full and complete transfer of ownership.

c. The officers and Board of Directors of THE XYZ CORPORATION shall continue in office until their successors are duly

Note: Missouri law requires that the Articles of Merger be filed.

Q: In Delaware, what must be filed, and at what point is the merger complete?

Note: In addition to the Plan and Agreement of Merger, you need to prepare and file with the Missouri Secretary of State in accordance with the General and Business Corporation Law of the State of Missouri, Articles of Merger, and we suggest the following form.

Form 46: Articles of Merger (continued)

elected and qualified under the provisions of the By-Laws of the Surviving Corporation.

d. The outstanding shares of WIDGETS, INC. shall be exchanged for shares of THE XYZ CORPORATION on the following basis:

Each share of Common Stock of WIDGETS, INC. that shall be issued and outstanding shall be forthwith converted into one (1) fully paid and non-assessable share of Common Capital Stock of THE XYZ CORPORATION.

e. The Articles of Incorporation of the survivor are (are not) amended (as follows:)

IN WITNESS WHEREOF, these Articles of Merger have been executed in duplicate by aforementioned corporations as of the day and year hereinafter acknowledged.

SURVIVING CORPORATION
THE XYZ CORPORATION

By: _____
    Albert Able, Pres.

ATTEST: _____
    Carl Charley, Secretary

ACQUIRED CORPORATION
WIDGETS, INC.

By: _____
    Don Douglas, Pres.

ATTEST: _____
    Ed Early, Secretary

Drafting Exercise 17

Prepare a Merger Agreement

A hotshot M & A partner that you have always wanted to work for comes into your office and asks if you want to help her on a new deal. Despite the piles of work you already have on your desk, you enthusiastically agree. The partner has just returned from a board of directors meeting with one of her biggest clients, XYZ, Inc. (the "Company" or "XYZ"), a manufacturer of microwave ovens. At the meeting, the directors decided to pursue a merger with ABC, Inc. ("ABC"), a manufacturer of frozen foods. Both companies are incorporated in Missouri.

The top executives at the Company have held several meetings with the ABC people, and they have started on their preliminary due diligence review. Things at ABC look pretty good—no obvious "smoking guns." After the board meeting, the partner had further discussions with the Company president. The Company president told her that XYZ really needed to do this deal, as soon as possible, but that she didn't want ABC to get a sense of that.

The partner gave you the following list of terms and conditions, including her queries, to help you prepare the first draft of the merger agreement. Draft an appropriate Agreement and Plan of Merger.

1. ABC will merge with and into XYZ, with XYZ as the surviving corporation. All of the corporate housekeeping documents of XYZ will carry over to the new company. The directors and officers of the new company will be Albert Able, President and Director; Bob Baker, Vice President, Secretary and Director; and Carol Charley, Vice President, Treasurer and Director.

2. The effective date of the merger has been targeted. Should we include a "drop dead" date? What kinds of delays can we anticipate (delays by the parties) and what kind can we not (e.g., regulatory approval delays, necessary consents from third parties).

3. XYZ has 30,000 shares of common stock authorized, with a par value of $1.00 per share, with 22,772 shares issued and outstanding; ABC has 300,000 shares of common stock authorized, with a par value of $1.00 per share, with 75,000 shares issued and outstanding.

4. The simplest conversion rate seems to be 15 shares of ABC into 1 share of XYZ. What should we do about fractional shares (i.e., where shareholders own shares that are not evenly divisible as per the conversion ratio)? Is our only choice to pay them cash?

5. The Company will arrange to have the ABC certificates cancelled and new XYZ certificates issued upon consummation of the Merger.

6. The directors of both companies seem to think that they will be able to get a majority of their shareholders to agree to the merger. Is this all that is necessary under Missouri law?

B.   ANTI-TAKEOVER DEFENSES

1.   Shark Repellent Provisions

There are various ways that management can make hostile takeovers more difficult. One method is to use what are called "shark repellent" or "porcupine" provisions in the Articles of Incorporation. Three examples follow in this chapter.

These provisions may either be adopted when the corporation is formed or by amending the Articles of an existing corporation. If the Articles are to be amended, the provisions generally must first be adopted by the board of directors. The business judgment rule will apply to this action, and the board may not adopt these provisions solely to attempt to entrench their own existing positions. Shareholder approval is then necessary for these amendments, and in soliciting proxies, management of reporting companies must be careful to comply with the 1934 Act proxy requirements including full disclosure of material information. It is very important to include in the disclosure that the amendments will make it less likely that a hostile takeover will succeed, and that they will discourage takeovers. This is because hostile takeovers can be beneficial for shareholders who might receive for all or some of their shares a price which is frequently higher than the prevailing market price at the time the takeover attempt is made.

Counsel for the Company should prepare a detailed memorandum for the board of directors setting forth the purposes, advantages and disadvantages of the proposed amendments which the board should study carefully before voting. This will help to establish the business judgment defense in the event of future litigation. One important aspect in measuring the reasonableness of the board's action is whether or not a hostile takeover was actually threatened at the time that the board approved the amendments, and recommended that the shareholders also approve them.

2.   Other Defensive Tactics

In addition to shark repellent provisions which may be added to Articles of Incorporation to make hostile takeovers more difficult, there are numerous other defensive tactics.

1.   Management may give senior officers "golden parachutes," which are lucrative employment and fringe benefit packages that are triggered by a successful hostile takeover.

2.   Management may attempt to set aside securities for purchase by friendly parties in order to defeat a takeover or to make it more difficult. This is called a "lock-up."

3.   Management may try a "scorched earth" defense in which it sells off attractive assets to make the target less desirable. These attractive assets may include the "crown jewels," the very assets of the target that the aggressor wants.

4. Management may also agree to pay the aggressor "greenmail" which is a premium for the aggressor's stock in the target company, if it abandons the takeover.

5. Finally, the target may have adopted a "poison pill." This is something dormant in its capital structure that is triggered by a hostile takeover. Typically, a company adopts a kind of shareholders' rights agreement as a takeover defense for its shareholders; these shareholders have rights to buy the company's stock at a lower than market price if a hostile takeover is instituted. The poison pill makes it much more expensive, and sometimes unfeasible, to take over the target company.

Note that a board of directors that utilizes any defensive tactic will be liable if its motivation was to entrench and protect its own position. The business judgment rule applies to takeovers and generally requires that defensive measures be reasonable in relation to the threat imposed.

Form 47: Shark Repellent Provision #1

FORM OF CHARTER PROVISION ESTABLISHING CLASSIFIED BOARD OF DIRECTORS

ARTICLE THIRTEEN

Note: Without this provision, the entire board could be replaced at one annual meeting of shareholders. This provision would mean that, because the corporation does not have cumulative voting, if an aggressor got voting control by buying shares, it could only elect one-third of the board each year, making it more difficult to make an abrupt change. By making a takeover more difficult, existing shareholders might lose the opportunity to sell their shares at a premium.

Note: In Delaware, an unclassified board may be removed without cause at any time, but members of a classified board may only be removed with cause. *See* Delaware General Corporation Law, §141(k)

The business and affairs of the Corporation shall be managed by or under the direction of a Board of Directors consisting of not less than eleven nor more than nineteen directors, the exact number of directors to be determined from time to time by resolution adopted by affirmative vote of a majority of the entire Board of Directors. The directors shall be divided into three classes, designated Class I, Class II and Class III. Each class shall consist, as nearly as may be possible, of one-third of the total number of directors constituting the entire Board of Directors.

As the 1994 annual meeting of stockholders, Class I directors shall be elected for a one-year term, Class II directors for a two-year term and Class III directors for a three-year term. At each succeeding annual meeting of stockholders beginning in 1995, successors to the class of directors whose term expires at that annual meeting shall be elected for a three-year term. If the number of directors is changed, any increase or decrease shall be apportioned among the classes so as to maintain the number of directors in each class as nearly equal as possible, and any additional director of any class elected to fill a vacancy resulting from an increase in such class shall hold office for a term that shall coincide with the remaining term of that class, but in no case will a decrease in the number of directors shorten the term of any incumbent director. A director shall hold office until the annual meeting for the year in which his term expires and until his successor shall be elected and shall qualify, subject, however, to prior death, resignation, retirement, disqualification or removal from office. Any vacancy on the Board of Directors that results from an increase in the number of directors may be filled by a majority of the Board of Directors then in office, and any other vacancy occurring in the Board of Directors may be filled by a majority of the directors then in office, although less than a quorum, or by sole remaining director. Any director elected to fill a vacancy not resulting from an increase in the number of directors shall have the same remaining term as that of his predecessor.

Notwithstanding the foregoing, whenever the holders of any one or more classes or series of preferred or preference stock issued by the company shall have the right, voting separately by class or series, to elect directors at an annual or special meeting of stockholders the election, term of office, filling of vacancies and other features of such directorships shall be governed by the terms of this Certificate of Incorporation applicable thereto, and such directors so elected shall not be divided into classes pursuant to this Article THIRTEENTH unless expressly provided by such terms.

No person (other than a person nominated by or on behalf of the Board of Directors) shall be eligible for election

Form 47: Shark Repellent Provision #1(continued)

as a director at any annual or special meeting of stock-holders unless a written request that his or her name be placed in nomination is received from a stockholder of record by the Secretary of the Company not less than 30 days prior to the date fixed for the meeting, together with the written consent of such person to serve as a director.

Form 48: Shark Repellent Provision #2

**FORM OF CHARTER PROVISION
REGARDING RIGHTS, POWERS AND
DUTIES OF BOARD**

ARTICLE FOURTEENTH

Except to the extent prohibited by law, the Board of Directors shall have the right (which, to the extent exercised, shall be exclusive) to establish the rights, powers, duties, rules and procedures that from time to time shall govern the Board of Directors and each of its members, including without limitation, the vote required for any action by the Board of Directors, and that from time to time shall affect the directors' power to manage the business and affairs of the Company; and no By-law shall be adopted by stockholders which shall impair or impede the implementation of the foregoing.

Note: This amendment would make it impossible for new controlling shareholders to amend the by-laws making it more difficult for the board of directors to act.

Form 49: Shark Repellent Provision #3

**FORM OF CHARTER PROVISION
ELIMINATING RIGHT OF
STOCKHOLDERS TO ACT WITHOUT
A MEETING**

ARTICLE FIFTEENTH

No action shall be taken by stockholder of the Company except at an annual or special meeting of stockholders of the Company.

Note: Absent this provision, pursuant to Delaware General Corporation Law §228, a majority shareholder could authorize significant corporate action, such as removing the board of directors, authorizing a merger or selling the corporation's assets, without a meeting of shareholders by signing a written consent.

Drafting Exercise 18:

Prepare Anti-Takeover Defenses Memorandum

Prepare a memorandum for the Company's Board of Directors, composed of non-lawyers, describing the three proposed anti-takeover amendments. Discuss their purposes and the advantages and disadvantages for the shareholders. Note that the directors will review this memorandum before exercising their business judgment and voting on the three proposed amendments to the Articles of Incorporation.

Practical Pointers

1. In preparing a letter of intent, it may be a good idea to prepare a balanced agreement from the beginning. If the lawyer for one party slants the first draft in her client's favor (e.g., suggesting that the other party pay all expenses), several unnecessary drafts may be required to reach the intended result. Provisions should probably be mutually beneficial.

2. It is a good idea to include a "drop dead" date by which the transaction should occur. If the deal is going well it can always be extended, if necessary.

3. Always identify brokers, or provide that there are none.

4. Make due diligence requests as specific as possible so that all necessary documents will be provided promptly. It is an irony of corporate practice that the most junior lawyer is often sent to do the due diligence investigation, even though that lawyer is the least likely to recognize a "smoking gun."

5. In preparing merger agreements be careful to keep the representations and warranties reciprocal. Also, do not leave anything of substance merely in the preamble (the "whereas" clauses); include it as a representation and warranty.

6. At the end of Form 45, Agreement and Plan of Merger, it might be a good idea to include three more "boilerplate" provisions:

   (h) This Agreement and Plan of Merger states the entire understanding by the parties with respect to subject matter hereof and supersedes all prior and contemporaneous oral and written communication and agreements with respect to the subject matter hereof.
   (i) This Agreement and Plan of Merger shall bind, benefit and be enforceable by and against the parties and their respective successors and assigns.
   (j) If any provision of this Agreement and Plan of Merger is construed to be invalid, illegal or unenforceable as to any party or generally, then the remaining provisions shall not be affected thereby and shall be enforceable without regard thereto.

7. In preparing Articles of Merger, be careful to track the relevant statute from the correct state.

8. Keep in mind that shark repellent anti-takeover defenses may be marginally useful because the directors will still, of course, owe fiduciary duties to the new owners.